The story of the emergence of
humans and humanity in Africa

Origins

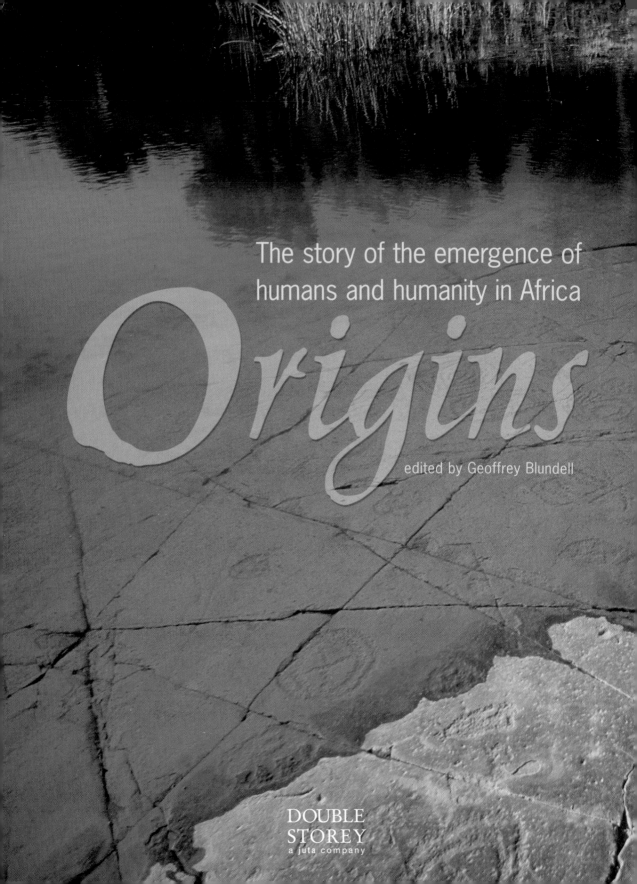

The story of the emergence of
humans and humanity in Africa

Origins

edited by Geoffrey Blundell

DOUBLE
STOREY
a juta company

The engraved pavement at Driekopseiland. The geometric images are thought to be the work of Khoekhoen peoples.

Published 2006
by Double Storey Books,
a division of Juta & Co. Ltd,
Mercury Crescent, Wetton, Cape Town

ISBN-10: 1 77013 040 3
ISBN-13: 978 1 77013 040 3

Editing by Priscilla Hall
Map by Susan Abraham
Design and layout by Jenny Young
Printing by CTP Book Printers, Parow, Cape Town

Acknowledgements
A number of people were very helpful with sourcing, collating and providing extra images. These include: Ron Clarke, Kathy Kuman, Ian Tattersall, Chris Henshilwood, Ghilraen Laue, David Pearce, Riaan Rifkin and Lara Mallen. Priscilla Hall meticulously copyedited the texts. Jenny Young prepared the layout. Susan Abraham produced the map for the volume. Russell Martin, Bridget Impey and Francis Gerard offered constant advice and encouragement.

COVER ILLUSTRATION: One of the hanging panels from the Origins Centre. The stitched panel is based on rock art imagery that depicts a trance dance. Seated women clap and sing around a fire, while men dance. On the right, a shaman climbs the ladder to the sky. Photograph by Ken and Amy Price.

BELOW: The main panel of eland at Game Pass Shelter in the Drakensberg. The site is one of the most spectacular and important painted shelters in southern Africa.

Contents

Seven million years of African history

At some point in the first two decades of the twentieth century – we can't be sure exactly when – Lindiso, a San (or Bushman), set out from his house among the Mpondomise people in south-eastern South Africa. He walked several kilometres through thick bush, following the Inxu River upstream, until he reached a secluded rock over-hang known these days as Ncengane Shelter. Here, in secret, he prepared ochre pigments with a binder before applying the paint to the rock surface. He created an image, possibly one of the horse and riders or wagons or even an antelope that can be found in the shelter still. It was the last time that rock paintings in the San tradition were ever made.

What makes Lindiso's last journey to Ncengane Shelter so poignant is that it brought to an end the world's oldest continuous art form. Before him, Lindiso's father was also a painter, and before him countless generations of San artists had painted on the rock shelters of southern Africa; the tradition stretches back at least 27 000 years into the past. Yet this estimate may be misleading. The recent discovery of two incised ochre pieces from Blombos Cave on the southern shore of South Africa, dated to 77 000 years before the present, suggests that the rock art tradition may be even older. The incised markings on the ochre are the world's oldest known images.

Together with other archaeological discoveries in sub-Saharan Africa, the Blombos ochre pieces have sparked a significant debate amongst archae-ologists. For many years, conventional archaeo-

Manqindi Dyantyi, Lindiso's daughter, walks towards the Inxu River Valley, where her father painted rock art. He was probably the last San rock painter.

logical wisdom has held that art and symbolic behaviour began in Europe about 35 000 to 40 000 years ago. In part, this acceptance was based on the spectacular rock art and material culture remains found in the deep limestone caverns of France and Spain. The entrances of many of these caves had collapsed after people had made the images, preserving their handiwork in a perfect 'time capsule'. The abundance of well-preserved images and artefacts seemed to suggest that it was in western Europe that humans had first become fully modern; it was in the deep, dark caves of France and Spain, many thought, that the proverbial light first switched on inside the human brain.

Some archaeologists, however, hesitated to accept the conventional wisdom. For them, there was always the nagging question: What about Africa? After all, that continent had yielded up rich fossil material that clearly showed that our pre-human ancestors had evolved on this continent. Moreover, there were certainly modern human remains in Africa that significantly predated those in Europe. The doubts became more insistent when radical developments in genetic research showed that our earliest common human ancestor had lived in Africa between 150 000 and 200 000 years ago. If the light switched on in Europe at only 40 000 years ago, this would mean that our ancestors had lived in Africa for a period of between 110 000 to 160 000 years without accomplishing very much. Such ideas smacked of older perceptions of Africa as the Dark Continent where nothing really happened, which troubled many archaeologists working there.

The Blombos ochre pieces and other archaeological discoveries did much to challenge such assumptions and soon a growing number of archaeologists turned their attention to the African Middle Stone Age period – the part of history dating to between 300 000 and 40 000 years ago – and especially the time period from 80 000 to 60 000 years ago, where the richest archaeological deposits seemed to be. This work, still ongoing, is likely to reveal important dis-

ROCK ART RESEARCH INSTITUTE

Images of antelope from Ncengane Shelter.

coveries in years to come that will change the way we understand the past.

While the Middle Stone Age period attracts most attention currently, there have also been significant developments in research carried out on earlier archaeological periods, which encompass our pre-human ancestors. Recent discoveries of new hominids have challenged long-held views about where and how our earliest pre-human ancestors took a different evolutionary course from the rest of the primate family. Southern and especially eastern Africa, where the majority of fossils have been found, are thought to be where the hominid and primate lines diverged. Central to this view is the distinction between forest and savannah

MZ (as he is known to academics), the son of Chitiwe, the first-born daughter of Lindiso. He still lives in the area where his mother practised as a rainmaker and his father painted the last rock paintings.

FRANCIS GERARD

Painting of dancing shaman, partly transformed into an antelope, as can be seen by the animal legs and hoofs. Such images are characteristic of the rock art of the area where Lindiso and his ancestors painted.

regions. As forested regions in Africa retreated over millions of years, our pre-human ancestors would have adapted and developed bipedal locomotion for more mobility, while the primates, who opted for a more arboreal existence, would have had no need for such adaptation.

The discovery in Chad of a 7-million-year-old hominid, *Sahelanthropus tchadensis*, however, challenges this view. Although Chad today is mostly desert, seven million years ago – when *Sahelanthropus* was alive – it was part of the great African rain forest. If it is our earliest-known hominid ancestor, why then is it found in a previously forested area and not on the grasslands, where the other hominids occur? While the answer to this question will be debated for years to come, there can be no doubt that the discovery of *Sahelanthropus* has shaken long-held convictions about where and how hominids and primates went their separate ways.

Debates among specialists on pre-human ancestors are often heated, in part owing to the fragmentary nature of the fossil evidence. In most cases, discoveries comprise only a few fossilised fragments of a cranium or some other bit of anatomy. From the morphology of these fossil fragments, researchers must infer the phylogenetic tree of evolution that takes us from seven million years to the point where we become anatomically modern – a difficult task when one considers the huge time periods between the various fossil fragments. In such a research discipline, the discovery of a complete or even near-complete fossil skeleton would be a truly spectacular achievement. Only a few years ago, Ron Clarke, a scientist at the University of the Witwatersrand, and two field excavators, Stephen Motsumi and Nkwane Molefe, through some remarkable detective work, discovered that a complete skeleton of *Australopithecus africanus*, one of our pre-human ancestors, was embedded in the breccia at the world-famous Sterkfontein Caves. With meticulous excavation, they have slowly uncovered the fossilised bones of what we now know as Little Foot.

Blombos, *Sahelanthropus tchadensis* and Little Foot are just some of the exciting recent discoveries that are shifting the traditional perceptions of our human and hominid past. Already an understanding is emerging of Africa as the place not only where humans originated but also where we first attained the key characteristics that give us our humanity. The archaeological evidence points to the origins of technology, image-making and symbolic thought on this continent long before it happened anywhere else.

The excitement at discovering the origins of humans and humanity in Africa should not, however, distract us from dealing with the more immediate issues of the recent African past. This past has included slavery, colonialism, exploitation, oppression and, in certain places, genocide. It is these factors, directly and indirectly, that ultimately led to the end of San rock painting. By the time Lindiso walked up the Inxu River, there were only isolated pockets of San who retained their language and culture. Indeed, Lindiso was one of the last speakers of !Gã !ne, a language of which only 140 words are recorded.

Some 150 years prior to Lindiso's last journey, in the 1770s, colonial farmers were wreaking havoc amongst San communities on the Eastern Cape frontier. Raiding parties went out regularly to abduct San children for slaves. Any resistance was brutally dealt with: one farmer claimed to have killed 2700 San personally, another that he had killed 3200. Throughout the nineteenth century this process of white aggression continued until, within South Africa, San communities almost entirely disappeared as distinctly recognisable groups with their own language. Today in South Africa there are only a handful of N/u speakers in the northern parts; all other San languages once spoken in the country are extinct. In Botswana and Namibia there are still large bodies of San whose languages are threatened to varying degrees.

Those San who were not killed or enslaved quickly merged with their Bantu-speaking and Khoe neighbours. The Bantu-speaking peoples had arrived in the southern part of Africa some 2000 years ago. Moving out of West Africa, they had slowly migrated southwards, bringing with them cattle, agriculture and iron-working. After their arrival in southern Africa they built some of sub-Saharan Africa's most impressive stone-walled urban centres and soon established trade networks that spanned eastern and southern Africa. Through Arab maritime trade, urban centres such as Mapungubwe and Great Zimbabwe, were connected to the vast Indian Ocean trade network, stretching all the way to India and China. Who the Khoe originally were and how they got to southern Africa, however, is a much more difficult question.

One school of thought holds that they moved into southern Africa from Central Africa, bringing sheep and pottery with them. Another argues

Anthropomorphic figure bending forward with an antelope head.

that the Khoe have always been in southern Africa and that they acquired sheep and pottery through a process of dispersal from central Africa. Recently, rock art evidence has been incorporated into the debate. There are rock art sites in southern Africa where geometric motifs are the principal subject matter – a form common in the rock art of Central Africa, where San rock art does not occur. In southern Africa, geometric motif sites are clearly distinct from San rock art sites; these sites are associated with Khoe peoples and are found along the rivers, which have been argued to be their migration routes. This seemingly supports the idea that the Khoe were people who moved into southern Africa as a distinct entity; but the debate, already ongoing for several decades, is far from resolved.

It is difficult to establish exactly what part the various San communities played in the trade networks established by places like Mapungubwe and Great Zimbabwe. They appear to have provided these and other urban centres with goods from hunting and mining. They seem also to have held a special place in various Bantu-speaking communities as rain-controllers and

intermediaries with the world of the spirits. Whatever the status of various San interacting or living with the diverse Bantu-speaking communities throughout southern Africa, their impact on those communities was significant. This is evident from the high percentage of San genes found amongst certain Bantu-speaking communities as well as the clicks in the Nguni languages, which were adopted from the San. Even today, traces of San religion, myth and belief can be seen in the rituals of a number of Bantu-speaking communities throughout southern Africa. While they have disappeared as independent communities with their own distinctive languages, San culture thus lives on through the Bantu-speaking peoples. Not only does San culture survive with Bantu-speaking peoples, but it is being actively reclaimed. Under the apartheid system, Khoe and San descendants were classified as 'coloured' – a term that actually robbed people of their identity. Neither black nor white, the term signified something betwixt and between. Today, many so-called coloured people are rediscovering their Khoe and San identity. In the process, they are finding that not all traces of the past were obliterated: fragments of ritual and religious knowledge persist, and so do memories of historical events.

While the recent African past is largely one of colonial oppression, it is also characterised by indigenous resistance to domination. The evidence for this resistance is found in history texts – and also in rock art images. While battles and other encounters between colonists and San

ABOVE: Bored stone. Such stones were used to weight digging sticks in order to dig up roots and bulbs but they were also used to bang on the ground in order to summon the spirits of the dead.   DAVID PEARCE

LEFT: The finely-detailed head of an eland, a favourite subject of San rock artists in many parts of southern Africa.

ROCK ART RESEARCH INSTITUTE

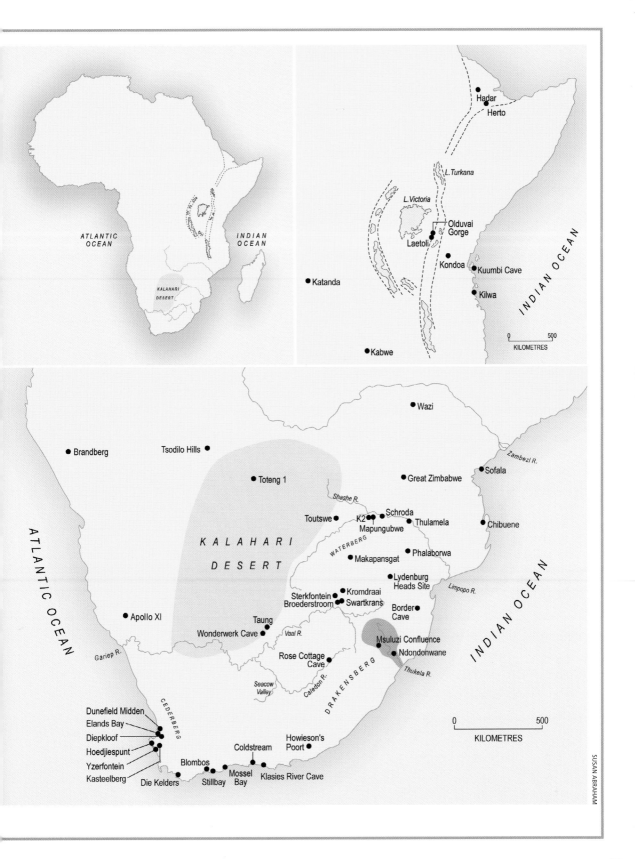

ATLANTIC OCEAN

INDIAN OCEAN

KALAHARI DESERT

● Hadar
● Herto
L. Turkana
L. Victoria
Olduvai Gorge
● Laetoli
● Kondoa
● Kuumbi Cave
● Kilwa
● Katanda
● Kabwe

INDIAN OCEAN

0   500
KILOMETRES

● Wazi
● Brandberg   Tsodilo Hills ●
● Toteng 1
Zambezi R.
● Great Zimbabwe   ● Sofala
Shashe R.
● Toutswe   ● K2   ● Schroda
● Thulamela   ● Chibuene
Mapungubwe
KALAHARI
DESERT
WATERBERG
● Makapansgat   ● Phalaborwa
● Lydenburg Heads Site
Limpopo R.
Sterkfontein ●   ● Kromdraai
Broederstroom ●   ● Swartkrans
● Border Cave
● Apollo XI
Taung ●
● Msuluzi Confluence
Wonderwerk Cave ●   ● Ndondonwane
Vaal R.
Gariep R.
Rose Cottage Cave ●
Seacow Valley   *Caledon R.*   *Thukela R.*
DRAKENSBERG

ATLANTIC OCEAN

INDIAN OCEAN

Dunefield Midden ●
Elands Bay ●   *CEDERBERG*
Diepkloof ●
Hoedjiespunt ●
Yzerfontein ●
Kasteelberg ●
● Blombos   Coldstream ●   Howieson's Poort ●
Die Kelders ●   Stillbay ●   Mossel Bay ●   Klasies River Cave ●

0   500
KILOMETRES

SUSAN ABRAHAM

11

are painted quite widely, it is in the Pedi rock art of northern South Africa that one finds the most detailed accounts of resistance. In site after site, images of Boer commandos on horseback are painted in thick white pigment. These images refer to the Maleboho War of 1894, when the Hananwa people resisted the invasion of their land by Paul Kruger's forces. Images such as these are testimony to the violent past and also to resistance against colonial oppression. In post-apartheid South Africa and more broadly in postcolonial Africa, it is liberating to realise that Africa is the home of humans and humanity, and that the more recent past of oppression, resistance and ultimately political freedom is documented by Africans themselves in the innumerable rock shelters of the continent.

In celebration of humanity's origins in Africa and the rich archaeological heritage of the continent, a new museum, the Origins Centre, opened in Johannesburg in 2006. The museum's motto is: 'We are who we are because of who we were.' This book, as the official publication of the museum, is very much about who we were and who we are today. It is not a catalogue, although many of the objects that are described in word and image in this book have some form of representation in the museum. Instead, it is a collection of essays, written by some of the world's foremost authorities on African history in a manner that is easily accessible to the nonspecialist.

The book has three parts. The first, African Genesis, considers the earliest pre-human ancestors and their associated material culture all the way through to the appearance of genetically modern humans between 200 000 and 150 000 years ago. The second part, called The Creative Explosion, considers the surge of development in Africa during the Middle Stone Age period, which takes us through to about 40 000 years ago when the Later Stone Age begins. The final part of the book carries us on from the start of the Later Stone Age all the way through to the very recent past, to the time when Lindiso made his last journey to Ncengane Shelter up the Inxu River valley. The scope of the book thus covers the period from the time of *Sahelanthropus* through the immense human creativity of the Middle Stone Age to the disappearance of rock art production on the continent – seven million years of African history.

CONVENTIONS USED IN THIS BOOK

Dates Dates up to AD 1000 are given in the standard archaeological format as BP. This stands for 'Before the present', a point in time taken as 1950. A date given as 2000 BP would thus mean 2000 years plus the number of years since 1950, to indicate what we know in Christian terms as 50 BC. Where BP might be confusing and the conventional Christian chronological terminology is better known, BC and AD are retained.

Although every attempt has been made to ensure consistency of dates through the various texts, it is important to understand that dates are often contested issues in archaeology. This is especially true of dates for the origin and termination of periods and events.

San The click-speaking former hunter-gatherers of southern Africa were previously known as Bushmen. The name, however, derived from earlier, colonial pejorative phrasing. For this reason, some researchers prefer the word San. Unfortunately, this is a Khoe word for the Kalahari peoples, which is also pejorative. The present Kalahari peoples largely prefer to be called Bushmen, arguing that the term has lost its negative connotations. In South Africa, where the recent history of racial prejudice and segregation is still fresh in people's minds, the word Bushmen retains negative connotations. The term San is thus preferred and is used throughout the book; any negative connotations are rejected.

Khoekhoen Another diverse collection of peoples in southern Africa who speak click-languages are the Khoekhoen. Typically, they are described as a pastoralist people and it is thought that they were responsible for introducing fat-tailed sheep into southern Africa. Formerly, these peoples were called 'Hottentots' by the European colonists, a pejorative term. The noun Khoekhoen carries the adjectives Khoekhoe and Khoe, as in 'the Khoe language'. In an older orthography, but one that is still sometimes used, the word is spelled Khoi. Although Khoekhoen and San are often grouped together as one family and labelled Khoesan or Khoisan, the nature of the relationship between Khoe and San is disputed and still widely debated in archaeology and anthropology. The modern spelling of Khoekhoen is used throughout the book.

Clicks In several places in the book, words with clicks are used. The clicks are represented thus:
- ≠ (alveolar click). The front part of the tongue – not just the tip – is placed against the alveolar ridge and then drawn away. It is a softer-sounding click than the alveolar-palatal click.
- ! (alveolar-palatal click). The tip of the tongue is placed against the alveolar ridge where it meets the hard palate. By snapping the tongue down sharply, a loud pop results. The technique is sometimes used in English to mimic the sound of horse hoofs on paving.
- / (dental click). The tip of the tongue is placed at the back of the upper front teeth and then pulled away to create a fricative sound. The same technique is used in English in gentle reproof.
- // (lateral click). The tongue is placed more or less as for the alveolar click but is released from the side of the mouth. The same technique is sometimes used to spur horses on in English.

Hominid and hominin Generally, 'hominid' refers to all the human and pre-human species that ever evolved, including the extinct ones. In strict taxonomic terms, however, chimpanzees and gorillas are also hominids. For this reason, some writers prefer the term 'hominins', which means the same as 'hominids' but excludes chimpanzees and gorillas. In this book, unless the author indicates otherwise, both terms refer only to human and pre-human lineages. (Humans and apes share only one common ancestor at about seven million years ago. After that, the families go their different ways.)

Stillbay and Still Bay In archaeological practice it is usual to name new technological industries after the place where they were first discovered. One such industry that is discussed in the book was first described near the South African town of Still Bay. In order to make a distinction between the place name and the stone tools from there, the portmanteau 'Stillbay' is used for the lithic technology.

African
Genesis

Painted stone from the Origins Centre, depicting a row of people carrying digging sticks.

Human evolution in Africa

IAN TATTERSALL

The human story reaches almost infinitely back, to the very origins of life on earth not much short of four billion years ago. And while for many of us the most fascinating part of this story concerns specifically how we became our remarkable if familiar selves, with all the attributes that make us the extraordinary creatures we are today, it remains true that we are the end result of a process of evolutionary accretion that took place over a very long period of time.

In turn this means that, if we are fully to appreciate how we came to be what we are, we have to know something of our remoter past. This chapter is devoted principally to recounting the story of human evolution in a modestly broad sense, starting with the earliest members of our own family, Hominidae. But to create some perspective it is desirable to begin a little earlier with a brief glance at the history of the order Primates, the greater group of mammals to which we belong.

The complete fossilised skeleton of an *Australopithecus africanus* lies embedded in the breccia of Sterkfontein Caves.

Man's place in nature

The modern human species, *Homo sapiens*, is classified in the order Primates, the large group of mammals that also includes the lemurs, lorises and bushbabies, the tiny and enigmatic tarsier, the monkeys of the Old and New Worlds, and the apes. Because a great deal of time has passed since the common ancestor of this diverse group existed, there has been so much evolutionary change in the various primate lineages that it is difficult to pin down many features which all of them uniquely share.

Thus, instead of seeking diagnostic features of the order, primatologists have tended to characterise it by pointing to a number of general evolutionary trends that are exhibited to one extent or another by all of its members. These include the preservation of a fairly generalised body plan; enhancement of the mobility of the digits of hands and feet; the replacement of claws on the tips of those digits by nails backed by sensitive fleshy pads; the progressive abbreviation of the snout and reduction of the sense of smell, together with an elaboration of the visual apparatus; and a tendency towards increase in the size of the brain, and particularly of its cerebral cortex.

In general, in living primates these trends are least accentuated among the 'lower' primates, the lemurs of Madagascar and the lorises and bushbabies of Asia and Africa, which in spite of exhibiting a wide range of locomotor, dietary and other specialisations thus retain more in common with the ancestral primate. They are more pronounced among the 'higher' primates, consisting of the New and Old World monkeys, the apes, and humans, and are particularly noticeable among the last two.

Extremely archaic primates are known as fossils from the very beginning of the age of mammals, some 65 million years ago (MYA), when such creatures were apparently widespread throughout Eurasia and North America. These early primates are placed in their own suborder Plesiadapiformes because no direct links are discernible with any later primate group, and unlike all later primates they had specialised front teeth and most of them retained clawed hands and feet. However, it has recently been shown that at least one of them did have an opposable thumb with a nail, and many at least were probably forest-living, possibly adapted to feeding in the terminal branches of trees.

'Primates of modern aspect', or euprimates, appear with the Eocene epoch 54 to 34 MYA. The

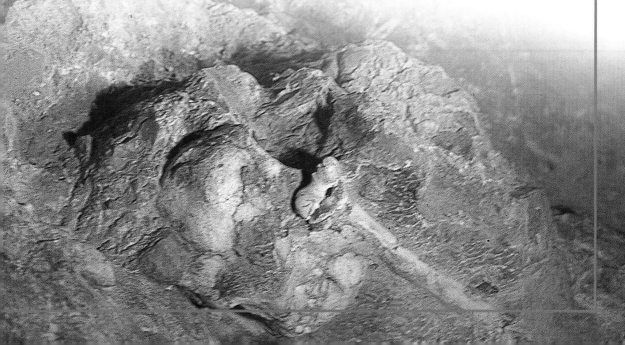

primates of the Eocene were clearly tree-living, with reduced snouts, grasping hands and feet, forward-facing eyes, somewhat larger brains, and many of the other hallmarks of today's lower primates. And although it is not certain that direct ancestors of any contemporary primates have yet been found as early as the Eocene, it was clearly within this exuberant primate radiation that the origins of later primate groups are to be sought. By the end of the Eocene lower primates had all but disappeared from North America, but by not long afterwards early relatives of modern lower primates begin to be found in Asia and Africa.

Fossils from the Fayum region of Egypt announce the appearance of ancient higher primates 35 to 33 MYA. The Fayum desert is now a sandy waste; but at that time, like most of Africa, the region was covered by tropical forest through which sluggish rivers flowed. This forest supported a diverse fauna of higher primates, including members of a group (the propliopithecids) that may lie close to the common ancestry of all the living Old World higher primates. Precursors of living New World and Old World monkeys begin to appear in the fossil records of their respective continents by between 28 and 20 MYA.

Hominoidea, the superfamily that contains today's greater and lesser apes and humans, first appears in the fossil record of Africa about 23 MYA, early in the Miocene epoch. One of the earliest hominoids is Proconsul, which is known from most of its skeleton and which, like living apes, may have lacked a tail. Otherwise, it generally lacked the specialisations of today's apes; species of Proconsul were apparently quadrupedal runners, lacking the mobile shoulder that is so much a hallmark of hominoids today.

Indeed, fossil hominoids even of the later African Miocene do not include any forms that are clearly ancestral to the modern African apes, the gorilla and chimpanzee. Still, they all lived in what seem to have been fairly heavily forested environments, though at this time the formerly rather low-lying continent of Africa was beginning to rise along the more or less north–south line of what is now known as the Great African Rift.

Further east, fossil relatives of the modern orang-utan (which was formerly widespread in eastern Asia but is now found only in Sumatra and Borneo) are present in India and Pakistan by about 13 to 12 MYA, although members of the genus *Sivapithecus* appear, like their African cousins, to have remained primitively quad-rupedal in their body skeletons, lacking the suspensory adaptations developed by today's African and Asian apes. Or possibly they had specialised towards a certain amount of ground-living in response to more open woodland environments than those their ancestors had inhabited.

Early hominids, hominid relatives

Together with its fossil relatives, today's species *Homo sapiens* is classified in the family Hominidae. Used in this sense, Hominidae excludes the living apes and their fossil relatives. However, to indicate their close relationship to us, some palaeoanthropologists prefer to include the apes in Hominidae, and they therefore use the subfamily Homininae, or even the tribe Hominini, to denote the smaller group containing just humans and their fossil relatives.

The result is that trawling through the literature on human origins can be extremely confusing, with the same terms varying wildly in their inclusiveness, depending on the author. There is, sadly, no way round this, and no general consensus is yet in sight. Still, although the choice here is largely a matter of philosophy, by now the variety of fossil human relatives known is so diverse (some twenty species and counting) that clearly the non-ape group fully warrants family status on its own. I thus prefer to continue using the term Hominidae and its derived adjective 'hominid' for the 'human' grouping and its members, excluding any apes.

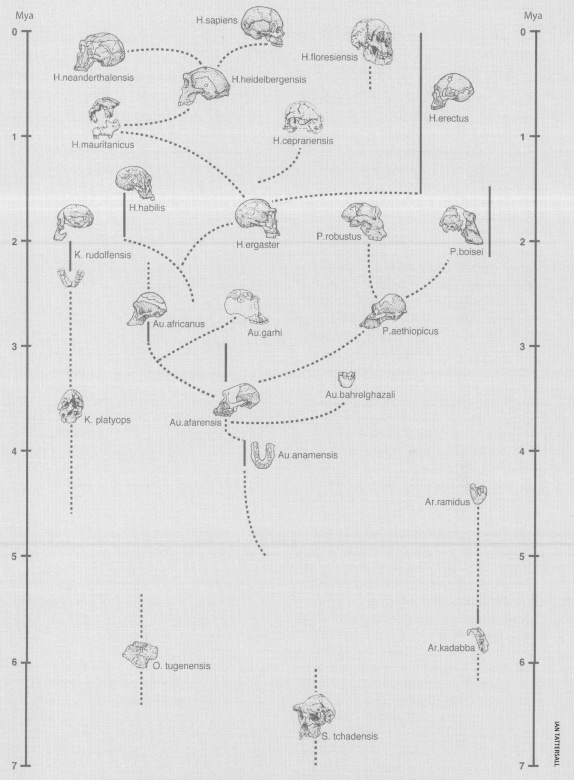

Mya

H.sapiens
H.neanderthalensis
H.floresiensis
H.heidelbergensis
H.erectus
H.mauritanicus
H.cepranensis
H.habilis
H.ergaster
P.robustus
P.boisei
K. rudolfensis
Au.africanus
Au.garhi
P.aethiopicus
K. platyops
Au.bahrelghazali
Au.afarensis
Au.anamensis
Ar.ramidus
Ar.kadabba
O. tugenensis
S. tchadensis

IAN TATTERSALL

One possible family tree of relationships among generally recognised hominid species.
Almost all of the suggested relationships are highly tentative.

From Greek localities dating to the later part of the Miocene, around 10 to 8 MYA, come fossils assigned to the genus *Ouranopithecus* (or *Graecopithecus*). It is believed by some that this form may lie close to the point at which the human lineage diverged from that leading to its closest ape cousin (it is disputed to which living ape modern humans are most closely related, though many opt for the chimpanzee).

It has even been argued that *Ouranopithecus* may postdate the ape–human split and represent a very early hominid, especially since its molar teeth have very thick enamel, a trait thought to have characterised the earliest hominids. Whether or not either is the case still awaits consensus, but certainly *Ouranopithecus* lies more or less in the time range when both palaeontologists and molecular systematists believe the ape–human split occurred.

Still, there is no doubt that the hominid story in its strictest sense begins in Africa, and that it was in this continent that our lineage was born. Unfortunately, though, we do not have a very good notion of what the earliest hominid *ought* to look like, so it is hardly surprising that there is a great deal of dispute surrounding the oldest fossils – all of them African – that have been claimed to be definitively hominid. Over the fifteen decades since Charles Darwin published his groundbreaking *On the Origin of Species* and thereby introduced the concept of evolution into Western thought, a number of different features, perhaps most notably the possession of a large brain, have been proposed as the defining attribute of Hominidae.

In recent years, though, as our knowledge of the human fossil record has expanded, a general consensus has developed that the fundamental characteristic of Hominidae is upright walking on two legs. As a result, claims of bipedalism have predictably enough been made for all the early contenders for this honour. This is so even though, in the drying and increasingly seasonal climates of Africa after about 10 MYA, it seems quite likely that several lineages of hominoids

Discovery in Chad, Central Africa

Towards a new paradigm for the cradle of mankind

MICHEL BRUNET

The idea of an ascendance for our species is quite recent.[1] In the last 150 years or so, we have discovered unexpected ancestors and numerous close relatives, revealing our deep prehistorical roots. The overarching question has always been: Who was our earliest ancestor?

Palaeoanthropologists had debated whether our earliest ancestor arose in eastern or southern Africa . Then in the early 1980s the discovery of the oldest known hominid fossil in East Africa led

archaeologists to propose what is known as the 'East Side Story' palaeoscenario. At that time scientists believed that early hominids appeared during the Pliocene epoch (5.3 to 1.8 million years ago) in the savannah regions east of the Rift Valley, while early African apes remained in the rain forest west of the Rift Valley. This idea was accepted by many palaeoanthropologists until 1994.

In 1995, however, to the east of Koro-Toro in Chad, researchers from the Mission Paléoanthropologique Franco-Tchadienne (MPFT) found the lower jaw of a new australopithecine variant, dated between 3.5 and 3 million years ago. This discovery was the first ever made of a hominid fossil west of the Rift Valley. The new variant is named *Australopithecus bahrelghazali* or, more colloquially, Abel – it is the western cousin of the famous fossil Lucy, an *Australopithecus afarensis*. The find spurred research and survey, and between 1994 and 1997 three more fossiliferous areas were located in the Djurab desert. These areas were dated to the period between 7 and 4 million years ago, raising the possibility that even older hominid remains existed there. If such a hominid came to light, it would be significantly older than those found east of the Rift Valley, where the oldest known hominid fossil was 3.5 million years old.

In 2001 the MPFT made a truly remarkable discovery at the site of Toros-Ménalla, locality TM 266, some 2600 km west of the Rift Valley. They found a well-preserved and near-complete cranium of a hitherto unknown hominid. The hominid was named *Sahelanthropus tchadensis*, or Toumaï. The fossilised fauna at this site date it close to 7 million years ago, which puts it in the Miocene epoch. This date makes Toumaï the earliest known hominid ever found and the discovery overturns the received wisdom that our earliest ancestors had an exclusively southern or eastern African origin. Now, early hominid history must be studied within a completely new paradigm.

MICHEL BRUNET

ABOVE: Lower jaw of *Australopithecus bahrelghazali*.
BELOW: The desert landscape of Chad, where *Sahelanthropus tchadensis* was discovered.

JEAN-LOÏC LE QUELLEC

may have been forced to the ground by the climatically-induced thinning of the ancestral forests.

Since the hominid family can only have had one ancestor, if more than one such hominoid group adopted an upright posture on the ground it would of course follow that bipedalism alone cannot be an infallible indicator of membership in Hominidae. On the other hand, in our present perspective bipedalism would still appear to be a necessary qualification for membership in Hominidae, even if it might not be a sufficient one.

Over the past ten years or so, three newly described African fossil genera have been claimed to throw new light on the origin of Hominidae. Probably the oldest of these is *Sahelanthropus*, described in 2002 from Chad in Central Africa by Michel Brunet and his Franco-Chadian team, and dated to about 7 to 6 MYA. As described so far, this putative early hominid is known only from a cranium and some bits of a mandible, but its discoverers infer that the creature was an upright biped because of the forward position of its foramen magnum, the large hole in the base of the skull through which the spinal cord passes from the braincase to the vertebral column.

This same characteristic is also the primary basis for the claim that the rather younger *Ardipithecus*, a motley collection of fragments from Ethiopia dating from 5.7 to 4.4 MYA, was an upright biped and thus an ancestral hominid. The position of the foramen magnum is significant because in quadrupeds it points somewhat backward, whereas in upright walkers it lies further beneath the skull and points downward. This is because in a biped the cranium has to be balanced atop a vertical spine. Still, most authorities would probably agree that a forwardly-placed foramen magnum is an indirect indicator of posture rather than a proof of upright bipedalism.

Slightly younger than *Sahelanthropus* is the 6-million-year-old *Orrorin*, quite recently described from deposits in northern Kenya. This primate is also claimed to have been a biped, but this time principally because of the structure

The Late Miocene Chadian hominid

To date, two Late Miocene species other than *Sahelanthropus tchadensis* have been found that can lay claim to being among the earliest hominids. Both are from East Africa: *Ardipithecus kadabba*, described by Yohannes Haile-Selassie and his team, dates to between 5.8 and 5.2 million years ago and comes from Middle Awash in Ethiopia; and *Orrorin tugenensis*, described by Brigitte Senut and her team, is about 6 million years old and comes from Lukeino in Kenya. Neither of these two fossils is as old as *Sahelanthropus tchadensis*.

Sahelanthropus tchadensis displays a unique combination of primitive and derived characters which clearly shows that it is not related to chimpanzees or gorillas, and suggests that it is related to later hominids and is close in time to the last common ancestor between chimpanzees and humans. The principal anatomical hominid features of *Sahelanthropus tchadensis* are: relatively flat face with short premaxilla (the two bones in the upper jaw that bear the incisors); forward-positioned foramen magnum (the opening at the base of the skull through which the spinal cord passes) linked to a shortened basioccipital (back, lower part of cranium) and a sub-horizontal nuchal plane (the area at the nape of the neck giving attachment to the muscles of the back of the cranium); non-honing canine-third premolar complex; small-crowned canines that show wear on the top; and post-canine teeth that show maximum radial enamel thickness that is intermediate between chimpanzees and australopiths.

Late Miocene hominid environments

In Chad, the Late Miocene evidently had successive wet and arid periods, at least from 7 million years ago. The rock strata are alternately aeolian (windblown) sandstones from arid times and sedimentary sandstones from perilacustrine and true wet periods. *Sahelanthropus tchadensis* and associated fauna have been uncovered from the perilacustrine sandstones. These data fit the kind of mixed environments you would get in a vegetated perilacustrine belt between lake and desert. We can see the same sort of diversity today in the Okavango Delta of the central Kalahari Desert in Botswana: a mixture of lake and river waters, swamps, patches of forest, wooded islets, wooded savannah, grassland, and desert areas.

Exactly where Toumaï lived in this range of available environments is still being explored, but probably it was in woodland. Two other hominids, *Ardipithecus kadabba* and *Orrorin tugenensis*, are also associated with wooded environments, so perhaps the savannah played less of a role after all in favouring the development of hominid bipedal posture. In fact all three of these Late Miocene hominids are probably bipedal — this observation forces us to reconsider the significance of the savannah in the development of hominid origins.

Towards a new early hominid history

The models for hominid evolution have been modified — and sometimes overturned — by successive discoveries in the last 150 years. This points to the importance of ongoing fieldwork, as our understanding of evolutionary history has, at most, a life expectancy to the next fossil discovery.

In the twentieth century, available fossil hominid remains led us to consider first South Africa and then East African savannah as the cradle of humankind. Now it appears that the earliest hominids inhabited wooded environments and were not restricted to southern or eastern Africa but lived in a wider geographic region including at least Central Africa.

In the last decade the number of hominid species has doubled and the date for the appearance of our earliest hominid ancestor has been pushed back even further. *Sahelanthropus tchadensis* indicates that the split between chimpanzee and human lineages occurred over 7 million years ago.

In addition, the MPFT results prove that Central Africa was, at least between 7 and 3 million years ago, a crossroads marked by intermittent faunal exchanges with northern and south-eastern Africa. Knowing more about the migratory patterns and the faunal exchanges in Africa during the Mio-Pliocene is vital for understanding the origin and dispersal of the earliest members of the human group and therefore its evolutionary history. We need still more data from these geographic areas and notably from Central and north-eastern Africa (Chad, Libya, Egypt, Sudan). Overall, palaeontologists and palaeoanthropologists have to conduct more field surveys to understand the first steps of humankind.

1 This essay is greatly indebted to all the members of the field team from the Mission Paléoanthropologique Franco-Tchadienne. The mission is an international scientific collaboration between the University of Poitiers, the University of N'Djamena, and the Centre National d'Appui à la Recherche (N'Djamena). It now includes more than fifty researchers from ten countries.

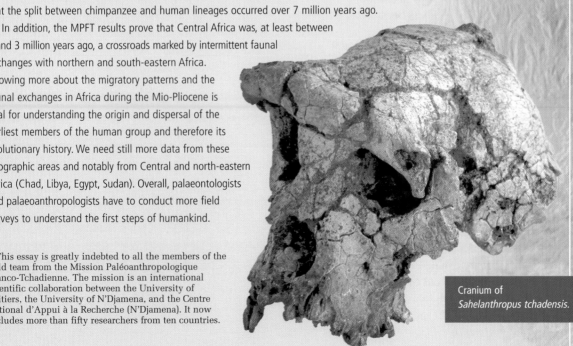

Cranium of *Sahelanthropus tchadensis*.

Entrance to vertical shaft at Sterkfontein.   RON CLARKE

Dr Broom
and the skeleton in the cavern

RONALD CLARKE

In 1925, after Raymond Dart had published in *Nature* his discovery of the Taung child skull that he named *Australopithecus africanus*, Robert Broom published an article about the fossil in the journal *Natural History*. Broom's article is significant for three prophetic statements. First, he provided his drawing of how he thought an adult *Australopithecus* would appear when eventually discovered. Secondly, he referred to a 1774 statement by James Burnett, Lord Monboddo, who not only maintained that humans had descended from apes but that it would be in Africa, if it were well searched, that 'all the several types of human progression might be traced and perhaps all the varieties of the species discovered.' Thirdly, Broom ended with the following statement: 'It seems to me not at all improbable that an adult *Australopithecus* will yet be obtained and possibly a perfect skeleton. Should such a discovery be made, it would be difficult to overestimate its importance.'

All three of these prophecies have been fulfilled. It was to be Broom himself who, in 1936, would discover the first adult *Australopithecus* at Sterkfontein caves, and who in 1947, assisted by John Robinson, would uncover a skull (called Sts 5) that closely resembled his drawing of the predicted adult.

It was to be Broom also who uncovered some of the other 'several types of human progression and some of the varieties of the species' with his discoveries of *Paranthropus* at Kromdraai (1938) and Swartkrans (1948), and *Telanthropus* (now called *Homo ergaster*) at Swartkrans (1949).

of the shaft of its upper leg bone. But while, as we shall shortly see, some aspects of leg bone structure are indeed telling in terms of locomotion, the preserved parts of *Orrorin* unfortunately do not offer us the most diagnostic of indicators, although the claim that this primate was upright is certainly far from implausible.

Rather younger, at maybe as much as 4 million years old but still a member of the early hominid group, is the extraordinary skeleton from Sterkfontein Member 2 that is currently being excavated by Ron Clarke of the University of the Witwatersrand, following a saga of palaeontological detective work and deduction without parallel in the history of palaeoanthropology. Rummaging through some unidentified bones that he believed had been found in Sterkfontein's Silberberg Grotto many years previously, Clarke found some pieces of a rather primitive hominid foot that has been immortalised with the name of 'Little Foot'. These, he eventually discovered, connected with the preserved lower end of a tibia, the lower leg bone. The tibia was broken off just above the ankle; and, since the break looked fresh, Clarke suspected that the rest of the skeleton might still

Further discoveries that fulfilled Monboddo's prophecy on human progression were indeed to be made in Africa – ranging from the 7-million-year-old *Sahelanthropus tchadensis* in Chad, through to the 6-million-year-old *Orrorin tugenensis* in Kenya, the 5.7- to 4.4-million-year-old *Ardipithecus ramidus* in Ethiopia, the 4.2- to 3.9-million-year-old *Australopithecus anamensis* in Kenya, and the 3.6- to 3.2-million-year-old *Australopithecus afarensis* in Ethiopia. For the fulfilment of the third of Broom's 1925 predictions, that of the complete *Australopithecus* skeleton, the world would have to wait 72 years until it was discovered in 1997 in the Sterkfontein Caves.

Interestingly, Broom was 72 years old when in 1938 he wrote as follows: 'If I live another 8 years, I may be able to do a little more. I think it is very likely that within the next couple of years we shall find other specimens of Pleistocene apes and perhaps much of his skeleton. If we could find a pelvis, a foot and a hand of either the Sterkfontein or Kromdraai ape the importance of the discovery would be greater than all the previous discoveries put together.'

Broom, of course, could not have meant that last sentence literally but only wanted to emphasise the importance he placed on the pelvis, foot and hand. He knew that the pelvis would confirm whether or not *Australopithecus* walked upright, and that the foot and hand might demonstrate the kind of anatomy that makes humans unique among primates. When Broom and Robinson discovered a pelvis in 1947, it did indeed show that *Australopithecus* walked upright, but the hand and foot were not destined to be discovered in Broom's lifetime.

Nevertheless, when the complete skeleton was found at Sterkfontein in 1997 it was through the clues provided by its feet. I had in 1994 found in a box of fossil animal bones at Sterkfontein four conjoining bones from the left ankle and foot of an *Australopithecus*. These had been chiselled out 14 years previously from breccia blasted out by lime miners in the 1920s or early 1930s from the lowest deposits in the cave in the Silberberg Grotto. Unfortunately they had not been recognised as hominid when they were exposed in 1980.

Next, in 1997, I found in a box of monkey fossils more bones from the same hominid left foot and leg and a lower right tibia fragment. I then remembered a small fragmentary foot bone I had found in the 1994 box but which I could not match with the left foot. When I looked at it again,

Broom's prophecy of how an adult *A. africanus* would appear when found (left, courtesy of *Nature*) and his drawing of Sts 5, the Adult *A. africanus* found in 1947 (courtesy of the Transvaal Museum).

RON CLARKE

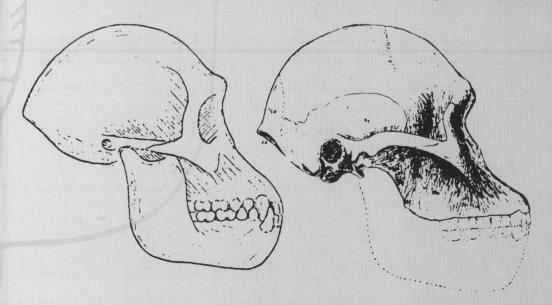

be in place in the gloomy and cavernous grotto, where matrix containing bone was still found lining the cave's walls.

In June 1997 he showed a cast of the bone fragment to his two colleagues Stephen Motsumi and Nkwane Molefe and asked them to scour the cave to see if any bones exposed in its walls might show the same cross-section as the tibial fragment. As Clarke himself admitted, this was equivalent to asking them to find the proverbial needle in a haystack. But Motsumi and Molefe uncomplainingly took on the task. Within two days, scrutinising the walls of the dank, gloomy cave inch by inch with hand-held torches, the indefatigable searchers miraculously found the match to Clarke's tibial fragment that had been blasted away by lime miners and collected by palaeontologists many years earlier, leaving the rest of the fossilised leg still in the rock.

What Motsumi and Molefe found exposed on the wall of the cave was no more than a vague circle of bone, where the base of the tibia had been broken away from the shaft higher up by the force of the miners' explosion. But painstaking dissection away of the rock-hard matrix sur-rounding the bone showed that the best part of the entire skeleton of an early hominid, including the skull, remained enclosed in the rock, from which Clarke is still extracting it today with infinite patience, and under very difficult conditions.

This astonishing rarity will certainly turn out to be one of the most important early hominid discoveries known, and it is already clearly different from anything else so far discovered, anywhere. What it will eventually wind up being named is anybody's guess at this stage, but for the time being Clarke is referring to this amazing skeleton, technically known as Stw 573, as an archaic form of the classic South African hominid genus *Australopithecus*.

If it is as old as suspected, Stw 573 is of approximately the same age as the 4.2- to 3.9-million-year-old Kenyan fossils that have been allocated to the species *Australopithecus*

I found that it was a hominid bone from the right foot, a mirror image of one of the newly discovered bones of the left foot. The fact that we now had foot and leg bones of both sides of one individual meant that the whole skeleton had to be there embedded in the breccia of that lower cave, the Silberberg Grotto. I gave a cast of the tibia frag-ment to Stephen Motsumi and Nkwane Molefe and asked them to search, with hand-held lamps, the deep dark cavern to see if there was any bone exposed to which that tibia would fit.

After one and a half days they located a section of bone to which the tibia end fits perfectly. I knew then that, encased in that steep slope of ancient cave infill, we would uncover something that palaeoanthropologists had wanted for so long – a complete skeleton of

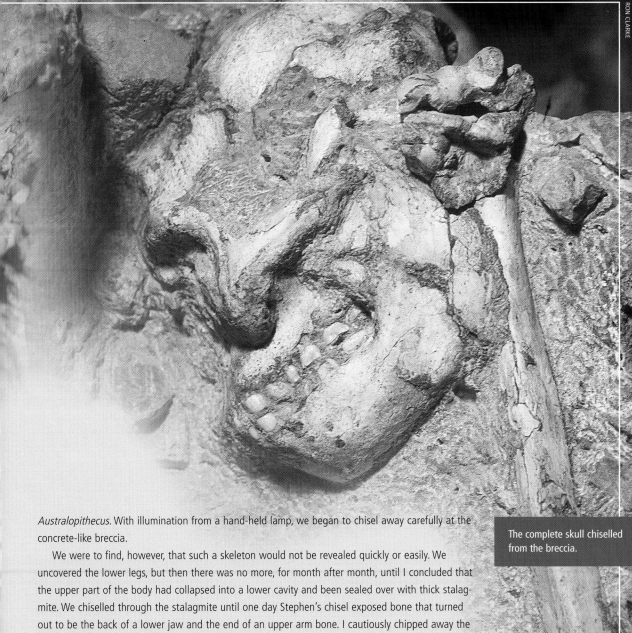

The complete skull chiselled from the breccia.

Australopithecus. With illumination from a hand-held lamp, we began to chisel away carefully at the concrete-like breccia.

We were to find, however, that such a skeleton would not be revealed quickly or easily. We uncovered the lower legs, but then there was no more, for month after month, until I concluded that the upper part of the body had collapsed into a lower cavity and been sealed over with thick stalagmite. We chiselled through the stalagmite until one day Stephen's chisel exposed bone that turned out to be the back of a lower jaw and the end of an upper arm bone. I cautiously chipped away the rock to reveal more of the bone and then the glint of tooth enamel sent a shiver down my spine. It was an upper molar which, together with the lower jaw, told us that we had located the skull. And what a magnificent skull it proved to be! It was complete, with only some minor cracking and displacement. Much later and further up slope, Nkwane's chisel chipped away a piece of breccia to reveal a perfectly preserved end of a radius and ulna, the forearm bones. Many weeks of chiselling away rocks large and small, as well as the careful removal of encasing breccia, revealed the whole left forearm and a perfectly preserved hand with fingers clenched.

Because the breccia is like concrete, full of small stones and large rocks, and because the bone is soft and we cannot be sure where any piece might occur beneath the encasing breccia, the work has to be slow and very, very cautious. Hence the uncovering of the skeleton has taken a long time.

anamensis – though it is clearly not the same thing, thereby emphasising the diversity of hominids that existed even at this very early stage of hominid evolution. Although it is known mostly from jaws and teeth, for the first time *Australopithecus anamensis* provides us with firm evidence for upright bipedalism in the form of a partial tibia that this time includes the upper end, the part that forms the lower half of the diagnostic knee joint. In this specimen the twin joint surfaces are elongated from front to back, concave, and approximately equal in area, rather as in ourselves.

It is also quite large, indicating an individual who in life may have weighed as much 50 kg or even more. A wrist bone indicates that this structure had been capable of powerful flexion so that, while the knee was that of a biped, the wrist seems to have been that of a climber. This combination of new features indicates bipedal locomotion on the ground, together with the retention of a spectrum of ancestral tree-climbing characteristics, and seems to have produced a successful overall adaptation that endured in its essentials for millions of years.

Why bipedality?

As we have just seen, the very early hominids seem to have been a fairly motley crew, united principally by a common tendency to upright locomotion. This supports the scenario whereby our family Hominidae was born, in the period about 8 to 6 MYA, as ancestral hominoid populations were obliged to cope with a new set of African environments induced by climatic and environmental change. Forced to spend more time foraging on the ground by the gradual trans-formation and the beginnings of fragmentation of their dense tropical forest habitat, formerly forest-dwelling hominoids found terrestrial locomotion becoming ever more of an issue for them.

As Elisabeth Vrba has repeatedly emphasised, initially as a result of analysing faunas from a

We still have far to go, but we have now also revealed some vertebrae, ribs, a badly crushed pelvis, the upper legs, and a badly crushed and displaced right arm and hand.

The age of this fossil based on palaeo-magnetic dating is about 3.3 million years. The foot, as Broom had hoped, does show the uniqueness of *Australopithecus*, for it is neither fully human nor fully ape, but a mixture of the two – with indications of humanity and upright walking, but also with anatomical features that show it could slightly abduct its big toe, which would have helped in tree-climbing. It shows the morphology of the kind of foot that could have made the 3.6-million-year-old Laetoli footprints in Tanzania, which have been attributed to *Australopithecus afarensis*.

But it is the complete hand which is most revealing about our ancestry. It does not have the long palm and long fingers of the modern ape. Instead its hand is like that of a modern human in proportions, but much more muscular: it has a short palm and long thumb with relatively short fingers. Such a hand with a long and very muscular opposable thumb had apparently evolved in our ancestors for the purpose of firmly grasping branches during tree-climbing. This, together with the almost equal arm and leg lengths and the slightly opposable big toe, is consistent with a human ancestor that climbed cautiously in trees.

The modern apes have long arms and long hands and fingers with short thumbs. This anatomy developed so that they could suspend themselves beneath branches and move by arm-swinging from branch to branch. When they had occasion to walk on the ground, they used the long arms as supports and walked on their knuckles. Our ances-tors did not go through such a knuckle-walking stage, but instead retained a primitive hand that was specialised only in its opposable thumb for branch-grasping. It was this long opposable thumb

and relatively short palm and fingers that provided the necessary manual ability for tool-use and tool-making. It is the combination of this hand and the large complex brain that has enabled humans to develop into the only advanced cultural animal on earth.

The complete left hand of the skeleton.

Alun Hughes, who was field director of PV Tobias's Sterkfontein excavation for 25 years, used to tell me of a recurrent dream he had of his breaking into a cavern and finding a complete skeleton lying there. Sadly, for some reason he didn't see the 1980 foot bone pointers to that skeleton. Happily though, the complete skeleton of Broom's prophecy and Alun's dream has now become a reality. It lies on its back on a slope with its left arm extended above it head, its right arm by its side, and its legs crossed. The completeness of the skeleton shows that it fell into the cave and was not a carnivore meal. The complete left hand indicates that the body was mummified in dry conditions before a change to constant wet climate formed the thick stalagmite that sealed it into its rocky tomb for 3.3 million years.

Eventually when it is removed entirely from the encasing rock and after it is reconstructed and studied, it will be possible to determine to which species of *Australopithecus* it belongs. At present, it does not seem like that of *A. africanus* but seems to have more similarity to *A. afarensis*. All we can say for now is what Broom probably thought in 1925 – 'time will tell.'

variety of South African hominid fossil sites, the evolutionary histories of multiple mammal lineages have been deeply affected or even determined by environmental changes that were entirely external to them and that occurred entirely without regard to the adaptations they happened to possess. Indeed, when environmental changes are sufficiently acute, whole faunas – and not just individual species – tend to come and go quite abruptly in the fossil record. And it seems pretty certain that the earliest hominids and their successors were not immune to such processes.

Terrestrial locomotion by former forest dwellers is one thing; if you're forced to the ground then you have to get around somehow. But why exactly the process I have just described should have resulted in a population (or populations) of hominoid upright bipeds is quite another question, one that has been very energetically debated. Many different advantages of this very unusual form of locomotion, which might have led to its adoption, have been suggested at one time or another. Among them are:

- the freeing of the hands for purposes other than locomotion or foraging, such as for carrying objects
- improved economy of locomotion; greater efficiency of movement
- improved ability to scan an open horizon for predators
- social factors, among them phallic displays by males, directed at females
- reduced absorption and better dissipation of solar heat, important in cooling the body and particularly the heat-sensitive brain, in open tropical environments.

Well, it is easy to make up a story about all these possible factors, and doubtless each of them has its importance. However, it is clear that the main consideration is that, once you have stood up, *all* of the advantages (and, for that matter, all the disadvantages) of upright posture are yours; the really important thing is to have stood up in

the first place. Essentially, you have to buy the entire package.

So why did the earliest hominids stand upright? No matter what its theoretical advantages might be, upright posture is not going to be your choice if you are not comfortable with it. The simplest explanation of hominid bipedality is that upright posture was already preferred by the hominoid ancestor in its arboreal phase, while still living in the trees. Indeed, some living hominoids engage in extensive arboreal foraging in erect postures; and in Uganda there is a population of chimpanzees, living in a woodland setting where trees are pretty low and scattered, that spend a lot of time foraging in low branches while standing upright on the ground.

But while they can move bipedally if it is necessary or convenient, chimpanzees are basically quadrupeds when they are moving around on the ground; so much so that they have evolved a special form of terrestrial locomotion known as 'knuckle-walking' in which the long, grasping hands are folded over so that weight is borne on the outside of the knuckles. The centre of balance of the body is thus thrown forward, in classic quadrupedal style. In contrast, if the ancestral hominid was already most comfortable moving around more or less upright when in the trees, then a bipedal stance would have been the natural one to take when on the ground, and the transition to upright locomotion on the ground would not have been a radical one requiring special explanations of the kind I listed earlier.

The australopiths

The quite well-known early hominids classically known as the 'australopiths' (for the genus *Australopithecus* which was initially described from the South African site of Taung) form a very diverse group. But all had in common that they were upright bipeds, at least when they were on the ground. The australopiths are known from several African species – not all of them yet described, as in the case of Stw 573 – that date from the period about 4 to 1.5 MYA.

Evidently this period was one of busy exploration by our precursors of the apparently many ways there were to get by as a hominid in a period of accelerating climatic change, during which the African forests steadily yielded to more open woodland formations and ultimately in some areas to open savannah. Australopith remains have been found in sites that indicate environments ranging from closed liana-entangled forests to relatively treeless shrubby grasslands, and most of these creatures probably lived in a varied mosaic of settings, exploiting gallery forests along rivers as well as woodlands and, sometimes at least, the more open spaces in between.

Sculpted replica of the skull of *Australopithecus afarensis*.

The best-known species of australopith is *Australopithecus afarensis*, which serves as a pretty good general exemplar of this kind of hominid despite the diversity of species and genera that its group encompasses. The most familiar representative of *Australopithecus afarensis* is undoubtedly the partial skeleton from Hadar, in Ethiopia, popularly known as 'Lucy'. This remarkable find (even incomplete skeletons are vanishingly rare in the hominid record) consists of the fragmentary remains of

The contact between the foot and left lower leg bone found in 1997 by Stephen Motsumi and Nkwane Molefe.

a tiny individual, probably female, who lived about 3.2 MYA, weighed under 30 kg, and stood not much over three and a half feet tall. There seems to have been considerable difference in size between the sexes in *Australopithecus afarensis*, and some males at least may have weighed 45 kg or more, though none of them would have stood more than about four and a half feet tall.

Although these creatures were without doubt upright bipeds, the bodies of Lucy and her kind were not miniature versions of our own. The arms were relatively long and the legs relatively short, both compared to each other and to the trunk. The hands and feet were long, and their bones were a little curved and well suited for powerful grasping. Indeed, the skeleton was full of features, retained from an arboreal ancestry, that would have been useful in climbing – narrow shoulders, for example, permitted easier coordination of the arms above the head for suspensory purposes. But the pelvis and knee joint were distinctly those of upright bipeds.

The knee joint of *Australopithecus afarensis* shows a distinct 'carrying angle', which is a reliable tip-off to upright bipedal locomotion. This is because if you prefer four-legged terrestrial locomotion, as chimpanzees do, your arms and legs are going to function more or less like movable table legs, one at each corner of the body, with the feet widely separated from each other. So when a chimpanzee stands on two legs and walks, his widely separated feet will describe a forward arc as one leg pivots around the other. His centre of gravity will shift from side to side, exhaustingly, as he moves forward.

In contrast, in a human being the legs, instead of descending vertically from each hip, converge at an angle towards the knees. The lower leg then descends vertically to the ground, the feet together. Thus when we walk we swing our

feet forward in a straight line, which is exactly followed by the centre of gravity. This is made possible by the angle formed at the knee between the upper and lower segments of the leg, and of course this produces a highly recognisable knee shape that is clearly visible in *Australopithecus afarensis*.

Similarly, Lucy and her kind had a bowl-like pelvis well adapted for supporting the viscera, which in upright animals lie above the pelvic girdle. In apes the iliac blades of the pelvis are long and vertical, whereas in Lucy they are wide and flaring, supporting a musculature well

The footprints of *Australopithecus africanus* embedded in the soft, wet volcanic ash at Laetoli, Tanzania, 3.6 million years ago.   RON CLARKE

adapted for stabilising the pelvis and legs during bipedal locomotion.

Indeed, in Lucy the pelvis flared sideways substantially more than ours does, although the significance of this flare is actively debated, since it is distinctly un-apelike. However, it may be that among all hominids it is actually *Homo sapiens* that is unusual in having a fairly narrow pelvis, and that what we see in Lucy is actually the more common hominid condition, even if possibly displayed in a rather exaggerated fashion.

Normally, when an organism is known only from fossils, one has to infer its behaviours from the form of its preserved anatomical structures. But an amazing direct confirmation that these early australopiths walked upright on the ground comes from the Tanzanian site of Laetoli, where during the 1970s fossilised footprint trails were found of creatures who were without doubt upright bipeds. About 3.5 MYA, a nearby volcano puffed out clouds of volcanic ash which settled over the landscape. After one such event it rained, and the newly fallen ash was transformed into the consistency of wet cement. Shortly thereafter, a whole variety of mammals and birds, including a pair of australopiths, walked across this muddy scene, leaving footprints behind them that were then baked hard by the sun. Later ashfalls buried and preserved the footprints, which were eventually exposed again by erosion and spotted by a palaeontologist who had flung himself to the ground to avoid a ball of elephant dung hurled at him by a colleague.

There has been considerable debate over what exactly the australopith footprints of Laetoli tell us about the locomotion and the form of the feet of the hominids who made the trails. The long, unwavering tracks make it clear that the hominids were walking bipedally over the rather unusually open landscape of ancient Laetoli; but although some scholars have been impressed by the modern aspects of the scene, others have pointed to details of the footprints themselves that may indicate a relatively primitive foot form, perhaps something resembling Little Foot, whose ankle

was relatively modern but which may have had a rather divergent great toe.

The greatest variety of australopith fossils is known in South Africa, from a series of sites grouped principally in the Sterkfontein Valley, in Gauteng. Historically, these South African localities have played a pivotal role in our understanding of very ancient hominids; and it was from Taung, in North-West Province, that Raymond Dart, Professor of Anatomy at the University of the Witwatersrand Medical School, described the very first australopith fossil in 1925.

This was the small-brained skull of a juvenile, to which Dart gave the name of *Australopithecus africanus* ('southern ape of Africa'), and which he described as lying intermediate between apes and humans. On the basis of the shape of the brain, preserved as a natural endocast, Dart hazarded that, despite the small size of this structure, his creature 'had laid down the foundations of that discriminative knowledge of the appearance, feeling and sounds of things that was a necessary milestone in the acquisition of articulate speech'; and he pointed to the forward position of the foramen magnum as evidence that it had walked upright.

Dart was magnificently ahead of his time but, alas, his interpretations fell on deaf ears. British palaeoanthropologists, who at that time dominated their science in the English-speaking world, remained largely under the sway of the

Raymond Dart holding the skull of the Taung Child.

Ron Clarke excavating the Laetoli footprints.

large-brained Piltdown fossil (then believed very ancient, but later shown to be a fraudulent combination of a partial modern human cranium with a partial orang-utan jaw). In Britain in 1925, received wisdom could simply not admit that a tiny-brained fossil could represent an early member of the human lineage. Moreover, Dart's skull was that of a juvenile, with somewhat apelike proportions; and juvenile apes and humans anyway resemble each other more closely than adults do, largely because the large ape face remains underdeveloped early on in life.

Confirmation of the hominid status of *Australopithecus africanus* thus had to await further South African discoveries. These started coming in 1936, when Robert Broom began his extraordinary series of australopith finds at Sterkfontein and later on at Kromdraai and Swartkrans. In 1938 the influential American palaeontologist WK Gregory travelled to South Africa to see Broom's new material and became convinced by Broom's claims that these fossils, like the Taung baby, were

The fossil footprints of Laetoli

YVETTE DELOISON

YVETTE DELOISON

Preserved ancient footprints have the great advantage of providing information on soft tissues and stride lengths of hominids, which the study of bones alone cannot do. Up to now, the oldest known footprints are those discovered by Mary Leakey in 1978 at Laetoli in Tanzania. The footprints were made by hominids 3.6 million years ago as they walked over volcanic ash, which was probably wet and therefore preserved the shape of the feet.

Ron Clarke allowed me to study the casts of ten footprints that he made when he excavated the originals with Mary Leakey. These ten footprints are divided into two tracks, labelled G/1 and G/2. The footprints of G/1 are smaller than those of G/2. The photos above show three successive footprints of track G/1. They are much more detailed than the nearby larger ones of G/2. These three footprints are a series, of the right, left and right foot again, representing a double step of 46 cm multiplied by two, for a total of 92 cm. The preservation of these footprints of G/1 differs from that of G/2, which suggests that the two tracks were not made at the same moment, but at different times by people following the same path.

The position of the three small footprints differs from that of the big ones. They are respectively at angles from 20 to 30 degrees from the displacement line. The prints are of the same individual. The foremost footprint makes a larger angle, indicating a change in the subject's direction on the

The excavations at Sterkfontein. RON CLARKE

indeed very primitive hominids, truly inter-mediate between ancient apes and modern humans.

But the Second World War intervened, and it was not until after the war was over that the British establishment, largely under the influence of the distinguished anatomist Sir Wilfrid Le Gros Clark, finally capitulated to the South African fossils. Dart himself returned to the fray after the war, when James Kitching found the first human fossil at the Makapansgat limeworks in the Northern Province, and under Dart's direction Alun Hughes was placed in charge of excavations there that ultimately produced a trove of australo-piths. More recent discoveries at sites such as Drimolen, Gladysvale and Jacovec Cavern indicate that there is plenty of potential for future discoveries of this kind.

By now, many hundreds of australopith fossils are known from half a dozen sites. These sites are all rather unusual in their origin. Most fossils are found in sedimentary rocks that cover the landscape and that occur in relatively easily discernible sequences. In contrast, the South African australopith sites consist of solution cavities formed by water flowing through ancient limestones. At various different periods in the past these cavities became filled with bone-containing rubble that was subsequently

displacement line. This angle of displacement is far greater than in anatomically modern humans and so the fossil traces almost certainly belong to another hominid species.

The shape of each of these footprints is intriguing. The outer (lateral) side is distinctly deeper on its entire length than the rest of the foot (medial side). This lateral pressure shows that the foot was displaced inwards towards the midline of the body – a feature characteristic of non-human primates. The outline of the back part shows a narrow heel; the sole is not flat as with humans, but concave and with a very deep point at the centre of the heel slightly displaced towards the inner side. The medial side of the footprint shows a distinct bulge in front of the heel that suggests a strongly developed abductor muscle of the big toe. The axis of the big toe slants towards the inside of the foot, from the longitudinal axis of the foot. There is a distinct space between the print of the big toe and that of the other toes. These latter toes make a single print whose foreside is oblique and rounded. In front of each footprint there is a trian-gular mark with the summit pointing forward.

These features of the shape of the three foot-prints show – particularly in the transfer of weight during walking – that, although bipedal, they were made by non-human feet. This observation is further supported by superimposing a single foot-print from Laetoli over one from a human and one from a chimpanzee. It is impossible to match it to the human footprint even if certain dimensions are adjusted, whereas it fits over the chimpanzee's print easily, having the same shape and size.

The displacement of the foot towards the midline of the body, indicated by the deep lateral impression, shows a stronger pressure on the outer side. This position is associated with the opening of the big toe, and the strong development of the abductor muscle of this toe is shown by the internal bulge. As the footprints were made on a soft (and thus probably wet) surface, it seems that the hominid that left these prints used specific

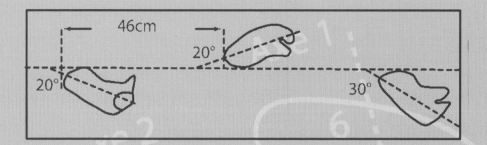

features to get a better grip on the yielding ground, suggesting that the hominid was prehensile.

The Laetoli footprints have the same non-human features as fossil foot bones discovered in Hadar, Ethiopia. Both the Laetoli prints and the Hadar fossil show the ability to spread the big toe substantially. The heel is not flat, as in human feet; we can deduce this from the hollow it makes, sinking into the ground. Importantly, the fossil footprints at Hadar were made by australopiths. This strongly suggests that the hominids that crossed the ashes at Laetoli were of the same genus. The toes, a least the four lateral ones, should have been long and curled up during the walk, but were in a peculiar position that produced the footprints as well as the trail of triangular shapes left on the ground in front of several other footprints at the same site. These marks, in front of but next to some footprints, may have been made by the unfolding of the lateral toes when the foot left the ground. The site of this track would originally have been a shallow stream – these footprints were conserved in the ashes because these were wet – and the hominids that walked there had to stand up on their hind legs as apes do when they go into water.

If the footprints at Laetoli were made by australopiths, they demonstrate that this particular hominid was capable of bipedal walking, but we do not know over what distance and for how long. Yet, their bipedalism was different from that of *Homo* and other primates, and appears to have been peculiar to them. The results from the bone anatomy of the australopithecine postcranial body, enriched with the analysis of the footprints of Laetoli, establish that these hominids were specialised for a locomotion more arboreal than bipedal, which would exclude them from the ancestral line of humankind.

ABOVE: Disposition of the three footprints, from left to right, G1/36, G1/35 and G1/34.
BELOW: Comparison of the outline of G1/34 with those of human (left) and chimpanzee (Pan) (middle) feet. The Laetoli and chimpanzee footprints are at the same scale.

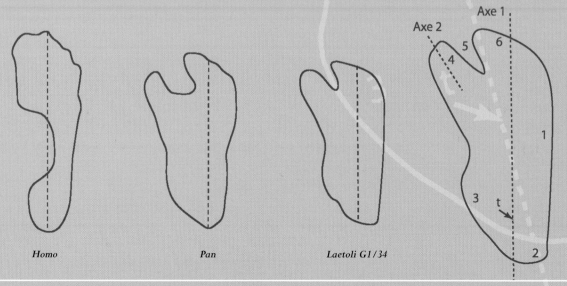

Homo   *Pan*   *Laetoli G1/34*

cemented together by redeposited lime. Most of the sites were discovered initially by miners who were after the pure lime and who discarded the rubble in dumps which thus became fossil sites in themselves.

Particularly because they have had complex histories of infilling, the sites have proved very difficult to date with any great precision, although several different new methods of chronometric dating are now being tried out. Historically, though, the approach to dating the australopith fossils from the various sites has principally been to compare the animal faunas with which they were found to faunas from other areas of Africa that can be directly dated. Since particular faunas are in general fairly characteristic of specific time periods, this is normally considered to be a fairly reliable though approximate process.

On the basis of such comparisons the South African australopith sites appear to date from as long ago as about 4 million years (Sterkfontein Member 2) to as recently as about 1.8 to 1.5 MYA (Swartkrans). The oldest fossils at Makapansgat may be around 3 million years old, while the bulk of those known from Sterkfontein, including Sts 5, the classic *Australopithecus africanus* cranium known as 'Mrs Ples', probably date from around 2.8 to 2.6 MYA. Taung itself remains vague in date, though a recent estimate has put it at 2.8 to 2.7 MYA.

As for the exact kinds of australopith involved in the South African story – how many species, how they are related – the plot is actively thickening. Early workers such as Broom and his colleague John Robinson discerned two groups among the fossils available to them. On the one hand lay the 'gracile', or lightly built, australopiths from Sterkfontein, Taung and Makapansgat; and on the other were the more massive and probably somewhat more recent 'robust' australopiths exemplified by *Paranthropus robustus* from Kromdraai and most copiously represented at Swartkrans by *Paranthropus crassidens*.

Today it is becoming clear that the picture is rather more complex than this simple division

The amazing Makapan

PHILIP BONNER AND
AMANDA ESTERHUYSEN

Makapan Valley, named after Mokopane, the chief of the Kekana people, was listed as a World Heritage Site in 2005 along with the Cradle of Humankind sites in Gauteng and the Taung skull site in North-West Province. All of these sites are renowned for their rich hominid-bearing fossil deposits which date to between 4 and 1 million years ago and which provide insight into the evolution and development of our early ancestors and their relatives (hominids). Makapan Valley, however, is exceptional in that the caves within the valley preserve a continuous record of hominid occupation from 4 million years ago to the present, and offer detailed information about climate and environmental change over this period.

The fossils from the lime works stimulated the early hypotheses about the activities and capabilities of our early australopithecine ancestors, while the Cave of Hearths — one of the most deeply stratified archaeological sites in the country — produced a near-complete stone tool sequence that plots a 300 000-year technological progression from Acheulean handaxes and cleavers to Middle Stone Age (MSA, from about 250 000 BP) points and blades and Later Stone Age (LSA, from about 20 000 BP) microlithic technology. This sequence also provides crucial information about the changes in cognition and behaviour that accompanied the emergence of our own species,

Homo sapiens, about 150 000 BP as it slowly developed a sophisticated hunter-gatherer social system. Other open sites and cave sites in the valley record the arrival of the first farmers in the area from about 1500 BP and provide evidence of a Middle and Late Iron Age transition and interaction with the colonial frontier.

The richness of the Makapan fossil, archaeological and historical record is the result of its location at a point of intersection, convergence and contact between distinct geologies, distinct ecologies, distinct botanies and distinct zoologies. The Makapan–Strydpoort highlands area – the quartzite escarpment and deeply eroded dolomitic uplands – form part of the 'Wolkberg hotspot'. This represents one of the world's most important areas of plant species that are native to a particular geographic region. The rich and varied vegetation covering Makapan Valley and the highlands range comprise a remarkable meeting of two distinct flora kingdoms, one a tropical flora of a northern origin, and the other a more temperate flora of more southern source. The Makapan faunal heritage is equally rich and diverse. It is the only place in South Africa that acts as host to all categories of primates as well as numerous other faunal species. An additional attraction to human habitation has been its strategic position along an ancient route of seasonal migration for hundreds of thousands of antelope through Makapanspoort.

The rich natural endowment of Makapan Valley has also placed it at the frontier of human interaction especially within the time frame of what is described as historical archaeology. Oral traditions extending back to the mid-seventeenth century plot the origins, migration and fission of dominant lineages (houses of chiefs) and record increasing intensity of interaction both among indigenous peoples and with trading centres along the east coast.

The valley was a site of repeated refuge from the conflicts arising from these linked processes of interaction and conflict, and constitutes a unique record of this opaque period of South African history. Many other archaeological sites are dotted around the entire region but the level of preservation is poor. The caves in the Makapan valley stand in stark contrast to this broader pattern. The highly alkaline deposits have allowed for the exceptional preservation of plant, animal and human material, in addition to a wide range of other artefacts, offering unique insights into the socio-economic and political life of this period.

In the 1850s the Cave of Gwasa (also known as Historic Cave or Makapansgat) became a refuge for the Kekana chiefdom from Voortrekker aggression. The land to the north and east of Mokopane suggests. It is true that some australopiths appear to have been more massively built than others, and especially that some had particularly large chewing teeth that may indicate that they had acquired a tendency to pulverise very tough vegetation. But the more closely you look at the fossils involved, the more blurred the gracile–robust distinction seems to become.

What's more, it is becoming evident that there was not a simple 'one site, one hominid' correspondence, as was often believed at earlier times. At Sterkfontein, for example, Ron Clarke suggested not long ago that at least two different hominids were present in the same member (Member 4); and more recent work indicates that the variety of australopiths at just this one site may be still greater. At Swartkrans, fossils allocated both to *Australopithecus* and to *Homo* have been reported throughout the deposits. If one thing can be confidently predicted, it is that the South African australopith sites will keep palaeoanthropologists busy for many years to come, and that the diversity of species found at them will probably in the end be truly astonishing.

Outside South Africa, australopith fossils later than *Australopithecus afarensis* (hence in the time frame from about 2.6 to 1.4 MYA) have mostly been allocated to the robust species *Paranthropus aethiopicus* and *Paranthropus boisei*. Of the latter species, the most famous representative is the 1.8-million-year-old type cranium, originally described as *Zinjanthropus boisei*, from Olduvai Gorge in Tanzania, while the most spectacular *Australopithecus aethiopicus* specimen is the 2.6-million-year-old 'Black Skull' from west Turkana, in northern Kenya. Another very early (3.5-million-year-old) *Australopithecus* species, *Australopithecus bahrelghazali*, was also named not long ago on the basis of a fragmentary jaw from Chad, in Central Africa; some believe that this specimen actually represents a western *Australopithecus afarensis*.

On the whole, the more gracile hominids from East Africa that date to the period following the invention of stone tools some 2.5 MYA have been

(formerly Potgietersrus) was at that time settled and owned by numerous African chiefdoms, kingdoms or states that jostled for dominance.

After the Voortrekker parties arrived in the Transvaal in the late 1830s they fanned out across different areas and split up into separate republics. As they thinned out, their power diminished. African chiefdoms notably in the Mokopane region challenged their authority and demands. The trekker communities in this area were mainly engaged in hunting and trading for ivory and animal skins.

These groups of 'trekker hunters' who spread through this area consequently depended on the assistance of the African communities among whom they moved to enable them to hunt and trade, or resorted to force to make them comply with trekker demands. Since the Voortrekkers were perennially short of labour, one of these demands was for African children, whom they would apprentice to work on their behalf and whom they sometimes traded from African chiefdoms or otherwise seized in raids or war. The balance of power seesawed between black and white groups in the

1840s and early 1850s, often precipitating conflict.

Conflict reached a peak in 1854 when wars broke out on all sides. One of these conflicts was between Chief Mokopane's Kekana and trekker parties led by the Potgieters. In retaliation for the alleged seizure of children, Mokopane's group massacred a party of trekkers at a place thereafter called Moorddrift (on the road leading south of Mokopane, a few hundred metres beyond the T-junction leading to the N1 road, where a monument now stands). Chief Mokopane and members of his chiefdom took refuge in the Cave of Gwasa. The subsequent siege of the cave, which lasted a month and ended in the death and surrender of its occupants and their dispersal among trekboer farms, has been accorded iconic status in Afrikaner public history, and became a central prop of the ideology of apartheid.

OPPOSITE: Entrance to the Cave of Gwasa.
ABOVE: The monument at Moorddrift.

An elaborate mythology was constructed that produced heroes – Paul Kruger, long-time President of the Republic, allegedly retrieved the body of Piet Potgieter after he had been shot dead by a Kekana marksman, a feat of bravery that is memorialised in a panel at the foot of the Kruger memorial statue in Church Square, Pretoria – and portrayed the trekboers as a chosen people. Africans in general were presented as treacherous and uncivilised, thereby producing a rationale and imperative for the separation of 'races'. Ironically (but conveniently) this obscured one of the central and enduring realities of South Africa's past, namely interaction and interdependence, in this case for hunting, trade and the provision of labour.

In the early twentieth century the large lime deposits in the limeworks attracted the attention of lime workers. At this time lime was a highly marketable product because it was required for extracting gold from ore. Thousands of tons of lime were therefore blasted out of the limeworks cave (and also at Sterkfontein and Taung) between 1907 and 1937. In the course of extracting the lime, fossil-bearing breccia (cave infill) was exposed at each of these sites. The fossils were recognised by amateur fossil collectors, local teachers in particular, but their full significance was not realised until 1936.

The mining opened the way for Makapan Valley to be situated at the frontier of palaeontological, archaeological and palaeoenvironmental research. It was here that Raymond Dart developed the first ideas about the nature of early hominid behaviour. From this point the valley generated many of the central hypotheses directing and guiding subsequent palaeontological and archaeological research through the work of Phillip Tobias, Bob Brain and Revil Mason. In a sense, it has occupied a central place in the history of ideas and continues to do so.

The continuity of hominid occupation, which is Makapan Valley's chief claim to fame, has recently been complemented by the most complete record of rainfall and temperature patterns to have been uncovered in the southern hemisphere. It takes the form of the palaeoenvironmental and palaeo-climatic data captured within cave features such as stalactites and stalagmites (also called speleothems) which are created when slightly acidic water seeps through dolomite and frees and then deposits calcium carbonate inside the cave. This documents the tail end of the Makapan sequence, providing a detailed and continuous picture of climate change in southern Africa over at least the last 10 000 years. The human and other histories of this period are now being rethought in the light of these data.

allocated to the genus *Homo*. One exception is the genus *Kenyanthropus*. This new genus was established not long ago on the basis of a 3.5-million-year-old skull from northern Kenya, but it has been extended to include the famous 1.9-million-year-old ER 1470 cranium discovered in the late 1960s to the east of Lake Turkana by Richard Leakey and initially attributed to an early form of *Homo*. Clearly, reconciling the southern and East African early hominid records remains a major task for the palaeoanthropological future.

Australopith way of life

Crude stone tools are known from several of the australopith sites, but they all derive from the rather late period (about 2.0 to 1.5 MYA) that follows both the apparent disappearance of *Australopithecus* species (although *Paranthropus* was still around) and the putative appearance of *Homo*. What is more, they cannot in any event be positively associated with any particular type of hominid. But at Swartkrans Bob Brain, a former director of the Transvaal Museum and the site's long-time excavator, has identified fragments of horn cores and animal bone from the same time period that appear to have been worn, in a way that suggests they were used for digging tubers out of the ground. They certainly show a polish identical to that acquired when experimental archaeologists use similar materials for the same task today.

Since the vast majority of the hominid fossils at Swartkrans belong to *Paranthropus*, the statistical likelihood must be that it was this species that wielded these implements. The tools themselves were probably not deliberately shaped for use in digging; suitable fragments were selected instead. But the fact that they are worn in the way they are suggests that these late *Paranthropus* used bone tools, even if they did not make them. Certainly, digging in the rough earth for tubers is consistent with the large flat chewing teeth typical of *Paranthropus*, for these strongly suggest that a tough, gritty diet was being processed.

Randall Susman of the State University of New York at Stony Brook even believes that hand bones from Swartkrans, which he assigns to *Paranthropus,* indicate sufficient manual dexterity for hominids of this kind to have made the scattering of stone tools present at this site. Interestingly, what is possibly the earliest evidence for the deliberate control of fire also comes from this site, although this innovation certainly did not become standard among hominids until very much later.

Still, this juncture is nonetheless relatively late in time, and there is no compelling reason to believe that, at least for the vast majority of their tenure on earth, any

Quartz may have been chosen as a raw material for stone tools because of unusual natural properties. When pressed together and rubbed, quartz produces light. The effect is called triboluminesence. DAVID WHITLEY australopith species made stone tools, which as we will see later first turn up in East Africa at about 2.5 MYA (although it may be significant that some of the earliest stone tools known, from Ethiopia, were found in sediments that also yielded the remains of a species known as *Australopithecus garhi*).

Without an artificial tool kit the small-bodied and relatively slow hominids would have been fairly defenceless, and it was probably because of this that these creatures appear to have been more or less confined to forest and woodland settings. Indeed, the early hominids not only remained anatomically well equipped for moving around in the trees but in all probability were still heavily dependent upon them for both shelter and security.

Some australopith sites are actually indicative of pretty densely forested conditions: Sterkfontein Member 4, for example, has yielded the remains of lianas that could only have grown in full-blown forest. And while more typical sites indicate at least somewhat more open conditions, the early hominids would certainly have been relatively vulnerable moving around in woodlands and grassy areas that teemed with large predators. Trees or cliff faces were probably thus particularly important as sleeping sites; and this alone would have tied the australopiths to places with a reasonable supply of trees, however much they may have ventured during the day into the riskier, more open habitats.

Although in the beginning they were almost certainly largely fruit eaters, some australopiths seem to have gravitated, as we have just seen, towards a diet that consisted increasingly of plant resources, such as tubers, which were found on the ground. At the same time, though, stable-isotope studies of fossils from South African sites seem to indicate that most australopiths were dietary generalists: they fed opportunistically on a whole variety of foods, including some meat.

How this meat would have been acquired is problematic; in some places today's chimpanzees hunt small mammals – colobus monkeys, baby bushpigs, and so forth – and devour their meat voraciously (with a complex system of sharing that reflects the subtle system of alliances within the social group); but in energetic terms animal protein is not a significant part of their food intake. And chimpanzees do not scavenge dead carcasses, which is the route by which it is widely thought that early hominids incorporated meat into their diet.

Indeed, it has been suggested that some australopiths may have capitalised on their climbing skills by specialising in stealing the remains of leopard prey – leopards still routinely stash carcasses in trees to protect them from other predators and ground-bound scavengers while they are away patrolling their territories. A dangerous occupation to be sure: Bob Brain has shown that two holes in the skull of an adolescent *Paranthropus* from Swartkrans match perfectly with the twin dagger-like canines of a leopard, and were probably acquired as the leopard was dragging the australopith carcass away for storage.

The typical australopith body form carries the unmistakable anatomical stamp of postural uprightness, a mode of carriage quite unlike what we see in the quadrupedal apes. And, as I have

Reconstruction of leopard attacking an australopithecine, Transvaal Museum.   BRUCE RUBIDGE

long canines. And this was something that was certainly important for australopiths such as *Paranthropus*, in which it is notable that absolute reduction in canine size was taken to an extreme.

In any event, at this stage in hominid evolution there is no reason to suspect that there was any significant difference between hominids and apes in the domain of cognitive function. And it is perhaps above all because of this that many palaeoanthropologists have taken to describing the australopiths as 'bipedal apes'. Not until the invention of stone tools does the current record give us any reason to suspect a significant advancement in cognitive function among the hominids compared to today's great apes, even though their behaviours were clearly different. Which makes it, perhaps, all the more remarkable that the first stone tools were probably made by a hominid of rather archaic build, as we will shortly see.

It is tempting to view the typical australopith body structure – and even way of life – as a sort of temporary halfway house on the way to modern body form. This, however, would be a mistake. The basic australopith formula was actually a very stable and successful one, and even though evidence of australopith skeletons following the time of Lucy is rather sparse, it seems as if the essential australopith body plan remained unaltered in its essentials over several million years, even as many new australopith species came and went, and as African climates and landscapes fluctuated.

Nonetheless, as the constant arrival and departure of actors in the hominid evolutionary play indicates, the long period of australopith tenure was clearly a busy one of ongoing evolutionary experimentation as these hominids energetically explored the ecological opportunities available to them. And although we cannot at present nail down a specific relationship between any known australopith species and the earliest members of our own genus *Homo*, it was evidently out of one such experiment that our genus eventually emerged.

already noted, we have direct evidence of upright bipedalism in the famous hominid trackways from Laetoli that date from about 3.5 MYA.

But for all the innovations that they displayed in the structure of parts at least of their body skeleton, above the neck these ancient creatures remained very apelike indeed. Just as in modern apes (with brains that are larger relative to body size than those of other primates, but are barely a third the size of ours), the australopith brain was housed in a small braincase which was hafted behind a large and forwardly projecting face that contained generally big teeth. One difference, though, is that these early hominids resembled later ones in having markedly reduced both the absolute size of the canine teeth and the size difference between these teeth in males and females.

It has been suggested that these differences may reflect changes in certain aspects of social organisation, but it is important to note that canine reduction has an important mechanical consequence: it allows the jaw to move from side to side in a grinding pattern during chewing rather than being guided up and down by the

Human language
and human origins

CHRISTOPHER EHRET

Human beings have a unique talent not found in any other creature, the capacity for fully syntactical language. Many animals, of course, have cries that warn of danger, for example, or attract mates, or convey readiness to attack. But only humans have the inborn ability to present and interpret their knowledge and experience in an infinite variety of meaningful sentences. This is what we mean by 'fully syntactical' language.

This capacity is what makes us fully human. It allows us to formulate abstract categories for our knowledge and experience so that we can use and build more effectively on what we know. With fully syntactical language we can envisage, talk about, and plan for things that have not yet happened. We can organise our concrete experience of kinship into abstract systems of relationship and then metaphorically extend relationship to wider groups of people, and in so doing build reciprocal relations among individuals and create communities. And because we can arrange our words in an infinite variety of sentences we can tell stories, construct ideas, and articulate beliefs to give meaning to why we are here.

But when did our ancestors first gain this capacity? Africa is the home continent of all human beings, and as recently as 60 000 BP the ancestors of every one of us still lived in Africa. Scholars agree that our forebears had fully syntactical language in Africa by then, but they differ on how long before. During the first age of language expansion, our earliest fully human ancestors spread out across Africa, bringing about the extinction of all those anatomically modern human populations elsewhere in the continent who had not developed the capacity for full language. We suspect that these first expansions of language-bearing humans emanated out of the eastern side of Africa, possibly during the 10 000–15 000 years preceding 60 000 BP.

Some scholars conclude that language was present between 200 000 and 170 000 years ago, because significant advances in toolmaking took place then among our distant ancestors in Africa. In addition, the skeletal evidence from a number of sites in eastern Africa dating between 200 000 and 120 000 BP reveals the presence of anatomically modern humans, whose skull shapes in particular were modern in appearance.

But the more probable period in which the human capacity for full syntactical language finally evolved lay between 90 000 and 60 000 BP. This was similarly a period of new advances in human culture, indicative of the further evolution of human mental capabilities. However, the most important indication that our common ancestors of that time were finally beginning to develop the capacity for full language rests on another kind of evidence. Possession of syntactical language gives us the essential grammatical structures for thinking abstractly and metaphorically. The first tangible evidence we have of this uniquely human kind of thinking comes from symbolic markings etched into artefacts in human sites dating to around 77 000 BP in southern Africa.

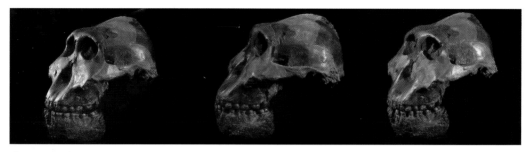

Three views of *Autralopithecus boisei*.

The first toolmakers

Ever since the discovery of the original Neanderthal fossil in 1856, it has been known that our species *Homo sapiens* is but one species of the human genus whose origins go quite far back in time. Just how far is debated, largely because, despite all the reams of scholarship devoted to the subject, we really do not yet have a consistent and agreed-upon set of criteria for assessing membership in *Homo*. Still, in the African fossil record between about 2.5 and 1.8 MYA, there is by now a quite wide variety of very fragmentary fossil contenders for the title 'the earliest *Homo*'. None of these fossil forms are very well known, however, and together they make a pretty motley assortment.

Indeed, it is hard to see why most of them have been distinguished from the australopiths, if it is not because the old idea of Man the Toolmaker is still so deeply entrenched. Long before it was known that there were fossil hominids of any kind, antiquarians in Europe were already finding reasons to infer an extremely remote human past in the existence of stone tools which were clearly ancient but whose precise origins were entirely unknown. In a very real sense, behavioural palaeoanthropology developed out of this branch of antiquarianism, in which being human was associated from the very beginning with making tools, much as in early days biologists considered having a large brain to be a crucial component of humanity.

One profound believer in the notion of Man the Toolmaker was Louis Leakey, who was effectively the founder of palaeoanthropology in East Africa. For years he and his wife Mary scoured Tanganyika's Olduvai Gorge for the remains of the makers of the crude stone tools found eroding from the canyon's walls, and he was naturally just a little bit disappointed when, in 1959, the spectacular cranium he called *Zinjanthropus* was found there; for this massive fossil, as magnificent as it might be, was clearly much more closely comparable to the *Paranthropus* fossils from South Africa than to anything that could be described as *Homo*.

Imagine Leakey's relief, then, when a couple of years later he found the jaw and some other bones of a much more lightly built hominid who made a far better candidate for an early representative of *Homo* – and which, he believed, showed indications in a couple of skull vault fragments that its brain was a little bit larger than that of the South African australopiths.

With two colleagues, who included Phillip Tobias (by then Dart's successor as Professor of Anatomy at Wits), Leakey in 1964 described his rather slender handful of new fossils from Olduvai as representatives of a new species of *Homo*: *Homo habilis*, which translates as 'handyman'. This new species, Leakey felt, was the true maker of the crude stone tools found at the bottom of the gorge. And it was a toolmaker of incredible antiquity, for in the very first application of the newly developed technique of

There is another even more telling reason for thinking that fully syntactical language did not emerge before this time. During the period of warmer climate that began after 110 000 BP, some anatomically modern humans were able to spread a short distance out of Africa, into the warmer parts of the Middle East. There they successfully displaced the previous Neanderthal inhabitants of the region, who were physically adapted for living in cold environments. But when a colder climate returned a bit before 70 000 BP, the Neanderthals returned to the Middle East too, while the anatomically modern humans disappeared from the region. Clearly, the early people of modern appearance who lived in the Middle East after 110 000 BP had not yet developed the capacity for coping with the re-advance of the Neanderthals or with the arrival of a colder climate.

In striking contrast, by 60 000 to 50 000 BP, when fully modern human beings first began to spread out of Africa into other parts of the world, language had become the essential marker of humanness. The capacity for syntactical language made all the difference. It allowed our ancestors to think abstractly and hence to plan ahead and to envisage and build a sense of community with people who were not close kin. Because our direct ancestors had these capabilities, conferred by language, they were able to out-compete and gradually drive into extinction all other closely related species, among them the Neanderthals of Europe and the Middle East, and they were able to settle in almost all the world except for Antarctica. As they spread into new areas, they carried their languages with them.

Some scholars have proposed that the language families of the world can be divided into two primary branches. In their view, one branch consists today of just a single remaining language family, Khoesan, found in eastern and southern Africa. Better-known Khoesan languages include Nama, spoken today in Namibia, the extinct /Xam language of the interior Cape regions of South Africa, and Sandawe, spoken in central Tanzania. All the rest of the language families of the world, according to this view, belong to the second primary branch. If this idea is correct, the Khoesan languages descend from the languages of those early true humans who remained behind in eastern and southern Africa during the first era of the spread of people with language across the rest of Africa.

After 60 000 BP human populations first began to spill out of Africa into other continents. Some scholars have suggested that two concurrent expansions of language may have accompanied these population movements. They conjecture that one group of language families, related to the Niger-Kordofanian and Nilo-Saharan families of Africa, may have been spread by people who followed the southern coasts of Asia eastward as far as Papua New Guinea and Australia. The second group of families, according to this conjecture, would have spoken languages ancestral to the Afrasian family (also called Afroasiatic) of Africa as well as to most of the language families of Asia, Europe and the Americas.

For now, these proposed episodes of early language expansion remain intriguing theories for future scholarly investigation. What is already certain, however, is that the evolution of the capacity for full syntactical language took place wholly in Africa before 60 000 BP, and that the spread outward from Africa of true humans, with language, began only after that time. That defining development in the evolution of our ancestors while they were still in Africa gives us our scope for commonality as human beings today, wherever we are.

Dr Louis Leakey around 1970.   PHILLIP V. TOBIAS

potassium-argon dating (which dated volcanic rocks associated with the fossils) to the human fossil record, both *Homo habilis* and *Zinjanthropus* had turned out to be around 1.8 million years old – far older than anyone had dreamed, and three times the age that Leakey had himself guessed when *Zinjanthropus* first showed up.

There was not an awful lot about the bones themselves that Leakey and his colleagues had to hand in 1964 to suggest that they should be allocated to a member of the genus *Homo*, and many commentators at the time pointed to resemblances with some of the more gracile South African australopiths. But the name stuck, and *Homo habilis* has become a convenient catchall name for many of the hominid fossils associated with the earliest stone tools. Such tools, generally called Oldowan for the place where they were first recognised, are now known from several sites in East Africa as old as 2.5 million years or so; and it is the appearance of such implements that marks the beginning of the archaeological record, the archive of ancient human behaviour.

Interestingly, at 2.5 MYA there is absolutely no evidence, at least so far, that there were any hominids around who did not still fit the definition of bipedal apes. All, as far as we know, still displayed small brains housed behind large faces, and short stature and archaic body proportions. The first stone-toolmakers thus physically resembled non-stone-toolmaking hominids of the kind that had already been around for millions of years, and this introduces a theme that we find consistently repeated throughout the palaeoanthropological record: the appearance of new kinds of technology or behaviour never seems to be associated with a new kind of hominid.

In other words, we cannot explain the arrival of new ways of doing things simply by the arrival of a new kind of hominid. At first thought this may seem a little counterintuitive or at least disappointing; but in fact it makes good sense. Any technological innovation has to be made by an individual; and that individual obviously cannot differ too much from his or her own parents. Quite simply, innovations have to be made *within* species because there is simply no other place where they can be introduced.

The earliest manufactured implements are not very impressive in themselves. They consist principally of tiny stone flakes only an inch or two long, chipped from small river cobbles which might also have been used as pounding tools once a few flakes had been removed. A simple flake doesn't sound like much, but the razor-sharp edges that such flakes bear when they are chipped from the right kind of stone must have revolutionised the lives of those who made them: as cutting tools, they are remarkably efficient – experimental archaeologists have managed to butcher entire elephants using nothing else – and they would, for example, have allowed the early stone-toolmakers to detach limbs or other body parts from carcasses they found. A meaty carcass is highly attractive to predators and scavengers of all kinds, and thus is a dangerous place for a hominid to be; and the ability to cut away hunks of an animal would have allowed such food to be carried away to a safer place for consumption.

Perhaps most interestingly of all, for all their simplicity the early stone tools also constitute the first unequivocal evidence we have for a cognitive leap forward among their hominid makers. There are several lines of evidence for this. For one thing, extensive experimentation on the matter has shown that no living ape has been able, even with extensive coaching, to comprehend that to detach a sharp flake, the original stone core has to be struck at exactly the right angle. Apes can get the idea of fracturing stones, but the niceties of flake production elude them.

What's more, it is clear that the toolmakers anticipated needing the implements they were going to manufacture, for they carried suitable kinds of stone around with them for long distances before making the tools themselves as required (often in places where no appropriate kinds of rock were available). We know this because the earliest archaeological sites are usually places on the ancient landscape where animals were butchered (as witnessed by the cut-marks left on their bones by the cutting implements); and at some of these sites archaeologists have been able to piece together entire rock cores from the flakes and other detritus of flake production found right among the butchered bones.

At one time it was widely believed that sites of this kind represented home bases to which hominids repeatedly returned (a pattern characteristic of later hominids), but nowadays this view is out of favour; as is, for example, the interpretation of a ring of stones found at Olduvai as a windbreak. It is becoming clear that early hominids had their own ways of doing things, and that trying to interpret them as junior-league versions of ourselves is not the most useful approach to understanding their lifestyles and ways of relating to the world around them.

Many studies have been made of landscape and resource use by early hominids, but the task of figuring out exactly how these early toolmakers exploited the environment around them is a difficult one. There are many reasons for this, of which one of the most important is that early archaeological sites tend to be found where circumstances were favourable for preservation rather than where the hominids were most commonly found.

Dense scatter of Early Stone Age tools (Acheulean Industry) from East Africa.

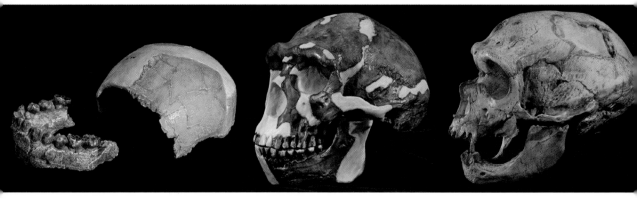

From left to right: *Homo habilis, Homo erectus* and *Homo neanderthalensis*   DAVID PEARCE

Most likely, the early toolmakers moved consistently throughout rather large territories in an opportunistic way. Some of the animals they butchered were large ones, such as hippopotamuses, which these diminutive creatures presumably found dead rather than hunting them; and it is generally believed that animal protein at this stage in hominid evolution was most commonly scavenged, although smaller mammals may have been hunted as well as lizards, tortoises and other small vertebrates, and presumably some invertebrates as well. Plant resources, possibly even including such atypical foods (for a hominoid) as sedges and grasses, presumably constituted the bulk of the diet. What we can be pretty confident of, however, is that the early hominids were pretty adaptable generalists, able to make a living in a fairly wide variety of environments.

The earliest hominids of modern body form

At about 2 MYA the fossil record of 'early *Homo*' picks up a bit, mainly because of discoveries made in the 1960s through the 1980s in the areas both to the east and west of Lake Turkana, in northern Kenya. As already mentioned, the renowned ER 1470 skull from east Turkana, once hailed as the classic cranium of *Homo habilis*, has recently been moved to the genus *Kenyanthropus*,

whose exact position in the hominid family tree is still rather obscure. Still often assigned to *Homo habilis* is the smallish-brained ER 1813 cranium, also about 1.9 million years old and from east Turkana. Some other east Turkana crania in the 1.9- to 1.6-million-year time range have, however, been described as 'African *Homo erectus*' or alternatively as *Homo ergaster*, a name originally given to a well-preserved lower jaw from the same region.

Homo erectus is a species described originally in the early 1890s from a site in Java, Indonesia. For historical reasons stemming from the fact that it was by far the earliest hominid known at the time of its discovery, it assumed centre stage in the human evolutionary drama and became the 'default hominid' of the 1-million-year time range throughout the Old World. As long as human evolution could be considered an Old World-wide phenomenon that proceeded everywhere through a more or less similar set of stages, this was a reasonable stance to take.

But it has become increasingly clear that human evolution has proceeded more in the manner of a series of pulses of new species of *Homo* emerging from the natal continent of Africa; and as more is known of *Homo erectus* and of human evolution in general, it is ever clearer that the Javan fossil represents a local eastern Asian evolutionary development lacking any direct relevance to what was going on in

From left to right: *Homo heidelbergensis*, *Homo ergaster*, and *Homo rudolfensis*   DAVID PEARCE

Africa. *Homo ergaster* is thus a preferable name for the Kenyan forms just mentioned: it clearly separates these very different African forms from the Javan hominids, although it is fair to say that there is quite a lot of anatomical – and possibly also species – variety even in this small collection.

What the tag *Homo ergaster* also does is to provide us with a convenient catchall term for a variety of African hominids (southern as well as eastern) of the 2.0 to 1.4-million-year period, the major exceptions being at least some of the fossils from Olduvai and elsewhere that have been assigned to *Homo habilis*, and certain robust australopiths of the genus *Paranthropus*, whose last representative, as the species *Paranthropus boisei*, is known from an Ethiopian site dated to around 1.4 MYA. With the disappearance of *Paranthropus boisei*, it seems, the last survivors of the australopith radiation had died out.

The east Turkana area has not only yielded crania that we can assign to *Homo ergaster*, but several isolated bones of the postcranial (body) skeleton, plus a partial skeleton that appears to have been affected by a major pathology. It is hard at this stage to know exactly what to make of the nonpathological postcranial elements simply because they are isolated and poorly described; but given the fact that the *Homo ergaster* crania show evidence of a fundamental reorganisation away from those of the australopiths and towards the modern condition, it is permissible to specu-late that the body structure of their possessors had been similar to that of the amazingly complete 'Turkana Boy' skeleton that was discovered to the west of Lake Turkana in the 1980s, also usefully assigned to *Homo ergaster*.

This extraordinary discovery, dated to 1.6 MYA, definitively announces the advent of an entirely new kind of hominid, one whose postcranial skeleton resembled our own in its essentials. This radical development was apparently sudden, and entirely unanticipated in the fossil record of the bipedal apes. In an admittedly sketchy record there is no suggestion of any gradual transition between the old form and the new one, which evidently emerged in an abrupt, short-term event that presumably involved a relatively straightforward change in gene regulation and development patterns.

The Turkana Boy comprises the bony remains of an adolescent who was probably 8 years old when he died, but who had already achieved the developmental stage of a modern 12-year-old. Indeed, this individual appears to have exemplified the relatively fast developmental pattern that seems to have characterised extinct hominids in general; today's *Homo sapiens* appears to be unusual in our family, let alone among primates, in the long-drawn-out nature of its developmental processes.

At his death the Boy stood about five feet three inches tall, but it is estimated that had he lived to maturity he would have topped six feet. This is a far cry from his diminutive predecessors, and here at last we have an individual of undisputedly modern body size. What's more, his principal body proportions were modern too: the Boy was slender-limbed and long-legged, a striding upright hominid fully equipped for life away from the trees, out on the grassy open sun-drenched savannah. He did retain a variety of archaic features, such as an upwardly-tapering ribcage a bit reminiscent of Lucy's; but to all intents and purposes he ushered in the era of bodily if not cognitively modern hominids, although some of his successors were a lot more robustly built than he.

Even so, though, above the neck he still differed substantially from *Homo sapiens*. His brain, while substantially larger than that of any australopith, was little more than half the size of ours; and his face, though reduced, was still large by later standards. It was forwardly hafted relative to the braincase, was decorated above with protruding browridges (though this feature is highly variable in the *Homo ergaster* sample we have), and possessed a dentition that was quite large. The chewing teeth, in particular, were substantially bigger than the modern average.

On the behavioural front, a dearth of relevant archaeological sites makes it hard to speculate how the lifestyles of the Boy and his kin may have departed from those of their more archaic predecessors. Still, it is almost certainly significant that at 1.6 MYA the Turkana Boy and his kind were still making stone tools that were little if any more sophisticated than those their predecessors had made a million years earlier.

Of course, stone tools by themselves give us only a very limited insight into the lives and cognitive abilities of their makers, but on the record as currently bequeathed to us there is very little reason to speculate that the new body form or even the somewhat increased brain size of *Homo ergaster* had materially reshaped the lives of the new hominids. On one level it is hard to believe that *Homo ergaster* was not a

behaviourally different entity from the stone-tool-wielding australopiths that had preceded it; but then again we have to consider the point, raised earlier, that novelties have to be introduced *within* species. If *Homo ergaster* was indeed a more effective operator than its predecessors on a technological level, the material record suggests that this was achieved by doing more or less what had been done before, but more efficiently.

Still, perhaps technology is not everything. The most notable consequence of the new body form seems to have been that, immediately it was acquired, hominids managed to spread beyond Africa, to which they had been confined for the millions of years since the origin of the family Hominidae. The site of Dmanisi, in the Caucasus, has already yielded evidence of hominids, perhaps even a diversity of hominids, that are 1.8 million years old. What is more, the hominid skulls from Dmanisi are quite small-brained, while the archaeological record at the site shows that the hominids made and used tools that were every bit as crude as those that were already being made in Africa hundreds of thousands of years before.

Clearly something must have occurred a little under 2 MYA that allowed hominids suddenly to spread beyond Africa and eventually throughout the Old World. And if, as the evidence from Dmanisi suggests, this something was neither an improved technology nor significantly larger brains and by extension improved mental functions, then only one possibility seems to remain, and that is the newly acquired striding body form.

Modern humans, we know, are walking machines, at least when necessary. And it seems that it was the new striding gait, which brought along with it unparalleled stamina, that finally freed hominids from the forest fringes and woodlands to which they had previously been confined, and allowed them to traverse vast distances and unfamiliar open territory to leave the continent of their birth. Of course, it would be unrealistic to imagine this spread of hominids of the genus *Homo* as the result of expeditioning or of any conscious form of exploration. Rather, it must have been the result of gradual population and range expansion, doubtless a complex process with many local advances and retreats, occupations and extinctions.

Again, it should be emphasised that the stone tool record gives us only the most partial glimpse of the lives and even the full range of technologies of our remote predecessors, and many important activities leave no trace whatever. Finds of post-cranial bones actively being made at Dmanisi at this moment may change the picture dramatically. But, based on what we know now, the new and fateful ingredient in hominid life that allowed all this to happen appears to have been vastly improved long-distance mobility.

More sophisticated tools and their makers

Crude stone-tool-making techniques continued to dominate on the Eurasian continent for a very long time; tools more sophisticated than the Oldowan barely penetrated east of India before the arrival of *Homo sapiens*, and the first archaic European colonists continued to use them long after they first managed to penetrate this difficult region almost a million years ago. But in Africa, only 100 000 years or so after the Turkana Boy's

time, at around 1.5 MYA, a new kind of tool type was finally invented. This radically new kind of tool was the 'Acheulean' handaxe, a larger implement usually eight to ten inches long, which, for the first time, was shaped carefully on both sides to a regular shape. This shape was most often that of a teardrop, though such tools were sometimes truncated into a cleaver with a broad surface at the end.

With the introduction of the handaxe, hominid toolmakers had begun to produce tools to a predetermined shape rather than simply going after a cutting edge regardless of what the flake actually looked like. So it seems that, for the first time, stone-toolmakers were acting according to a very precise template that existed in their minds before the stone-knapping started.

Such tools were often produced in prodigious numbers in 'workshops': at some South African sites, hundreds and thousands of more or less identical tools are found in deep piles. Sometimes they were apparently made playfully – occasionally, at sites such as Isimila in Tanzania, handaxes were produced on flakes almost half a metre long and were far heavier than could usefully be wielded.

Again, it seems that in the Acheulean we are glimpsing yet another cognitive advance, a more complex way of recognising the possibilities

Acheulean handaxes.

inherent in natural materials. Yet it remains impossible for us to know exactly how this advance might have reflected a larger change in the way the toolmakers viewed, experienced and interacted with the world around them.

At this stage in their demographic history hominids were still very thin on the ground, with extremely low population densities. Very little is known of hominid subsistence strategies then, though in a very general sense it would probably be justifiable to call these ancient precursors hunters and gatherers. Most authorities would be surprised to find evidence for highly advanced hunting techniques at this stage, and would be content to characterise hominids of this time as foragers who roamed opportunistically around the landscape exploiting resources they encountered. In this, these ancient precursors would have contrasted with historic hunters and gatherers, who have been collectors continually monitoring the resources around them and carefully planning their exploitation.

Unfortunately, in Africa – as elsewhere – the record is fairly thin between about 1.4 and 0.6 MYA; hominid fossils known from this period include the massive braincase from Olduvai known as OH 9, plus a couple of partial crania of fairly unimpressive brain size from Kenya, and crania from Buia in Eritrea and Daka in Ethiopia. None of these fossils particularly closely resemble any of the others – and indeed, the million-year-old Daka braincase seems more closely reminiscent of the slightly younger Italian specimen from Ceprano than of anything in Africa, while a trio of 700 000-year-old jaws from the Algerian site of Tighenif also seems to have its closest counterpart on the other side of the Mediterranean, at the Gran Dolina in Spain. Until the identities of these players and the complexities of their interrelationships are sorted out, which is far from being the case at present, exactly what was happening on the human evolutionary scene in Africa during this evidently eventful interval in human evolution will remain tantalisingly obscure.

At around 600 000 years ago, however, a new kind of hominid turns up about whose life and activities it is possible to say rather more. This new kind of hominid, known as *Homo heidelbergensis* (since it was first described from a jaw found in Germany), is most anciently known in Africa, specifically from a cranium found at the Ethiopian site of Bodo. The Bodo individual sported a brain of a size lying within the modern human range, although admittedly at its lower end. It is of particular interest in that the species it represents was apparently ubiquitous throughout the world, with representatives in Europe and China as well as in Africa, where the Bodo skull is joined by a fabulous cranium from Kabwe in Zambia and a braincase from Saldanha (Elandsfontein) on the west coast of South Africa.

Dating of the latter two specimens is tricky, but the 600 000 date for the Bodo skull seems pretty firm, as is the association of this new kind of hominid with stone tools of remarkably ancient aspect. As a result, it seems reasonable to conclude that the advent of the Acheulean in this region of Africa was significantly later than in certain other areas of the continent. This serves to emphasise the fact that cultural development in Africa was clearly no more linear and straightforward than hominid anatomical evolution seems to have been during this period, in this continent or elsewhere.

Homo heidelbergensis clearly first evolved in Africa. But because of a relative dearth of African archaeological sites in its general timeframe, we know most about its ways of life from European evidence, which shows that this species was already in residence in the subcontinent by around half a million years ago. The 400 000-year-old site of Terra Amata, in southern France, is particularly interesting in that it has produced the earliest generally accepted evidence of deliberately constructed shelters. These large oval structures consisted of closely spaced saplings that were embedded in the ground and brought together at the top. The periphery of the hut was reinforced by a ring of boulders, a break in which indicates where the entrance was.

Just within the entrance of one of the huts a depression was scooped into the ground and lined with stones. These stones, and associated animal bones, show signs of burning, indicating that this was the emplacement of a hearth within which a fire had burned. Following this time, hearths become an increasingly common feature of archaeological sites, indicating that it was at around this point in hominid history that the domestication of fire was finally becoming incorporated as a regular feature of the hominid behavioural repertoire.

At about the same time we find, at the German site of Schoeningen, the first direct evidence that we have of wooden tools. Wood is, of course, an incredibly useful material, of which hominids must have availed themselves at least from the early time at which they came into possession of the technology to cut and shape it. But it is a perishable material that rarely lasts for long except under the most extraordinary of conditions. Such conditions prevailed in an anoxic marsh at Schoeningen, from which excavators have recovered several long wooden spears, each measuring two metres or more.

There is some debate over the exact nature of these spears – whether they were used for thrusting or throwing – but their discoverers have argued that they were designed for throwing, with the weight concentrated up front, near the tip. If this is true, then the spears' makers were clearly indulging in ambush hunting, a process much less dangerous than thrusting from close up would have been. Compared to the rather crude stone tool kits made and used by early Europeans at that time, these are remarkably sophisticated weapons; and they serve to remind us just how indirect an indicator of wider aspects of culture the more indestructible stone-tool record is.

In any event, the European archaeological record putatively associated with *Homo heidelbergensis* shows us that, by half a MYA, largeish-brained hominids were regularly using fire in hearths and building shelters. Again, these inno-vations must be signs of cognitive advancements among the hominids who made them; but none-theless we have to wait until about 250 000 years ago before we begin to find, both in Africa and in Europe (most of Asia seems to have stayed strangely backward technologically over this period), evidence of a new style of stone-working.

This is the 'prepared-core' technique, in which a stone nucleus was carefully worked until a single blow would detach an effectively finished implement. Again, we are evidently seeing here a further cognitive refinement, one that involved the ability to see the potential in natural materials and to exploit that potential in new ways. And once the new 'flake' tools had been introduced, they seem to have replaced the Acheulean quite widely and rapidly throughout Africa and, perhaps somewhat later, in Europe too.

This technological innovation seems to have signalled some fairly fundamental changes in lifestyle, with a shift to what in Africa are called Middle Stone Age (MSA) stone-working cultures, among which archaeologists recognise rather more regional variation than had been typical during the long period of the Acheulean. What is more, the Stellenbosch University archaeologist Hilary Deacon has argued that MSA sites are more uniformly scattered over the landscape than Acheulean sites, which appear to have been restricted to stream valleys. This distribution is more or less the same as is found in later times, from which Deacon infers that with the advent of the MSA, hominid economic behaviours had shifted towards a distinctly more 'modern' pattern.

Further, while most authorities believe that stone tools of Acheulean kind were designed to be wielded directly by hand, it is becoming clear that some typical MSA tool types were intended to be hafted, either as spear points or as components of compound tools. This development may be paralleled by the evidence in this period for the active hunting in Africa of medium- to large-sized mammals, mainly members of Bovidae, the family of the antelopes and buffaloes and their relatives.

Once more, then, there are intriguing hints of cognitive and behavioural advancements as the MSA began to predominate in Africa – but who exactly it was that made those advancements remains frustratingly opaque. A scattering of fossil hominids is known from Africa between the time of Bodo and about 200 000 years ago. A 400 000-year-old cranium, probably associated with Acheulean tools, is known from Ndutu in Tanzania; a hominid face from Florisbad in South Africa is probably around 250 000 years old and is, in contrast, associated with MSA tools. Maybe around the same age is a very fragmentary cranium from Guomde, in Kenya, while a braincase from Salé, in Morocco, also lacking archaeological associations, may be as much as 400 000 years old. Some skull parts from Rabat, also in Morocco, may similarly be about 400 000 years old, and are associated with Acheulean lithics. A handful of skull bits from Eyasi in Tanzania remains inscrutable as to morphology, archaeology, and age.

All in all, these various pieces are hard to make a story out of at this point; and only two of them, the Florisbad face (sometimes known as *Homo helmei*) and the Guomde fragments, have been seriously portrayed as contenders for a close relationship with *Homo sapiens*. One of the problems in interpreting this diverse material has been the widespread tolerance among palaeoanthropologists of the idea of 'archaic *Homo sapiens*', a catchall category into which a huge assortment of fossil hominids, African and otherwise, has been swept. As long as this convenient dumping-place existed for a highly miscellaneous group of problematic fossil relatives, scientists were relieved of the huge difficulty of sorting it out. Now, however, it is clear that we are going to have to get a realistic grasp of the nettle of African hominid diversity and relationships in the later part of the Pleistocene epoch, because it is becoming ever clearer that it is out of this place and time that our own species, *Homo sapiens*, eventually emerged.

The emergence of *Homo sapiens*

In recent years the emerging discipline of molecular systematics has begun to contribute importantly to our knowledge of the origins of our own species, *Homo sapiens*. Our evolutionary histories are inscribed in the structure of our DNA, the hereditary molecule resident in the cells that compose our bodies. It is DNA that provides the blueprint on which each of us is constructed, and it is via this molecule that each of us transmits our genes to our children. DNA evolves through the accumulation of small changes in its molecular structure; and comparisons of DNA structure among species, and even among populations within species, can provide valuable information about the relationships of such groups.

Particularly favoured by molecular geneticists for such comparisons are mitochondrial DNA (mtDNA), which is passed from one generation to the next solely through the mother, and Y-chromosome DNA, which is passed only through the father. On the short timescale involved in the origin and evolution of *Homo sapiens*, these systems are especially useful because they have the advantage of changing fast and having a simple form of inheritance since they

The East African Rift Valley, where many of the hominid fossils have been found.

bypass the genetic mixing-up between each generation that is involved in biparental inheritance.

Studies of both mtDNA and Y-chromosome DNA are in remarkably close agreement on the origin of our species *Homo sapiens* in Africa. Africans, for a start, have the widest range of variation in their DNA, which suggests that members of our species have been accumulating new DNA conformations in that continent for the longest span (the accumulation of DNA changes is by and large a function of time). What is more, all the other human DNA conformations found around the modern world appear to be descended from just one subset of African genotypes. In other words, the molecular evidence points to a scenario whereby one African population is ancestral to all populations of modern humans living around the world today.

This is the genesis of the 'African Eve' hypothesis which has received so much play in the press of late, and which suggests that all living humans are descended from one female, or at least from one mtDNA type, that existed in Africa in the remote past. Further, from the genetic distances obtained from studies of this kind, scientists have inferred that this common ancestor of all living humans probably existed sometime around 200 000 years ago. As it happens, this estimate is in fairly good agreement with what we can infer from an admittedly scanty fossil record.

To tackle that record, we need some perspective. Although Africa certainly seems to have been the main centre of developments throughout the story of human evolution, in many ways we know more about what was going on in Asia and especially Europe during the past couple of hundred thousand years. Europe was occupied rather late by hominids, at around a million years ago; and it is only with *Homo heidelbergensis* that long-term occupation of the subcontinent was certainly achieved. As might have been expected, this occupation was followed by the development in Europe and western Asia of an endemic group of hominids, of whom the Neanderthals, *Homo neanderthalensis*, were the best known. Indeed, *Homo neanderthalensis* is by a country mile the best known of any extinct species of hominid.

It was the Neanderthals who had the misfortune to be in residence when the first *Homo sapiens* arrived in the region, having finally begun their journey in Africa. The confrontation of the European residents with these new people, known as the Cro-Magnons, rapidly resulted in the Neanderthals' extinction. Similarly, in eastern Asia, late populations of *Homo erectus* managed to persist in Java until 40 000 years ago or less – again, until the period within which it is reasonable to suppose that *Homo sapiens* had made its appearance in their domain. The same process of recent displacement and extinction appears to have obtained on the neighbouring Indonesian island of Flores, whence the extraordinary and diminutive *Homo floresiensis* was recently described. In other words, the pattern

outside Africa appears to have been a pretty straightforward one, of the fairly recent replacement of resident hominid species by newly arriving *Homo sapiens.*

In Africa the picture was not quite so simple. Certainly, to judge by the fairly miscellaneous nature of the African hominid record of the 600 000- to 200 000-year period that we have just glanced at, it is likely that a diversity of more archaic hominids was indeed eventually displaced in that continent by the emerging *Homo sapiens.* But there is in addition the origin of the latter to consider, and this is no simple question.

Living *Homo sapiens* has a highly distinctive anatomy, both of the skull and of the skeleton; and the first hominid fossils that show elements of that anatomical distinctiveness come from Africa. Among the most unusual features of the *Homo sapiens* skull are the ridges above the eye sockets. In modern people these ridges may be largeish or they may be vanishingly small; but in all living people the supraorbital areas have in common that they are bipartite, with a central component demarcated by a shallow oblique groove from a lateral plate below. Similarly, the modern human chin is very distinctive, not simply being a vague lump at the bottom of the midline of the lower jaw. It is actually a complex structure with a distinct vertical ridge above that is bordered by depressions on either side, and with a horizontal transverse bar below.

Where these features of the brow region and chin are missing, you do not have a 'fully modern' bone anatomy. Unfortunately, though, whether that in turn means that you are not *Homo sapiens*, a fully paid-up breeding member of our species, is anybody's guess. I say unfortunately because there is in South Africa a group of fossils, from sites such as Fish Hoek, Boskop, Border Cave, and (mostly) Klasies River Mouth, that have pretty standard *Homo sapiens* skull anatomy except for the absence of bipartite brows and modern chins. Some of these may be pretty late in time (Fish Hoek, for example, may be less than 10 000 years old), which makes the situation even odder.

Perhaps, then, it's best to start our discussion at the beginning of the chronological sequence.

In 2003 was announced the discovery, at an Ethiopian locality called Herto, of an adult skull, plus some other bits and pieces including a fragmentary child's cranium, that were reported to be effectively modern *Homo sapiens.* All were found alongside a stone tool assemblage that included elements typical of both the Acheulean and the MSA. The most remarkable thing about the remains themselves was that they were reliably dated to as much as 160 000 years ago, and were thus a great deal older than any other fossils that had yet been described as modern.

At the time, the closest contender for the earliest *Homo sapiens* was a fragmentary skull from the Omo basin of Ethiopia, which was apparently found in association with some MSA tools. It was then thought that this specimen might be as much as 130 000 years old, but since the Herto description was published it has been redated to about 195 000 years ago. Neither the (broken) brow ridge nor the chin region of the Omo skull is entirely modern in form; and the Herto adult cranium, lacking the lower jaw, has not yet been comprehensively published and illustrated, so it is not possible to be absolutely certain about all its morphologies. But on the strength of the Herto specimen, at least, it appears possible to say that modern human skull anatomy, or at least something very close to it indeed, had appeared in Africa by 160 000 years ago.

Other fossil hominids of this general time range include a rather odd-looking 130 000-year-old cranium from Singa, in the Sudan, which also lacks bipartite brows; and conceivably also the somewhat similar Eliye Springs skull from Kenya, whose brows are sheared off and which remains effectively undated. Two crania from Jebel Irhoud in Morocco may also be 130 000 years old or even more, and were found with stone tools that are the equivalent of MSA; these skulls are distinctly unlike *Homo sapiens* in a variety of features, as to a lesser extent is the probably 120 000-year-old skull from Ngaloba in Tanzania, again with MSA associations. Interestingly, however, the Tanzanian specimen has quite large brow ridges that are nonetheless bipartite.

Somewhat younger is a series of mostly jaw fragments from the Klasies River Mouth caves near the southern tip of Africa; these have usually been viewed as *Homo sapiens*, but in fact only one out of four jaw pieces preserving the symphysis (the midline where the left and right halves of the jaw come together) has a modern human chin, and the one piece of frontal bone that preserves any supraorbital morphology does not suggest a bipartite brow. Most of the Klasies hominids have MSA associations and date to around 100 000 years ago; there are also a few later bits from Later Stone Age (LSA) deposits.

In the period between about 200 000 and 100 000 years ago, then, there existed in Africa a fair morphological variety of hominids, a proportion of whom appear to have had some claim to lie at or close to the ancestry of today's *Homo sapiens*. Almost all these hominids had ties to the MSA, and the earliest of them had more archaic cultural associations yet. So, once again, we see a pattern in which the appearance of a new kind of hominid was unconnected with a change in technology.

In Europe, of course, we do see towards the end of the Pleistocene a clear pattern of abrupt change in which a hominid with sophisticated but archaic behaviour patterns was rapidly overwhelmed by an entirely distinct intruding competitor who was modern in every sense of the word, not only anatomically but behaviourally. But this was not the pattern in Africa, where invasion from outside by a new kind of hominid was not the issue. In this continent the flake implements of the MSA were not widely supplanted by the long, slender blades of the LSA until nearly 20 000 years ago, well after anatomical *Homo sapiens* had become ubiquitous in Africa (with the possible exception of the odd Fish Hoek–Boskop group, if they were indeed truly different).

In a limited sense this parallels what we see in the Levant, the region bordering the eastern shores of the Mediterranean and often regarded as a biogeographic extension of Africa. Here, in the period between about 100 000 and 50 000 years ago, there was apparently a long-term coexistence or at least alternation of some kind between Neanderthals (whose remains have never been discovered in Africa) and anatomically modern people. The earliest unquestionably fully anatomically modern human from the Levant – and just possibly from anywhere – is dated to almost 100 000 years ago, while the latest Levantine Neanderthal is only around 45 000 years old. In the Levant, the last Neanderthals disappeared only after the emergence of a new stone-working technology that was equivalent to the LSA.

Hilary Deacon has equated this latter stone-working tradition in Africa with virtually the whole panoply of 'modern' behaviours. Of these behaviours, which range from the economic to the spiritual, it is universally agreed that the most significant indicators of cognition are the symbolic ones such as ornamentation of the body and the creation of decorative objects. This is because symbolic activities of this kind are the most direct reflections we have of an entirely radical way of looking at and interacting with the world.

The importance of symbolic activities lies not simply in the external symbols themselves. Rather, those symbols are the expression of an internal life of the mind. By creating mental symbols and recombining them in new ways, modern humans remake the world in their heads. Instead of simply reacting to whatever nature comes up with, in more or less complex ways, symbol-minded modern humans are able to ask questions such as 'What if?' The asking of such questions is one of the most fundamental expressions of that mysterious quality that we call human consciousness, and it is this as well that allows us to invent creative solutions not only to practical but to imagined problems.

There is little doubt that the eventual worldwide success of *Homo sapiens* is attributable to this new and unprecedented form of cognition. But clearly the relatively late spread of LSA cultures in Africa does not denote a late acquisition in this continent of what has been called the 'human capacity'. Instead, what we see in Africa is the gradual acquisition during MSA times of the manifestations that we associate with that capacity today. Noting this pattern, the American archaeologists Sally McBrearty and Alison Brooks have recently argued with great force that there was no 'human revolution' in Africa of the kind that is so crisply defined in the European record. Instead, they point out that in certain East African sites blades were being produced as long ago as a quarter of a million years, that grinding stones were being used to process pigments not long thereafter, and that long-distance trade in materials and even the mining of flint were being carried out in Africa well

over 100 000 years ago, always in MSA contexts.

While this is certainly true, it is also the case that economic activities are not necessarily reliable indicators of symbolic cognition. *Homo neanderthalensis*, the best known of all extinct hominid species, was technologically highly skilled but still, in an extremely rich record, left nothing behind that could unequivocally be described as symbolic. This suggests that not all the components of the LSA package need be interpreted as evidence by themselves of modern cognition. And if we exclude technological activities from our list of criteria for inferring symbol-cognitive processes, then the evidence for modernity starts much more recently, though in Africa well before anywhere else.

The earliest non-technological evidence for symbolic activities is inferential. As a result of very painstaking excavation at the Klasies River

Middle Stone Age points.

Mouth caves on the southern African coast, Hilary Deacon believes that he can discern evidence for such activities by LSA peoples over 100 000 years ago, in their use of the living spaces they occupied. To him, the site was organised very much in the same way as sub-recent hunter-gatherer sites, indicating that traditional ways of life have not changed that much in a very long time. Deacon has also convincingly pointed to evidence for cannibalism among the fragments of hominid bone found at the site, although the record shows that in Europe such manifestations extend back in time well beyond the *Homo sapiens* record.

But, fascinating as Klasies is, to be absolutely certain that archaeological remains were produced by individuals with modern cognition you have to find objects that were overtly symbolic. To find very ancient objects of this kind you do not have to move very far from Klasies, either in space or in time. Blombos Cave is another coastal cave site in the southern Cape. Here Christopher Henshilwood and his colleagues have recently excavated a variety of objects that are dated to between 70 000 and 80 000 years ago and have a strong claim to be the world's most ancient symbolic pieces.

The most striking of these is a flat piece of ochre on which is engraved a regular geometric pattern. Not everyone accepts this piece as a symbolic production, but most authorities do, and it is pretty clear that a deliberate design was intended. What it meant is anybody's guess; but it fairly convincingly meant *something*, which is enough to place it in the symbolic category. A bone fragment of similar age from Blombos also bears marks that were intentionally engraved, and thus belongs in this category as well.

Finally, Henshilwood and his colleagues have lately reported finding pierced tick shells that may have been strung to make a necklace and may originally have been coloured red with ochre. Body ornamentation has a special significance among modern humans, having social implications that usually extend well beyond the basic notion of individual self-awareness that such decoration obviously implies. Thus, the ensemble of materials from Blombos suggests that the MSA people who made them may have been people of modern sensibilities and cognition. That this was not simply an isolated case is suggested by the finding of pierced (and presumably strung) gastropods far away in Ethiopia's Porc-Epic Cave, also in an MSA context and some 70 000 years old.

The arrival of modern cognition

In Africa, then, we have the earliest hints of the establishment of modern human cognition in MSA contexts at 70 000 to 80 000 years ago. And we have evidence of the early presence in that continent of anatomically modern humans, also in MSA contexts, quite probably as long ago as 160 000 years at Herto and certainly in Africa's Levantine extension at almost 100 000 years ago. But there is no consistent association between modern anatomy and modern behaviour. The LSA was almost certainly everywhere the product of modern *Homo sapiens*, but many of the most important characteristics of the LSA were already present in the MSA. The earliest hints of the LSA package go back a long way in the technological realm, but there are reasons to be dubious about equating advances of this kind with the shift to modern symbolic cognition.

Modern symbol-minded human beings were obviously derived from a non-symbolic precursor, and quite recently. It is hard to explain symbolic consciousness as a simple extrapolation of the evolutionary trends in cognition that preceded *Homo sapiens*, in other words as the end result of a continual burnishing of earlier intuitive forms of intelligence. Instead, our extraordinary species appears to be something truly new, the contrast with the old being most dramatically reflected in the confrontation between the non-symbolic Neanderthals and the symbolic Cro-Magnons in Europe.

So what does all this imply for the emergence of the both behaviourally and anatomically novel

entity that we are today? Are McBrearty and Brooks right in invoking a gradual transition to the modern condition that took virtually the entire timespan of the MSA? Or did events more closely reflect the discontinuity that apparently exists between non-symbolic and symbolic modes of thought?

One possibility that has been suggested is that a population of skeletally modern *Homo sapiens* acquired a neural adaptation that permitted symbolic thought, and that this newly equipped population subsequently displaced, worldwide, all the hominid populations lacking that adaptation. This seems inherently unlikely, though, especially in view of the rather small window of time involved. Instead it seems far more reasonable to suppose that a neural *potential* for symbolic thought was acquired, as a by-product, in the event that gave rise to the emergence of *Homo sapiens* as a (highly) distinctive anatomical entity.

This event probably occurred somewhere in Africa, and at least 100 000 years ago (the date of the unquestioned anatomical moderns from Qafzeh, in the Levant) or more probably closer to 200 000 years ago. The new cognitive potential initially lay unexploited, as it evidently also did in the Levant – in that region anatomical moderns and Neanderthals, wielding more or less identical Mousterian (MSA-equivalent) tool kits, somehow contrived to coexist for upwards of 50 000 years.

This coexistence ceased only when an LSA-equivalent tool kit was introduced, presumably by anatomical moderns who had added symbolic cognition to their repertoire. Something must thus have happened at that point to induce a switch to symbolic cognition, in a creature that had already for some time possessed the neural basis for acquiring it.

I suggest that the cultural or behavioural stimulus concerned was the invention of language. Language is the quintessential symbolic activity, and it is virtually impossible for us today to con-ceive of abstract symbolic thought in its absence. Hominids at least since Bodo times had possessed a vocal tract capable of producing the sounds we use today in articulate speech – and clearly this apparatus too, just like the language-enabled brain, had initially been acquired in some other context entirely. Nonetheless, the way would thus have been open for language – or something like it – to kick-start the human consciousness.

Not that this need at all to have been an instantaneous process. MSA hominids had presumably been laying the groundwork for it for quite some time. But initial forms of symbolic thought were clearly demarcated from those forms of comprehension of the world – whatever they were, and it is virtually impossible for us to fully imagine states of consciousness unlike our own – that had preceded them, and something must have happened to initiate the process of transition. The discovery of this new potential may have occurred on multiple occasions and in different places; indeed, the early signs of symbolic cognition at Blombos were promptly succeeded by a period of climatic severity that, it seems, almost entirely depopulated the most southerly part of Africa of hominids for several tens of thousands of years.

That is the long gap before we begin to pick up other evidence of bodily adornment and decoration further north, first in the East African Rift Valley and then shortly thereafter in the spectacular record of art and other forms of creativity left behind by the Cro-Magnons following their invasion of Europe at around 40 000 years ago. But what we see happening at Africa's southern tip some 80 000 to 70 000 years ago was evidently the beginning of a series of events that, for better or quite probably for worse, resulted in the population of the entire world by human beings possessing the admirable, and presumably also the deplorable, qualities that epitomise our kind today, everywhere.

Although most rock art is associated with the Later Stone Age in Africa, recent archaeological work has raised the intriguing possibility that image-making may have begun much earlier, in the Middle Stone Age period. ROCK ART RESEARCH INSTITUTE

Africa's creative
explosion

Engraved eland from the Origins Centre.

From neo-anthropes to modern people

The changing fortunes of the Middle Stone Age

JOHN PARKINGTON

John Goodwin invents the Middle Stone Age

Almost as an afterthought, John Goodwin and his collaborator C 'Pieter' van Riet Lowe entrenched the idea of a Middle Stone Age (MSA) between the more securely defined Earlier (ESA) and Later Stone Ages (LSA) in their classic 1929 formulation, 'The Stone Age Cultures of South Africa'. They intentionally set out to replace the then current European-derived terminology of Lower, Middle and Upper Palaeolithic because they saw that the later parts of the Stone Age sequence in Africa differed patently from those of Europe.

A strong migrationist theme permeated Goodwin's writing, with the most prominent metaphors for the appearance of new elements being the language of invasions, migrations and, most revealingly, waves of 'neo-anthropes' ('modern' human beings). He actually said that 'Africa is a pocket from which nothing tangible returns.' He clearly envisaged South Africa as a cul-de-sac, a bag into which things fell, never to be seen again. These things, arguably innovations, fell as if by gravity from north of the Sahara, where 'higher folk' lived.

Most of the assemblages and assemblage types he thought to be MSA were surface collections

Painted eland and rhebuck on stone from the Origins Centre.

dominated by flakes with faceted platforms and convergent dorsal scars, points either retouched or not, and radially flaked cores that closely resembled the Middle Palaeolithic of Europe. Already prominent in his reference frame for the MSA were two kinds of assemblage that were at once familiar yet intriguingly challenging. These were the Howiesons Poort Variation and the Stillbay Industry, both MSA yet with interesting novelties. These assemblages included artefacts that experience in Europe would suggest were not Middle Palaeolithic but rather Upper (later) Palaeolithic: large, backed segments and bi-facially retouched points. In Goodwin's terms, Variations were Industries in waiting, assemblage types for which more duplication and more context were needed before formal placement was possible.

Although the real waves of neo-anthropic 'folk' were reflected in the appearance of the LSA, the Howiesons Poort and Stillbay suggestively hinted at these developments. Goodwin was clear that the explanation of such precocious artefact types as the segments and bifacial points lay in the 'hybridisation' of incoming neo-anthropic folk with existing (presumably archaeo-anthropic) people. He argued that 'progressive hybridisation is more and more clear as we study the northern

Van Riet Lowe, Goodwin's collaborator, together with Prime Minister Smuts.

forms which have come down to us'. He saw, with his former teacher Miles Burkitt, 'possible neo-anthropic influence in the Stillbay' at least, and probably the Howiesons Poort too. Here is the introduction of the idea of an intermediate between ancient and modern, a concept given formal recognition for much of the mid-twentieth

century. Inevitably, perhaps, the contemporary model lying behind Goodwin's construct was provided by San (Bushmen), offering a seductively persuasive exemplar of what a neo-anthropic hunter-gatherer society could look like.

Goodwin and Van Riet Lowe's scheme was very much of its time and place, a version suffused with the feelings and expectations of archaeologists operating on the colonial fringe, writing as Europeans in deepest Africa. Despite this, the MSA narrative already contained the seeds of an idea that flourishes still. What is interesting is the persistence of many components of this idea: the language of migrations, the comparisons with Europe, the notion of precocious toolmaking, the significance of particular tool types, the grappling with the idea of intermediacy, and the role of recent southern African hunter-gatherers as referents for modernity.

There is, of course, a major difference between the version of 1929 and the many versions that compete for attention in the early twenty-first century. The direction of movement has been reversed, the tide has turned, the waves are now going not coming. Perhaps coincidentally, these are versions much more in tune with a post-colonial South Africa. Here is the potential birth of modern people in Africa, the signal of Africa's assertion of growing self-esteem. We are all, it seems, Africans, not Europeans.

In this essay I look at the changing fortunes of the MSA. I ask how and when the Afro-pessimism of John Goodwin became the Afro-optimism of Sally McBrearty and Alison Brooks, whether the influences came from new discoveries within archaeology or new influences from without, how the dominant position of the Cro-Magnons has been usurped by the denizens of the Dark Continent, whether the models in vogue today are best seen as metaphors rather than narratives, and what we can expect in the years to come. *Ex Africa semper aliquid novi*, maybe, but when, why and how?

Genetic evidence for our recent African evolution

HIMLA SOODYALL

The African continent has featured prominently in the history of our species from the very beginnings of human evolution to the present. Africa has also been the source and recipient of transcontinental movement of people at various times. For many years, discussions about the origin of modern humans revolved around two competing theories: the recent African origin hypothesis that modern humans first appeared in Africa about 150 000 years ago and then spread from there to the rest of the world; and the multiregional evolution idea that modern humans evolved over the past million years or so from archaic human populations across the Old World via a complex interaction of selection and migration.

Genetic data continue to unravel the mysteries of human evolutionary history, and the evidence in support of a recent African origin is compelling. These studies analyse patterns of genetic variation in living people and then attempt to deduce the likeliest evolutionary scenario to have given rise to them. In this essay we review the role of mitochondrial DNA (mtDNA) in uncovering the past, with some additional insights from other genetic data.

The mtDNA story

The first and still the most prominent source of DNA evidence on human origins comes from the mtDNA genome. The human mtDNA genome consists of about 16 500 base-pairs of DNA, or about 0.0006 per cent of the human nuclear DNA genome. Some properties of mtDNA make it useful for such studies: mtDNA is strictly maternally inherited, with no paternal contribution or recombination. This means that the only source of variation among mtDNA types is mutation, and hence the number of mutations separating two mtDNA types is a direct measure of the length of time since they shared a common ancestor.

Initial studies of human mtDNA variation led to what has become popularly known as the 'African Eve' hypothesis. It has three important points: first, all mtDNA types in contemporary populations trace back to a single ancestor; second, this ancestor probably lived in Africa; and third, this ancestor probably lived about 150 000 to 200 000 years ago.

Evidence for a recent African origin

Phylogenetic trees – ones depicting the evolutionary history of mtDNA types in human populations – invariably contain two primary branches, one consisting solely of African mtDNAs, the other of some African and all non-African mtDNAs. While other explanations are possible, the simplest one for this pattern is to suppose that the ancestor was indeed African.

In addition to phylogenetic analyses, all studies of worldwide human mtDNA variation have found that, on average, African populations have the greatest mtDNA sequence divergence, followed by Asian and European populations. The fact that Africans have the largest mtDNA sequence divergence indicates that they have accumulated the most mtDNA mutations – and the argument for an African origin states that the population with the most diversity is likely to be the ancestral population. Not only do non-African populations have much less mtDNA diversity, on average, but they also appear to

have a subset of the diversity present in Africa. Thus, the mtDNA type diversity in Africa appears to encompass all the diversity found outside Africa. Again, this is in keeping with the idea of an African origin.

The age of the human mtDNA ancestor ranges between 500 000 and 50 000 years, with most dates for the more comprehensive datasets falling between 200 000 and 150 000 years ago. The best dataset of complete human mtDNA sequences yields a date of about 150 000 years ago.

The breakthrough when DNA was retrieved from ancient specimens made it possible to examine mtDNA from contemporary humans along with archaic Neanderthal populations. A comparison revealed that modern humans and Neanderthals did not exchange genes but rather had diverged from a common ancestor about 650 000 years ago. These data added additional support to the Out of Africa model for human origins.

The research carried out on the mtDNA, suggesting an African origin, has been supplemented by investigation into the Y-chromosome. The Y-chromosome is the paternally inherited equivalent of mtDNA. Studies of Y-chromosome variation also point to an African ancestry, as phylogenetic trees of Y-chromosome types show the same pattern as mtDNA: the most ancient lineages are found in Africa, with lineages found outside of Africa having roots in Africa. Dates for the age of the human Y-chromosome common ancestor are also recent, ranging from approximately 200 000 to 40 000 years; again, the Y-chromosome appears to match the mtDNA evidence quite closely with respect to human origins.

Data from other nuclear genes have been accumulating rapidly over the past decade or so, and are also consistent with the African origin hypothesis.

Cro-Magnons rule, OK?

We need to remember that for most of the twentieth century France, not England, ruled the waves of palaeolithic studies. The dominant narrative was the *fossile directeur* approach that required archaeologists to define cultural units marked by assemblages with characteristic formally retouched tools. Upper Palaeolithic (UP) cultural stratigraphy prospered under this approach, establishing a rapidly changing, innovative period of technological and artistic achievement beginning as early as 40 000 years ago and ending only with the retreat of the glaciers at about 10 000 years ago. Prior to this period the Middle Palaeolithic (MP) appeared unimaginative and static.

The picture that emerged from many well-publicised excavations at French, Spanish and German sites was one of the rapid replacement of somewhat conservative Neanderthalers by clever, aesthetically inclined Cro-Magnon modern people, good candidates for the role of European, or perhaps universal, ancestor. They struck blades with soft hammers or punches, retouched tools by indirect percussion, developed a range of burins (chisel-like implements derived from a flake or blade) for working in bone, ivory, soft stone and presumably wood, spent much energy collecting shells and teeth to turn into ornaments, buried their dead with great ceremony, and carved, sculpted, painted, engraved and clearly thought like modern hunter-gatherers.

By contrast their predecessors, the Neander-thalers, apparently persisted with flake manufacture and direct percussion, made fewer, less standardised kinds of tools, hardly bothered with bone or ivory, rarely engaged in any nonfunctional marking of materials, didn't venture into dark caves, but arguably buried their dead. They made much less impressive potential ancestors and, conveniently, were eliminated by the smarter UP folk.

What has this to do with the MSA? Quite simply, the MSA looked like the MP but appeared from available radiocarbon dates to be a contemporary of the UP. Leaving aside the Howiesons Poort and Stillbay, to which we will return, MSA artefact assemblages are characterised by flake products struck from prepared, sometimes radial, cores but with little evidence of the use of punches or soft hammers. Decoration or ornamentation seemed rare or nonexistent. With the arguable exception of a young infant at Border Cave, there are no documented burials in the southern African MSA; even isolated fragments of human skeletons are rare.

For much of the twentieth century it was not understood that Neanderthal morphology is completely absent from the fossil record of sub-Saharan Africa. To many observers the cranium from Kabwe, then known as Broken Hill, and the calvarium from Elandsfontein, also known as Hopefield or Saldanha, with their associated postcranial fragments, were seen as African Neanderthalers, 'primitive' at that, dating apparently to the time of the UP in Europe. All the signs were that the MSA and its makers were best regarded as a backwater, both biologically and culturally, surviving in the 'pocket from which nothing returns' while Europe surged forward.

The key to this misperception lay not so much in the evidence as in the mindset and the available dating technique. The mesmerising effects of the classic UP sites and cave art of the Dordogne and elsewhere meant that few archaeologists, even those in South Africa, chose to judge the African evidence on its own terms. But far more importantly, the chronological playing field was not level. The radiocarbon results at this time seemed to place the end of the ESA at about 60 000 years ago, reflected in apparent ages for the Kalambo Falls Acheulean assemblages, and the end of the MSA at about 15 000 years at the Cave of Hearths. These seemed to show that, technological comparisons notwithstanding, the MSA and the UP were contemporaries. We would now recognise that these 'dates' were the result of the limitations of radiocarbon dating and not true ages at all. But at face value, the MSA did not appear innovative when compared with the UP artists and sophisticated toolmakers of the European caves.

If we return to the issue of the Howiesons Poort and Stillbay assemblages, we note that they have always appeared anomalous in the MSA. An idea that lasted for some time in the mid-twentieth century was that of a Second Intermediate, a period in which the MSA showed signs of becoming LSA. By the same token, assemblages with small, finely made handaxes labelled Fauresmith were considered First Intermediate, between ESA and MSA. The 'hybridisation' idea had faded but the struggle with a terminology for change or continuity persisted.

The Howiesons Poort was thought a likely candidate as a Second Intermediate Industry because it contained a substantial blade component, showed a greater interest in fine-grained raw materials, and had both burins and standardised backed segments, originally called crescents. We know now that it also has soft-hammer technique. Yet all of this was submerged in an undeniably MSA technology. At the time, prior to the late 1960s, the stratigraphic position of the Howiesons Poort was unclear because the type site had only Howiesons Poort assemblages, with nothing above or below, and Howiesons Poort assemblages at other sites were not *in situ*. To complicate this issue, attempts to date the Howiesons Poort by radiocarbon dating produced embarrassingly late and, with hindsight, clearly unacceptable ages of 10 000 to 20 000 years. The MSA, even in its most innovative manifestations, seemed to reflect the late survival of practices long abandoned in Europe.

A reversal of fortune

Desmond Clark gave a public lecture in London in the early 1970s which I was fortunate to attend, in which he championed the transition of 'African prehistory from peripheral to paramount'. He argued that, far from being a backwater, Africa

The cave site of Klasies River Mouth.

has long been in the vanguard of human cultural development. At about the same time John Vogel and Peter Beaumont reviewed the dating evidence for the southern African Stone Age and expressed confidence in the role of Africa as innovator rather than laggard. We are now in an even stronger position to make this case.

What caused so dramatic a reversal of fortune? First, it appeared that the Howiesons Poort, at least, is not stratigraphically Intermediate, though its formal intermediacy remained intriguing. Excavations at Klasies River main site by Ronald Singer and John Wymer showed beyond doubt that the Howiesons Poort was not the terminal MSA but was stratified beneath other apparently non-Howiesons Poort MSA assemblages. This was repeated in Peter Beaumont's excavations at Border Cave and prompted much head-scratching over the real meaning of the Howiesons Poort artefacts, of which more later.

Second, it has emerged that both the Howiesons Poort and the Stillbay are much older than previously thought. This was not yet clear from the radiocarbon dates from Klasies River in the 1970s because these included many apparently finite dates between about 35 000 and 40 000 years ago. With hindsight, and the wisdom of John Vogel, it is now obvious that all of these 'dates' are infinite and that all of the MSA assemblages there, including the Howiesons Poort, are beyond conventional carbon-14 dating. The development of new methods such as uranium disequilibrium, electron spin resonance and luminescence dating, and particularly the application of single-grain optically stimulated luminescence procedures, has generated age estimates of between 80 000 and 60 000 years for the Howiesons Poort and 75 000 years for the Stillbay at several sites.

These revised ages are part of a generally more reliable understanding of the great antiquity of the MSA as a whole. It is now conventional wisdom that the MSA began in Africa some 300 000 to 250 000 years ago and thus that the Howiesons Poort and Stillbay are relatively late in the MSA sequence. It is also obvious from newer dates in both Africa and Europe that the MSA and the MP began and ended at approximately the same times. Now the comparison between the MSA and the UP can be conducted with a more accurate understanding of their relative ages. This dramatically alters the conclusion, as we will see.

Third, the application of mitochondrial DNA (mtDNA) research to modern and fossil human skeletal and soft tissues from the mid-1980s shows that we should expect the ancestry of modern people to lie in Africa, not Europe. The advantages of mtDNA as a kind of genetic clock derive from the neutral nature of this part of the human genome, the rapid and apparently random nature of mutations, and the transmission of mtDNA material exclusively through the female line.

An assumption of the method, and one in some dispute, is that as changes are random and neutral they should accumulate proportionately

The Howiesons Poort within the Middle Stone Age

JANETTE DEACON

On a South African road map, Howieson's Poort is a pass west of Grahamstown misnamed after a Mr Howison who lived in the area about a hundred years ago. The Howiesons Poort (so called) in archaeological terms, however, is a distinctive period that lasted about 20 000 years within the Middle Stone Age (MSA), and the dig is a type site, giving its name to stone tools of this kind wherever they are found in Africa. To understand the significance of Howiesons Poort stone tools, it helps to know something about the history of the term, what makes the stone tools distinctive, how old they are, their geographical distribution, and what they can tell us about the people who made them.

History of the term

Between 1926 and 1928 a small rock shelter on the northern side of the Howieson's Poort pass was excavated by Dr John Hewitt, the director of the Albany Museum in Grahamstown, and a teacher at St Aidan's College, Father P Stapleton. They were immediately aware that the stone tools they found were different from those they had recovered from Later Stone Age (LSA) sites in the region. In the first place, there were no bones or other organic materials preserved and, secondly, there was no stratigraphy to speak of because the stone tools came from only one layer.

Crescents

What makes the Howiesons Poort distinctive?

The main characteristics that distinguish the Howiesons Poort stone tools from the MSA ones that were made before and after it are:

- a different range of raw materials that include finer-grained rocks such as silcrete, chalcedony, quartz and hornfels
- a significant number of stone blades with small striking platforms
- tools that have been retouched into geometric shapes such as segments and trapezes
- blades with notches along one or both sides
- rare bifacial points that have been retouched on both the upper and lower surface
- pieces of ochre that have been smoothed through use and sometimes notched.

The Howiesons Poort stone tool technology is characterised by a sophisticated technique that carefully prepared the domed upper surface of the core and also prepared an acutely angled striking platform. Blades about 40 mm long were then removed by using a 'soft' stone or wooden hammer against the prepared platform. This resulted in a characteristically small offset platform with a lip or overhang and diffuse bulb of percussion. Some blades were subsequently retouched to make D-shaped tools with a long, straight cutting edge and a curved, blunted back. They have been variously called crescents or segments. A variation on this theme is trapezoid in shape with blunting at the top and bottom edges.

The original collection of stone tools from Howieson's Poort also included unifacial and bifacial points characteristic of the Stillbay period, which we now know precedes the Howiesons Poort. These are usually triangular or leaf-shaped flakes with flat invasive retouch on both surfaces that reduces the thickness and strengthens the edges of the tool. This retouch is also used to reduce the size of the bulb of percussion and platform at the base of the triangle, and would have made it easier to fix the stone to a wooden handle to make a spear. Other formal tools include scrapers and various miscellaneous retouched pieces.

The tasks that the Howiesons Poort stone tools were made for probably did not differ significantly from those before and after: people continued to make stone tools for cutting, scraping and piercing. There is no difference in the animals they hunted or the environments they lived in. The contrast is in the way the tools were made and in their shape and size.

Backed Blades

Trapezoids

73

to the time since a last common ancestor. Briefly, geneticists argue that the extreme variety of mtDNA lineages among contemporary Africans and the pattern of convergence between them rule out a common female ancestor anywhere but in Africa. Eve, as they say, was an African woman who lived somewhere between 150 000 and 200 000 years ago. Greater resolution of this would depend on a more precise estimate of the rate of mtDNA change. Later DNA work on the Y-chromosome, illustrative of male lineages, shows that, as we might expect, Adam was also an African. But were they 'modern'? We return to this later.

This spotlight on Africa is, of course, substantially in line with the rather sudden replacement of Neanderthalers by Cro-Magnons in Europe, but does nothing to dampen the vociferous debate about how that replacement occurred. Clearly the modern Cro-Magnons came from outside Europe, most likely Africa, but were they so different, or so bloodthirsty, that they did not incorporate any Neanderthal genes in the ongoing modern lineage? This is an unresolved issue, though my impression is that most archaeologists and biological anthropologists agree that few Neanderthal genes persisted.

It is, of course, somewhat surprising that presumed Africans would be able to rapidly replace the Neanderthalers, who had evolved over many tens, even hundreds of thousands of years in temperate and often periglacial Europe. The competitive advantage held by Cro-Magnons was not specific habitat knowledge but a generally more flexible and insightful approach to resource exploitation and social organisation. This reference to increased intelligence will recur frequently in the discussion that follows. Neanderthalers were smart, but modern people were, somehow, smarter. The excitement and inconclusiveness of this debate should not hide the fact that the origin of modern people needs now to be sought outside Europe.

Dating the Howiesons Poort

In the 1950s the Howiesons Poort was placed in what was then called the Second Intermediate, a stage between the Middle and the Later Stone Ages. This term was dropped in the late 1960s because it became obvious from further excavations in southern Africa that the Howiesons Poort did not immediately precede the Later Stone Age. The precise age was difficult to pinpoint, however, because it was older than 40 000 years and therefore beyond the range of radiocarbon dating. In 1965 the name site was re-excavated to obtain charcoal samples for radiocarbon dating, but the results were unsatisfactory because the charcoal had become contaminated, possibly with younger carbon from the rootlets of a tree growing in the cave.

Over the next few decades, excavations at Klasies River, Boomplaas, Montagu Cave, Die Kelders, Diepkloof, Border Cave and Blombos used new and more appropriate dating methods such as electron spin resonance, uranium disequilibrium and luminescence, as well as palaeoenvironmental data. Collectively, these strands of evidence confirm that most of the Howiesons Poort stone tools were made between 80 000 and 60 000 years ago.

The Howiesons Poort always occurs above, and is therefore later than, both the MSA 1 and 2, and the Stillbay. It is also always below, and therefore earlier than, the final MSA, MSA 3 and 4. All of these stages are typologically and technologically different from the Howiesons Poort, which is the only one in the MSA that has backed tools like segments and trapezes.

The Howiesons Poort was therefore not a bridge between the MSA and LSA, but was a distinctive penultimate stage within the MSA.

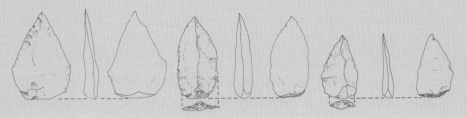

Unifacial points

Geographic distribution

The Howiesons Poort has been found stratified in about twenty rock shelters in Namibia, South Africa, Lesotho and Zimbabwe. This distribution indicates that the technological or social reasons for its persistence over less than 20 000 years were widespread and that active social networks kept them in operation. In other words, people throughout the region were communicating with each other and copying their stone-toolmaking methods. The geographic spread is very similar in extent to that of the LSA and to San rock art in the last 12 000 years.

Howiesons Poort people

Fragmentary human remains found with MSA 2, Stillbay, Howiesons Poort and MSA 3 stone tools at Klasies River on the Eastern Cape coast and Border Cave in KwaZulu-Natal, and isolated teeth found at Die Kelders and Blombos in the Western Cape, all indicate that the people who made the Howiesons Poort stone tools were physically modern in appearance. As hunter-gatherers they hunted large and small game, ate shellfish and occasionally fish and marine mammals washed onto the shore, and they gathered a variety of plant foods, ostrich eggs, tortoises and other collectable foods. In terms of social life, they habitually lived in caves and rock shelters as well as in the open, and they cooked their food over family fires, just like their LSA counterparts.

There are compelling reasons for believing that they were also modern in their behaviour and had the capacity to express symbolic ideas. We don't know what language they spoke, but it seems very likely that they had developed language by this time. They engraved geometric patterns onto ostrich eggshell at Diepkloof and they cut grooves into pieces of ochre that were rubbed smooth at Klasies River and the name site. Their Stillbay ancestors at Blombos Cave engraved geometric patterns onto ochre and they used shells with natural holes in them as beads. David Lewis-Williams and David Pearce have argued that the Howiesons Poort artefacts reflect early signs of spirituality on account of their shiny quality. The refracted light from quartz crystals is known to have been valued by people in many parts of the world where it is associated with the hallucinatory experiences of shamans. A very small number of Howiesons Poort stone tools display this type of refracted light.

Crescents

Fourth, we know that the Kabwe and Saldanha hominin fossils are very old, probably at least 500 000 years old, perhaps much older, are probably associated with ESA tools, and are not Neanderthalers at all but are part of a long-term morphological shift toward modern people in Africa. The Florisbad material, for example, is often described as near-modern, shows none of the kinds of distinctively Neanderthal characters, and is almost 200 000 years old. It is associated with MSA artefacts. Many other African fossil hominins, such as those from Laetoli, Omo and Herto, increasingly well dated but not actually found in stratigraphic context, are modern in the sense of being indistinguishable from contemporary African morphology, and more than 100 000 years old.

Most importantly, every single fossil hominin fragment associated with MSA stone tool assemblages 50 000 to 120 000 years old from South Africa, including those from Klasies River, Border Cave, Die Kelders, Sea Harvest and Blombos Cave, is distinctly modern. Remember, Neanderthalers exclusively occupied Europe till about 40 000 years ago. Morphological and genetic evidence, in most experts' views, now reflects the appearance of anatomically modern people in Africa more than 100 000 years ago. A more difficult task is to define and identify modern behaviour.

The current debate about the MSA and modern human origins

The waves of neo-anthropic invaders, bringing innovative practices with them, have become waves of modern people exporting modern behaviour to the world. Talk of hybridisation has been transferred to the discussion of the fate of Neanderthalers. The stigma of backwardness has been transformed into the confidence of originality. But how are the current versions of modernity phrased, what is the evidence and why is there not agreement on a narrative? Let's begin with an obvious question: what do we mean by modern behaviour?

By anatomically modern we mean skeletal remains that would not be beyond the range recorded among living people, but the same option is not as easy for archaeologists dealing with cultural remains. Behaviourally modern cannot, obviously, mean assemblages of artefacts and foodwaste that would fall within the range known from modern human societies. At least, it could, but we have chosen not to see it in such narrow terms.

One option, favoured by some, is to use the well-known circumstances of the Neanderthal to Cro-Magnon transition as a guideline. If we list the behavioural practices of the Cro-Magnons, especially those not shared with the Neanderthalers, we could compile a trait list of modernity. This is because the Cro-Magnons were, skeletally at least, patently modern. This list, as indicated above, might include some stone-tool-flaking practices such as blade removal, soft hammer retouch and the use of a punch, the manufacture of tools from organic raw materials such as bone, the making of ornaments by piercing materials and stringing them or attaching them to clothing, the production of geometric or naturalistic images on some or other object or canvas, and some vaguely defined 'advanced' economic practices usually including shellfish-gathering and 'efficient' hunting of game using innovative devices such as spear throwers or even bows and arrows.

There is widespread objection to this approach. For a start, it appears to be a shopping list, possibly appropriate in some landscapes, Ice Age Europe perhaps, but unlikely to be so for tropical or subtropical Africa. In any case, there is no reason to suppose that this set of behaviours or practices appeared as a package. It may have gradually coalesced under the specific and changing circumstances of human evolution. Each component almost certainly has its own history and geography. This Eurocentrism is usually rejected.

Interestingly, it is often rejected in Europe too but for a different reason. Some European archaeologists argue that Neanderthalers were already engaging in practices on the modern trait list before Cro-Magnons came to Europe. This would mean that at least some archaic populations were, for example, working in bone, making decorative items or even carving images. Not only that, but some of the early Cro-Magnons may not have been doing these things. The UP model for modern behaviour is not as attractive as it might appear.

A second approach would be to look for behaviours that characterise all, or at least most, of the recent hunter-gatherer communities recorded by ethnographers. Surely, it might be argued, modern behaviour is usefully defined as what hunters and gatherers all do, since we know that earlier, potentially modern people were extracting resources this way. Such an approach has the advantage of generalising about modernity and avoiding a definition that is too closely tied to some particular geographic circumstance.

It does, however, produce another trait list and one not that different from the UP model. Again on the list are practices such as the making of items of personal adornment, decoration of artefacts, image production, ritualised disposal of the dead, gendered practices, complex social arrangements including kinship systems of various kinds, and some sophisticated equipment for hunting or gathering. Because these practices are observed among living peoples, they include more intangible components alongside more material ones. Underpinning these, of course, would be the planning and communication that are facilitated by language.

This approach seems to be getting nearer to the heart of what we might want to mean by modern behaviour. Perhaps because we are thinking here about our own fairly recent ancestors, we usually see increased smartness and language as underpinning a series of social and symbolic practices such as the construction of identity, the capacity to engage in complex planning, the ability to communicate abstract as well as concrete ideas, the awareness of past and future as well as

present, and the ability to construct a world that is properly accounted for. For these reasons there is an emerging consensus that the term 'modern' is far too vague and needs to be replaced by something like 'fully cultural' or, better perhaps, 'symbolically mediated' behaviour.

Language is the most quintessentially symbolic of all human behaviours, but its detection in the material record is notoriously difficult. The problem facing archaeologists is how to make use of concepts such as planning, symbolism and style. How are these manifested in the material remains and their associations that we might excavate and record? What do we expect to find as the residue of symbolically mediated behaviour? Most disagreements in the debates about modern behaviour derive from differing perceptions of what is or is not symbolism, or planning, or style.

Symbolic behaviour in the MSA

A popular notion of symbolism is that of the external storage of information, communication between individuals using artefacts that carry mutually agreed and interpretable information. Think of a distinctive mark on a bag or a quiver that everyone knows means 'it's mine', a particular design that differs from others on your or her bag or quiver, a meaningful choice from a set of available symbolic, not representational, markings. I could have a picture of me on the bag, but three crosshatched lines in a particular orientation can 'stand for' me. Alternatively, our group could agree to make and mark artefacts in a different way from the way your group does. These differences would not affect the functioning of the artefacts but would reflect a group 'style', the purpose of which was to represent the group and distinguish its products.

Individual and group identities can be reflected in, reinforced by, or challenged by these symbolic markings that operate as a nonverbal language. Language, though, may be needed for their effective implementation. The message may be 'hands off' or 'look how efficient we are' or 'your mother came from our group' or any other, but the key principle is readability – mutually agreed but arbitrary meaning imposed by consent. Could we discover these kinds of practice in the Stone Age record in the MSA perhaps?

A challenging arena is that of flaked stone, because most archaeologists are trained to see flaking as part of making rather than marking. We might think that the functional requirements of flaked stone artefacts are paramount, leaving little room for style. Clearly this is not so. Handaxes, the quintessential ESA Swiss Army knives, are often far more persistently flaked, far more symmetrically shaped than mere function might demand. There may well be information stored in this overdetermination and symmetry, clues that contemporaries of the maker could easily read. This is not a new idea, and is offered here just to remind us that any symbolic message discernible in MSA stone tools may be far from the first such in hominin evolution. The beautiful bifacially flaked points of the Stillbay and the extremely standardised backed segments of the Howiesons Poort have been seen as carrying symbolic information.

In addition, some archaeologists expect that modern people, like those in the Holocene, would make artefacts that vary markedly through time and across space as a reflection of stylistic differentiation among neighbouring groups. Rapid replacement of tool forms is taken as a sign of symbolic rather than simple functional aspects of equipment. Could the reportedly brief durations of the backed segments or the bifacial leaf-shaped points be examples of this? They could – but as far as we can tell, the pace of tool-form replacement is still very slow through most of the MSA, quickening perhaps after 100 000 years ago.

Are these the clues we have been looking for? Are the supposedly precocious artefacts of the Howiesons Poort and Stillbay signs of an emergent modern mind? Is the apparently slow replacement or development rate of the ESA

Modern humans and symbolic behaviour

Evidence from Blombos Cave, South Africa

CHRISTOPHER HENSHILWOOD

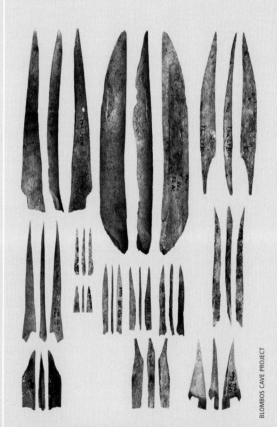

BLOMBOS CAVE PROJECT

Worked bone from Blombos Cave.

Once symbols appeared, we know we're dealing with people with advanced cognitive skills who could not only invent sophisticated tools, weapons and develop complex social networks for mutual security but could also marvel at the intricacies of nature and their place in it, people who were self-aware.
– Mitchell Leslie, 'Suddenly Smarter', *Stanford Magazine*, July–August 2002

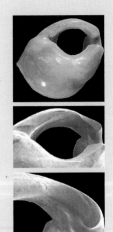

The evolution of symbolically driven behaviour

When and where humans first behaved in a 'modern' way ranks among the most important questions archaeologists ask about our past. Closely linked is when and where humans first became anatomically modern. The second question is perhaps easier to answer as palaeoanthropologists are occasionally lucky enough to uncover human remains dating to the period when humans first looked like us.

Recent finds of anatomically modern humans by Tim White and his team and also by Ian McDougall in Ethiopia may date back more than 150 000 years. Skeletal evidence is backed up by that of mitochondrial DNA (mtDNA). We know that mtDNA is passed on through the maternal line only, and the greatest diversity in mtDNA occurs in Africa – suggesting that the 'mother' of all the world's populations, a 'mitochondrial Eve', lived in Africa between 200 000 and 150 000 years ago. On balance, combined evidence suggests that anatomically modern people originated in Africa and subsequently radiated out to populate the world. All other hominids became extinct during this expansion process.

So what was it that made these new African hominids so successful? How were they able to replace earlier hominids that had successfully occupied specialist environmental niches for hundreds of millennia – the Neanderthals in Europe and *Homo erectus* in Asia? Being anatomically modern – the equivalent of having the right hardware – must have helped, but a more crucial role must have been that of behaviour. It seems likely that a rewiring of the human brain – the software – was linked to physical modernity, and almost certainly that a capacity for syntactical language and for other 'modern' behaviours was possible by perhaps 200 000 years ago, although the evidence for this is not easily detectable in the archaeological record.

If anatomically modern *Homo sapiens* evolved first in Africa, it suggests that behavioural 'modernity' also first developed on the continent. Until recently, archaeological evidence from Africa and Europe did not support this scenario. The markers of 'modern'-type behaviour that are recoverable from archaeological sites typically include evidence for art, personal ornaments,

Nassarius kraussianus shell beads from Blombos Cave. The keyhole perforations made with a bone tool inserted through the shell mouth are clearly visible. Close inspection of the beads reveal wear facets caused by friction against thread and other shells after stringing.

CHRISTOPHER HENSHILWOOD AND FRANCESO D'ERRICO

Christopher Henshilwood alongside the stratigraphy at Blombos Cave.

formal bone tools, and sophisticated subsistence behaviour. Great discoveries of abstract and representational wall paintings, personal ornaments such as perforated animal teeth, marine shell beads, and decorated bone tools all seemed to come from Europe and many were dated at around 35 000 BP. There was no apparent evidence for 'behavioural' modernity in Africa at this early date. A consequent assumption made by many archaeologists was that 'modern' behaviour evolved first in Europe and not in Africa.

The entrance to Blombos Cave.

BLOMBOS CAVE PROJECT

Discoveries in Africa of objects associated with 'modern' behaviour were initially few and far between; but by the 1980s evidence was accumulating that *Homo sapiens* in parts of Africa may, in fact, have been 'modern' long before they reached Europe. Part of the problem lies in the recognition of what constitutes 'modern'. The European evidence, based on material culture, was long presented as the benchmark of behavioural modernity. This explanation was not universally accepted: why should modernity in Europe present in the same way in Africa, some argued. The vast differences in climate alone suggested that the material culture of Europeans would look very different from that of Africans. It seemed clear to some that a new paradigm for measuring modernity in Africa was needed.

A milestone in the evolution of human cognitive abilities occurred when humans were first able to store concepts or information outside the human brain with the aid of material symbols, and to locate or even anchor memory outside the individual brain. The use of modern language was essential for the operation of symbolically driven systems because modern language is the only communication system with a 'built-in' meta-language that allows the creation of symbolic codes.

Once humans store information outside their brains, the society or social systems in which they operate will be mediated by symbolically driven behaviour – perhaps one of the great turning points in human evolution. Symbolic material culture, the one marker undeniably associated with behavioural modernity, whether in Europe or Africa, is providing archaeologists with a strong theoretical model for identifying early modernity. Taken together with the 'hard' evidence, with some of the artefacts recently recovered from Middle Stone Age (MSA) sites in Africa, the evidence is building that 'modern' behaviour first evolved in Africa.

The Blombos Cave evidence

Blombos Cave, located on the southern Cape coast near the village of Still Bay, is one MSA site contributing to a better understanding of the origins of symbolic behaviour. First excavated in 1992, the MSA levels – dated to at least 75 000 years by the optically stimulated luminescence method – have yielded a range of artefacts unusual for this time. In 1999 and 2000 respectively, two slabs of ochre were recovered with abstract designs visible on both pieces.

handaxe and most of the recognisable early MSA forms a sign of their manufacture by archaic minds? Perhaps so, but it is also possible that we are not reading the signs properly, that there are key developments that we barely detect.

At least this kind of analysis draws attention to the drastically altered pace of change in the later MSA. It is also noticeable that these later distinctive tool forms are often much more geographically restricted than earlier MSA and ESA forms. Another sign of intentional use of design in differentiation, this time between spatially separate groups? There is meat to argue over here but little resolution.

The distinction between stone-flaking characteristics that are functional and those that may carry symbolic meaning is not merely academic. Improvements that offer real competitive advantages to the innovators may be expected to survive and flourish until replaced by better ideas, whereas technical but primarily symbolic innovations might come and go in more capricious ways, with little connection to environmental or subsistence patterns. Because these issues are very difficult to resolve, visible stone-toolmaking changes such as the use of punches, or bones as soft hammers, or an emphasis on blade production are enigmatic, borderline perhaps between the clearly symbolic and the distinctly functional.

Most archaeologists believe we are on safer ground relating the non-flaked stone component of MSA assemblages to developments in symbolic behaviour. Take ochre, for example. Pigment-generating rocks and minerals such as ferruginous shales, various kinds of weathered iron oxides often called ochre, or manganese dioxides are abundant in the South African Stone Age. The common name in English for some of the iron oxides – haematite, also called bloodstone – underscores the highly symbolic uses of this pigment in modern and recent hunter-gatherer societies. We can trace the use of pigment-generating materials (let us for simplicity sake call them ochre) back far into the ESA at Wonderwerk

Ochre is a mineral rich in iron oxide and when rubbed yields a streak of pigment or if scraped produces a powder. The colour of ochre ranges from yellowish to deep red. At Blombos Cave 75 000 years ago, the inhabitants preferred the deep red ochres. They collected more than two thousand pieces from at least 20 kilometres away and brought them to the site to be worked as a pigment.

Most ochre pieces show evidence of use, but two pieces of ochre were treated differently. First, a surface on each was repeatedly scraped or rubbed to form a flat facet. Using a stone flake with a sharp point, an abstract design was then deliberately engraved on that surface. On one piece the design consists of a series of oblique lines in one direction and a lesser number of lines that cross over these. The design is indistinct, almost as if repeated rubbing or abrasion occurred after the original design was created. On another piece a distinct crosshatched pattern was engraved and, as if to emphasise the design, three further lines were engraved across the top, through the middle and at the bottom of the pattern. There appears some evidence that an earlier design was made on the same surface that is now indistinct. It is possible that the later prominent engraving served to reinforce the muted design.

These designs were engraved with deliberate symbolic intention and had meaning for the maker and very likely for a wider social grouping, although the exact meaning of these symbols is no longer understood. The Blombos ochre engravings are perhaps two of the earliest known examples of abstract designs that represent symbolic systems stored outside the human brain.

More than thirty bone tools, some finely worked and polished, more than 300 leaf-shaped bifacially worked stone points, and well-preserved evidence of terrestrial animals hunted and gathered come from the levels dated at about 78 000 to 75 000 BP. Marine resources were extensively exploited including seals, dolphins, large fish and shellfish.

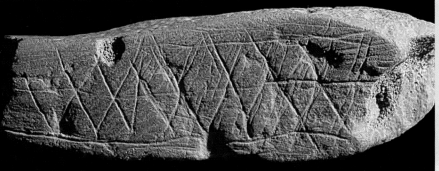

A surprising find in these levels was more than sixty shells of the estuarine gastropod *Nassarius kraussianus*, the tick shell. Too small to be food items, these animals were collected from river mouths at least 15 kilometres from the site. Resembling small, pearly white molars, each shell was carefully pierced by inserting a small bone tool through the mouth and then with pressure creating a keyhole aperture. The shells were then strung, perhaps using plant or animal-derived thread, and worn as a personal ornament. Wear patterns on the shells from the thread and also from repeated contact with human skin tell us that some of these 'necklaces' or 'bracelets' were worn for considerable periods of time, and very possibly for more than a year.

The recovery of discrete shell groups in different parts of the site suggests that a number of different personal ornaments were lost at the site. In particular, a concentration of more than twenty beads recovered in one level, all showing extensive wear and similar in colour and size, indicates the loss of a single beadwork item probably worn for a long period by an individual.

Personal ornaments, particularly beads, communicate cultural values in a symbolic language that expresses social, personal and ethnic identity in modern hunter-gatherer societies. Fully syntactical language is arguably an essential prerequisite for sharing and transmitting the symbolic meaning of each beadwork item. The discovery of personal ornaments in the approximately 75 000 BP levels at Blombos adds an unambiguous marker of symbolically mediated behaviour to the list of innovations already identified in the MSA.

The Blombos Cave finds are adding to the data from a number of African sites older than about 50 000 years that incontrovertibly point to an early African origin for human behaviour mediated by symbolism. It now seems certain that not only did our common ancestors evolve in Africa but also the roots of our contemporary behaviour.

Engraved ochres from the Middle Stone Age levels (ca. 75 000 years ago) at Blombos Cave.

Cave. Ochres are very common in the later MSA at many South African sites, much more common apparently than at any MP sites in Europe and the Near East. We can also show that lots of these ochreous fragments have been intentionally ground, because they are often bevelled, striated or faceted. Sometimes the ground shapes are quite pointed, leading to the term 'ochre crayons' and suggesting a use for them as marking tools. I believe Lyn Wadley is probably correct in suggesting that the crayons are but one extreme of a range of shapes that ground ochre can take, and that all of these pieces are simply bits of rock that had been scraped to produce pigment powder.

It is more difficult to know why the pigment powder was being used. Because the iron oxides have antibacterial qualities that might have been recognised by our early ancestors, the pigment may not have been paint but a component of hide preparation or a skin cosmetic, although neither of these uses rules out some symbolism. The archaeological context of the ochre doesn't preserve the context of use closely enough to

resolve this, so we have to resort to more indirect lines of inquiry. Ian Watts has argued that the preference shown for saturated hues in many assemblages is evidence for selection of symbolically loaded pigment-making. Modern hunter-gatherers do this. The nonsymbolic use of ochres draws on hues that are common but not specially chosen. This certainly supports the point that the colour of the pigment was a crucial part of its attraction, likely to imply, as in later times, a reference to blood or life. Unfortunately we do not have the more explicitly symbolic scattering of ochre on burials, as in the European UP, until much later in the South African record.

An extension of this argument is enabled by the geometric markings on several ochre pieces from the Stillbay layers at Blombos Cave in the southern Cape. This is a clearly MSA context with reliable single-grain, optically stimulated luminescence ages of about 75 000 years. While it is, even here, not possible to rule out completely some functional purpose in the markings, the complexity of the design seems to be strong evi-

View of Diepkloof Rock Shelter.

NEIL RUSCH

dence for symbolic intent. In the clearest example the cross-hatching is very obviously framed by three parallel engraved lines, altogether too constructed to be merely striations from use. Other fragments from the same layers are less persuasive, but supportive. The combination of design and pigment generation is good evidence for some kind of 'symbolically mediated behaviour', especially given the widespread and regular collection of pigments from the surrounding landscapes. We will return to the stratigraphic context of these pieces later.

Equally persuasive are the intentionally marked ostrich eggshell fragments excavated from the Diepkloof Rock Shelter in the Western Cape by Cedric Poggenpoel. Working with myself and French colleagues Jean-Philippe Rigaud and Pierre-Jean Texier, he has identified more than 170 small fragments of eggshell that have been scored and incised, at least five of them clearly parts of ostrich eggshell flasks. The rounded perforations made in the eggs are incorporated into the radiating designs, which we think might mean that all of the pieces were once intentional markings on the upper parts of flasks. Designs include parallel and intersecting marks, parallel lines with hatching, and fully cross-hatched sets of lines. When we have fully understood the placement of these markings on the eggs, we will assuredly have the component parts of a complex, fully abstract signalling system.

The Diepkloof evidence adds to the case for symbolic mediation by showing that marking was very common at some times, that it included a range of designs from which people chose, and that it was applied to objects of lasting value. It is likely that the differentiation of eggs by distinctive marking was aimed at fellow group members, a communication device located outside, but linked to, the human brain. This is the core of Merlin Donald's notion of symbolic practice. Every single marked piece comes from the uppermost layers of the Howiesons Poort part of this important sequence. Preliminary single-grain optically stimulated luminescence dates of 63 000 years come from these layers. No intentionally marked pieces come from below or above the Howiesons Poort layers, although there are many ostrich eggshell fragments there.

The ostrich eggshell flasks, also recorded from the Howiesons Poort levels at Apollo XI Cave in Namibia, are suggestive evidence for both storage and transport. The ethnographic records of flasks in hunter-gatherer communities extending back to LSA times allows us to speculate that water was collected, transported and stored for use in these containers. This is their sole function in recent times, though they are not always 'decorated'.

It seems that several of the operational expectations for symbolism, including planning, are observable at Diepkloof and Apollo XI. It would also seem likely that, once invented, ostrich eggshell containers would remain permanently as part of people's technological repertoire and coping strategy, though marking might be optional. All the more strange then that the marking is not found consistently from Howiesons Poort times on. We could also wait for more excavations to be sure the absence of evidence is, indeed, the evidence of absence. The preservation of material in the deposit at Diepkloof is very good, as we noted above, and the disappearance of both marking and flask mouths requires some other, presumably behavioural, explanation.

Beads and pendants are very common in the LSA of South Africa, made from a wide range of materials including ostrich eggshell, marine shell, bone, seed and, later, glass and metal. Until very recently, however, none were known from the MSA. Christopher Henshilwood and Francesco d'Errico have recently reported 41 beads, all but two from the Stillbay layers at Blombos Cave, made by perforating the shells of an estuarine gastropod snail, *Nassarius kraussianus*. The bead-makers seem to have chosen large specimens, transported them more than a dozen kilometres, and carefully perforated the shells near the margin. Because they were excavated in groups of several closely associated beads, they may have been strung on necklaces and worn around the neck.

These shell beads are dated to about 75 000 years ago and are easily the earliest objects of ornamentation from anywhere in Africa, and arguably anywhere at all. From UP sites in Turkey, there are shell beads some 40 000 years old, and others in Europe may be that age too. All were made by modern people after their arrival in Europe. Beads or pendants are singularly rare before the UP. The only exceptions are perforated teeth from the very final MP in northern France, made by some of the very last Neanderthalers (possibly copying the incoming Cro-Magnons, though this is disputed).

The Blombos beads are extremely important. If the arguments for their purposeful transport and manufacture are sound, and they appear to be, these beads represent unambiguous evidence for the modification of materials for symbolic use. The most likely explanation is that the beads served to identify some particular maker and to 'stand for' an individual identity. They were presumably worn in such a way that they became a readable part of an individual's personality, an outward display that probably 'spoke' both to the wearer and the viewer. It is hard to think of a purely functional or utilitarian explanation that accounts as well for the 41 perforated shells.

Bone tools are also extremely rare in European MP sites but very common in later UP ones, a major factor in the idea that modern Cro-Magnons were more imaginative, inventive and innovative than their Neanderthal predecessors. For this reason, regular manufacture of bone or other organic tools is usually included in the trait list of modern behaviour. In South Africa, bone tools are rare in the MSA but a finely made point was found, albeit in an uncertain stratigraphic context, in the MSA at Klasies River by John Wymer. Most archaeologists dismissed this bone point in the light of the rarity of bone tools elsewhere from MSA contexts. At Blombos Cave,

The origin of complex burial in southern Africa

DAVID PEARCE

'Really marvellous it is.' These were the words James Drury recorded in his notebook in 1911 upon his discovery of a finely painted grinding stone covering a human burial. He found it in the Coldstream rock shelter in the Eastern Cape Province of South Africa. It is the most detailed of the painted stones so far found. The grave it comes from was that of a Later Stone Age (LSA) person, and formed part of a complex of burials that is probably the most elaborate expression of southern African LSA culture yet found.

In contrast to this elaboration, earlier evidence for human burial is scant. The first anatomically modern humans in southern Africa are represented by only a few small fragments of bone scattered through cave deposits dating from as early as 120 000 years ago, although most are not that old. The sites where the early evidence was found include Klasies River main site, Border Cave, Die Kelders Cave 1, Blombos Cave, and Equus Cave. None of the early skeletal fragments were the product of formal burial.

Human burials from more recent periods are still rare. Indeed, throughout the LSA, except in the Eastern and Western Cape Provinces, finds of human burials are unusual. The reason is that southern African LSA people seem, like modern San in the Kalahari during the last century, to have buried

their dead in unmarked graves in the open (not in rock shelters) with few, if any, grave goods. The Kalahari San then moved their camp away from the burial place. LSA people seem to have done the same.

The situation along the Eastern and Western Cape coasts and adjacent interior was different. Between about 10 000 and 2000 BP people buried their dead in rock shelters. Why this change took place is not yet clear. It is, however, because of the change that so many burials are known in the area: archaeologists find them in the course of routine excavations of rock shelters.

The change was profound. Not only was there a change of burial location, but also a shift in ideology. The dead were no longer placed in graves in the open, and avoided; they were buried in rock shelters in which people continued to live. In addition, some of these graves seem to have been marked: painted stones have been found covering a number of them. Many others were covered with unpainted stones. Because of the internal collapse of many graves and the continual accumulation of deposit over them, it is uncertain whether the stones were originally visible on the surface or not, but it does seem likely that some were.

The painted stones are important because they provide a clear link between the burials and the paintings that adorn the shelter walls. The imagery on the painted stones is, unsurprisingly, remarkably similar to the wall paintings. Indeed, all the human postures recognised as characteristic of the trance dance, and recorded frequently in the wall paintings, occur on the painted stones. This similarity is valuable for two reasons. First, it provides information on the type of beliefs held by the people who painted the stones and constructed the graves. Secondly, it gives an indication of the antiquity of the

The painted stone from Coldstream shelter that so moved James Drury is the most detailed of the painted stones yet found. It contains depictions of three polychrome human figures with blood smeared back from their noses across their faces.

however, there are several well-made, stratigraphically well-provenanced bone artefacts, including two points that would not be out of place in the LSA, that settle the matter. Again associated with Stillbay bifacially flaked points, they demonstrate that at least some MSA people regularly worked bone.

Here we should mention a series of barbed 'harpoon' points made of bone, from the site of Katanda in the Democratic Republic of Congo, described by Alison Brooks and John Yellen. These remarkable artefacts, including both single- and double-rowed types and showing a range of technical manufacturing details, were excavated from buried stratified layers at several sites in association with arguably MSA stone tools and a complex animal bone assemblage. According to Brooks and Yellen, the whole assemblage is at least 90 000 years old on the basis of electron spin resonance ages from hippo teeth and other luminescence age estimates on the enclosing sediment.

From the time of the announcement of these ages, some archaeologists, including the late Desmond Clark and the very much alive Richard Klein, expressed doubt about the associations. Klein, in particular, voiced concern that the harpoons may not be contemporary with the hippo teeth or the sediments in which they were found. His scenario is that much later fishers stood on a gravel bar and, in the course of harpooning fish, lost some of their bone tools, which became inextricably mixed with much older sediments and faunal remains. He points out that some, but not all, of the bones are now so rolled that they resemble bone pebbles, whereas the harpoons appear much fresher. The excavators respond by assuring us of the stratigraphic integrity of the site, pointing out that there are three such assemblages of harpoons and noting that all diagnostic material is MSA.

Some independent observers have noted with surprise that the range of bone harpoons is remarkably similar to other such assemblages

painting tradition and associated beliefs in the area: at least 8000 years.

The inclusion of stones was not the only addition to the graves. Their contents became extremely elaborate with large numbers of grave goods of diverse types included. Ground ochre was often sprinkled in graves. Beads made from ostrich eggshell or seashells commonly adorned bodies, sometimes numbering in the thousands of individual beads. Grinding stones, bored stones, seashells, ostrich eggshells and tortoise shells were also frequently placed in graves.

In addition to this 'core' of common inclusions there are also a number of ancillary items that have each been found in only a single case. In the grave of an elderly man at Oakhurst rock shelter, for instance, a bored stone plugged at one end with black resin was found. Within the cavity of the stone was the complete vertebral column of a small fish. Another burial at the same site is, perhaps, the most touching of all those yet found: the skeletons of two children, aged between three and four years,

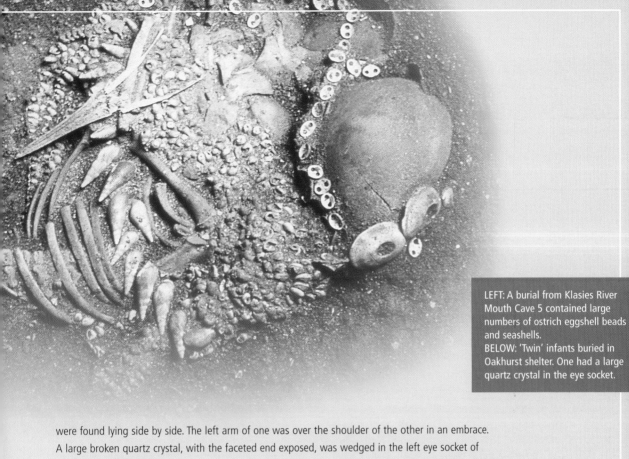

were found lying side by side. The left arm of one was over the shoulder of the other in an embrace. A large broken quartz crystal, with the faceted end exposed, was wedged in the left eye socket of one of the children.

The objects included in the burials, both the core and ancillary items, and the very structure of the graves were far from random. In fact they were highly symbolic. The symbolism related primarily to entrance to the spirit world and water (going underwater was itself thought to be a way of entering the spirit world). The dead were put, literally and symbolically, underground into the spirit world. It seems likely, however, that the burials were not only a means of inserting the dead into the spirit world, but also played an important role in the lives of LSA communities at the time.

Drury was right, and not just about the burial and painted stone he had uncovered. The graves and the adornment of the dead were clearly very special and important for the people who made them. For modern researchers too, they form a marvellous resource to help us understand the lives and, indeed, humanity of people who lived in southern Africa's distant past.

UNIVERSITY OF CAPE TOWN LIBRARY

from several sites across a large part of Central Africa and fairly reliably dated to the very late Pleistocene or early Holocene, exclusively later than 20 000 years. It would indeed be surprising, but not impossible, for artefact types in the past 100 000 years to last more or less unchanged in a narrow geographic region for 70 000 or 80 000 years. There is apparently not enough organic material in the harpoons to allow the excavators to radiocarbon-date them. In my view we need to wait for further supporting evidence before accepting these Katanda harpoons as securely MSA.

The Katanda harpoons are an excellent reminder of the difficulties of interpreting the archaeological 'record'. Very often, too often it seems, crucial information is rendered at best awkward and at worst inadmissible because of some doubt about age or correct association. This has been a problem with many of the examples already discussed here. As a cautionary tale we might consider what has happened to claims of early domestic animal bones in southern African LSA sites. In almost but not quite all cases where surprisingly early sheep were claimed on the basis of association between radiocarbon-dated charcoal and sheep bone, direct dating of the sheep bone showed the bones to be much later.

Nassarius kraussianus shell beads from Blombos Cave.

They had lodged lower down the stratigraphic sequence than their original correct position, no doubt due to gravity, undetected disturbances or excavation error.

We should also note that these effects almost always work to give erroneously high ages, though examples of the opposite no doubt could occur. This generates problems primarily because many archaeologists believe they are engaged in an Earlier Than Thou competition, in which earliest is best. No one is clamouring to record the latest sheep bone, the latest harpoon or the most recent decorated ostrich eggshell fragment. Gravity and the egos of archaeologists conspire to generate an ongoing, no doubt endless, stream of claims for 'the earliest', some of which have subsequently to be retracted. My own position, somewhat tongue in cheek, is that the first recorded instance of anything should be seen as a mistake, the second as coincidence and the third as evidence. Others are less cynical.

The real significance of these bone tools, notwithstanding a few residual doubts about some of their ages, is not clear. Although rare, there is no doubt that archaic occupants of Europe as far back as 300 000 years ago were perfectly capable of making tools out of organic raw materials. The wooden 'spears' from Clacton, Lehringen and, recently found, Schoeningen demonstrate this. The idea, then, that until modern people appeared, hunter-gatherers somehow didn't recognise the potential of organic raw materials as suitable for toolmaking is clearly wrong.

This is clear from the African record too, although the shadow of the ambitious, subsequently disproven claims by Raymond Dart for an osteodontokeratic 'culture' of bone, tooth and horn artefacts still haunts us. From Swartkrans, for example, Bob Brain has excavated a large number of pointed bone objects that appear, from microscopic analysis of their tips, to have been used to dig termites out of their mounds. Even if some other use is eventually discovered for them, it appears these are bone tools, although their shape may have accrued from use rather than deliberate manufacture. The Blombos Cave bone tools have clearly been deliberately shaped.

In sum, the evidence that MSA people constructed readable signals for their fellows by shaping, marking, piercing and otherwise modifying artefacts and natural materials of various kinds is undeniable. The pieces are not isolated, but appear to be part of everyday life, implying that the original sample may have been far more substantial than the one preserved and recovered. Although quantification is difficult, it does appear that the density of ochre, marked objects and beads in the MSA is far higher than in the MP in either Europe or the Near East. What we may need to recognise is that almost all of these enigmatic but interesting items in Africa come from the later MSA and specifically from Howiesons Poort and Stillbay contexts. If supported by larger and more numerous excavations, including clear cases of early MSA without them, or more enigmatically latest MSA without them either, this pattern would be extremely significant. With this in mind, I now summarise the distribution of MSA assemblages and sites across South Africa.

The MSA at sites in SA

Hilary Deacon has reminded us that there is useful information in the changing distributions of sites across the landscape through the Stone Age. His point is that the distribution of MSA sites is far more like that of the LSA than either is like that of the ESA. Whereas ESA sites are closely tethered to water sources such as the streams, rivers, pans and lake basins of Africa, MSA sites are more likely to be away from these places, often on bluffs, sometimes in caves and rock shelters. LSA sites are very frequently located at rocky outcrops, also often in overhangs of some sort.

There seems to be an increasing interest in rock shelters through this sequence, though this

Klasies River Main site after excavation.　　JOHN PARKINGTON

needs to be phrased carefully and is far from a statistically tested statement. There are certainly more open sites than cave sites of all ages. The nature of population distribution and site location across the landscape is, though, an important point. How is the MSA cultural stratigraphy distributed across open and cave sites? Where and when are the Howiesons Poort and Stillbay assemblages?

Most landscapes have particular kinds of repositories that contain and preserve the archaeological record, at least those parts of it that are deemed worthy of investigation. The most obvious examples from southern Africa are the dolomite cavern systems in the north that house and conserve early hominin skeletal remains in association with many other animal bones and some stone tools. No one believes that these hominins hung out exclusively, or perhaps ever, in the caverns; but their remains, and indeed all record of their being and behaviour, are located there. The caverns represent the archaeological opportunity in this part of the landscape.

In the Cape, the repetitive onshore transport of shelly sands generates the dune plumes and dune fields that present a similar opportunity to find later hominins. The mechanism is likely to be related to lowering and rising of sea levels. At lower sea levels sand supplies are exposed, dry out and are transported inland by the strong winds, particularly the southerly summer winds. Because sand supply is determined by shoreline shape and topography, these dune plumes regularly overlie earlier ones. Plant colonisation and the process of soil development lead to cementation of sand bodies into calcretes and aeolianites which, because of the alkaline shelly sands, lead to good bone preservation. Almost all coastal MSA sites around the Cape coast relate in some way to these onshore sand movements.

Cape south coast

A key and most frequently quoted reference is the site complex at Klasies River. Wymer and Singer did us an enormous favour in recovering such massive assemblages of bone and stone, but at the expense of resolution and completeness. Many have bemoaned the fact that sieve mesh sizes were large and, as a result, many small bones and artefactual debris slipped through. They also decided that many of the apparently (to them) unidentifiable bones, not to mention all of the shells, need not be kept and discarded them. Fortunately, Hilary Deacon returned some twenty years later and carried out small but

The rock arts of sub-Saharan Africa

BEN SMITH

South of the Sahara we find three separated rock art zones: one spreading throughout southern Africa, one throughout Central Africa and one in central Tanzania. There is a hiatus division in formal characteristics between each zone and, with only a handful of recorded overlaps in distributions that contain tens of thousands of sites, there is a remarkable physical separation of the traditions. These divisions imply that there were major cultural divisions between early hunter-gatherers in sub-Saharan Africa. Such a pattern is a direct contradiction of the received wisdom that San populations once extended as far up Africa as the Ethiopia and Sudan.

I discuss each of the rock art traditions in turn. I begin with those rock arts known to have been made by groups ancestral to the modern San in order to determine the degree of variation within these traditions and therefore the extent to which we might explain the three hiatus divisions in terms of regionalism in San artistic traditions.

Southern African San rock art

Some writers have proposed that San rock art should be divided into sub-regions based on certain differences in subject matter and manner of depiction. The groupings developed by these writers were not clearly defined and seem to split more along natural gaps in the distribution of

San fine-line rock painting from the Western Cape, South Africa.

rock art than along lines of significant change in manners or subjects. That the number of groupings and their boundaries varies in each of the proposed distribution maps shows that San rock art does not divide as neatly into regional groupings as other aspects of material culture, such as stone tools. None of the many divisions proposed have been taken up by other researchers. Rather, work on regionality now emphasises a change in art through space and has moved away from the search for the kind of strong horizons that would warrant formal division.

The repertoire of animals chosen for depiction and the relative frequencies with which they are painted or engraved can be seen to change in San art across southern Africa. Eland, for example, dominate Drakensberg rock art as well as the paintings and engravings of the Free State and North-West Provinces in South Africa. Also in South Africa, elephant and sheep take on numerical importance in the Western Cape; and further north, in the Waterberg of Limpopo Province, the hartebeest becomes the most painted animal; it is then overtaken by kudu, giraffe and elephant in the art of the Limpopo Flats in South Africa, and in Zimbabwe. To the north-west, in the Brandberg in Namibia, springbok become the most painted animals. The relative proportions of the animals therefore vary significantly between regions, but there are no sudden changes — the shift is progressive.

Similarly, the manner in which the human form is depicted varies progressively, as does the ratio of male to female figures. Within South Africa, for instance, as one moves north from the Drakensberg

ROCK ART RESEARCH INSTITUTE

meticulous excavations carefully placed through the 20 metres of deposit. We now have a much better idea of the age of these shelly sediments, their contents and associations.

The depositional pile at the main Klasies River sites consists of a very large cone of occupational debris banked up against a cliff, substantially shelly but with massive quantities of bone fragments and stone artefacts associated with many hearths and fireplaces. As the cone piled up it infiltrated, blocked and in some cases filled a series of small caves and overhangs. A single, complex stratigraphy accounts for all of the sites. Preservation of bone is generally good, especially near to the rock face, because there is a massive shelly dune atop the cliff, rendering percolating waters alkaline.

Based on their assessment of the changing stone tool assemblages Wymer and Singer divided the stack up into MSA1, MSA2, Howiesons Poort, MSA3 and MSA4, from earliest to latest. There is, significantly, no Stillbay assemblage at Klasies River. A small midden of LSA material had accumulated in Cave 1 on top of, but obviously much younger than, the MSA4. It is very important that we recognise that Wymer, who developed the scheme, never intended it to be applied to the MSA of the whole of South Africa, only to the cone at Klasies River main site. MSA4, for example, is located in Cave 1, whereas MSA3 is atop the Howiesons Poort in Shelter 1A.

In Wymer's view there were only minor differences between the MSA stone tool assemblages, a view that has contributed to the notion that MSA people were somewhat unimaginative, staid and conservative. The exception, of course, was the Howiesons Poort assemblages, whose makers showed a much greater interest in finer-grained raw materials such as silcrete, developed somewhat innovative blade production techniques including the use of soft hammers, and made very large numbers of highly standardised backed tools such as truncated blades, trapezes and segments. There were also burins in the

the massive dominance of male figures steadily reduces until, in the Limpopo Flats, depictions of women nearly outnumber depictions of men. The progressive nature of the change is clear in intervening areas such as the Waterberg, where the ratio is between the extremes of the Drakensberg and Limpopo Flats. One could demonstrate similar progressive change in a range of other painted features such as the nature of kit depicted, the use of colour, and the size of depiction. The overall nature of regionality in San art is therefore one in which certain features are general and pervasive but others are regional, or at least enjoy special regional emphasis.

The general features that pervade southern African San art are explained in terms of concepts that pervade the cognitive systems of San people in all areas. For all San groups the most important ritual is the Great Dance. The San say that through trance in this dance they harness a kind of spiritual power that is like electricity. They use this power for things such as healing, hunting, removing societal tensions, and making rain. It is aspects relating to this dance that are pervasive in San rock art, partly because the dance was of such great importance to the San but more immediately because the act of making rock art seems to have been integral to the process by which San ritual specialists harnessed and shared the power of the dance.

In all areas, therefore, rock art images depict aspects of the dance, most often just fragments of the dance rather than entire dance scenes. We see individual or small groups of dancers bending forward, wearing dancing rattles, holding wildebeest tails or dancing sticks and bleeding from the nose: these are all features peculiar to the dance. Around these fragments of the dance are placed animals, but not just a random selection. The animals that have special supernatural potency are the ones particularly chosen and repeated often.

It is from these animals that the San say they draw power in the dance, and the rock art sometimes shows this. Lines of power connect animals to dancers in the art. More than this, dancers are regularly depicted taking on features of powerful animals such as their hoofs or heads. The art also shows the magical otherworldly things such as rain animals, monsters and spirit people that are encountered by dancers on their out-of-body vision journeys. We thus understand San art as a deeply spiritual art, one that harnesses and shares with others the power of generations of San spiritual experience and enlightenment.

It is within this understanding of San rock art that most researchers have grappled with regional variability in San art. One emphasis has been to suggest that local beliefs and requirements (such as the need for rain in arid areas) led particular groups to draw on different animals as their symbols of potency. The varying natural distributions of animals must also have played a part.

Another emphasis has been that certain regional variations in the choice of animals and ways of depicting the human form reflect differing social relations, in particular differing experiences of cultural contact. In South Africa, for example, the progressive decline in the number of sheep painted as one moves from the Western Cape towards KwaZulu-Natal has been well explained by the changing nature and extent of contact with herder peoples; and for the human

Black and white re-drawing of a San fine-line rock painting of a trance dance, Kwazulu-Natal, South Africa.

form, researchers have explained the special emphasis on human facial features in the rock art of the Free State and Eastern Cape in terms of the rise of individual status and agency amongst the later San painters of this area.

From these findings it is readily apparent that a simple link between regionality and ethnicity can be ruled out for San rock art. The broad commonalities in San rock art, alongside steady and significant difference through space, stand in marked contrast to San ethno-linguistic groups as we know them. San linguistic boundaries were so firmly marked that neighbouring communities often spoke languages that were mutually unintelligible. The pattern of regionality does not fit well with either known linguistic or material culture groupings. It more closely matches the nature of variation within San cognitive systems, where certain cognitive fundamentals are held broadly but detail of ritual and symbolism varies locally.

For the period of San contact with Khoekhoe herders, Bantu-speaking farmers and colonial settlers, a wide range of factors have been proposed to explain the reasons for regionality in San rock art. Most researchers have focused on locally specific reactions to the Other. In the pre-contact period the picture is less clear. It does not seem that San groups used rock art to negotiate an identity in opposition to that of neighbouring San groups. The changes in subjects and manners are too gradual through time and space. Such intentional divisiveness would also go against the nature of intergroup relationships known among the later San groups of the Kalahari. Rather, it seems that the older regionality reflects the existence of longstanding and gradual variation in San beliefs through space or the application of commonly held San beliefs in different ways in different areas or, most likely, a combination of the two.

Howiesons Poort assemblages. 'Blade and burin assemblages' is a term often used to characterise the UP of Europe, as John Wymer would have known well. But the key observation at the time (the excavations were conducted in the late 1960s) was that the Howiesons Poort, very like the Howiesons Poort at the type site, was undeniably stratified beneath what Wymer called MSA3. It was the first clear demonstration of this and became the trigger for future MSA thinking.

Although well aware that Wymer had discarded many of the 'unidentifiable' bones, Richard Klein believed the remaining faunal assemblage was representative enough to support some extremely important, persuasive but ultimately arguable conclusions. He noted that there were almost no fish bones or flying bird bones in the Klasies River animal bone samples. Klein ascribed these absences to the inability of MSA people to fish or catch flying birds. Fish and flying birds such as cormorants and gannets are very common in nearby LSA shell middens, presumably collected from the same kinds of habitats available to the MSA occupants.

This comparison, and the conclusion drawn from it, formed one strand of an important hypothesis advanced by Richard Klein: that MSA people were technologically inferior to their later LSA descendants, effectively not modern in their behaviour. The other strands included the observations he made about differences in the species composition and age profiles of faunal assemblages from MSA and LSA sites along this south Cape coast. He thought that the relative abundance of eland compared to buffalo and wild pig in the MSA at Klasies, compared to the reverse in local LSA assemblages, meant that MSA hunters were less capable of approaching and killing dangerous prey, another sign of non-modernity. The age profiles of the eland at MSA and LSA differed in a way that Klein thought indicated a more effective, less opportunistic strategy in the later period. Although alternative views were offered by other analysts, Klein believed the MSA people could hunt but not

as efficiently as the obviously modern LSA ancestors of modern San.

These two points, the relative position and distinctiveness of the Howiesons Poort and the notion of non-modern MSA behaviour, were probably the key observations to come from the Wymer and Singer excavations. Richard Klein developed his hypothesis through the following decades and built further strands of evidence into it. It became clear with excavations at Nelson Bay Cave by Ray Inskeep and Klein himself, and at Elands Bay Cave by myself, that the seal bones at LSA sites differed substantially from the sample recovered by Wymer from the Klasies River MSA. The latter included lots of adults, including some aged individuals, whereas the LSA samples were all completely dominated by much smaller and more uniformly sized yearlings.

Klein has argued that this, too, reflects a less sophisticated strategy by MSA people, who some-how did not schedule their visits to the coast as cleverly as their LSA descendants. They may have scavenged adult seal carcasses from the shore. LSA coastal hunter-gatherers timed their visits so as to be able to cull lots of yearling seals washed ashore tired or dying from the winter swells.

These same LSA excavations at coastal sites had shown that limpets and other shellfish were always smaller at LSA sites than in earlier MSA ones, a feature Klein ascribed to smaller MSA populations making less regular use of the coast, or living at lower population densities, or both. This overall view is the most sophisticated expression of the idea that, right through the MSA, people's behaviour is easily distinguished from later times, and is not 'modern'.

One result of the very large exposures opened up by Wymer and Singer at Klasies River, and one they certainly hoped for, is the relatively substantial sample of human skeletal fragments from the sites. Relatively, because human remains are very rarely, if ever, buried in MSA sites and usually occur as extremely infrequent, broken, sometimes burnt elements of the MSA faunal record. Scattered amongst the other bones, the

Central African Geometric rock art

San rock art ends in line with the Zambezi River and the Namibia–Angola border area. North of this one enters a completely different art zone dominated by Geometric art. The Central African Geometric art differs significantly from the rock art made by peoples known to have been ancestral to the San in that it is finger-painted and dominated by geometric forms (more than 90 per cent). The fine brushwork animals and humans that characterise San art are absent. Those very rare animal forms that exist (less than 10 per cent) take bizarre and varied stylised forms. Often the stomach is hugely exaggerated and the limbs dwarfed or omitted altogether.

Geometric art uses various motifs. They are usually made using finger-width lines (either straight or curved), and by far the most common means of application is the finger. Red is nearly always the primary colour used, and sometimes the only colour; otherwise, white is used for filling and for secondary decorations in red and white bichrome paintings.

The designs are highly conventionalised. There is a limited set of basic defining boundary shapes and almost all motifs are variations based on additions to these.

Circles and concentric circles are very common, as are half-circles and concentric half-circles (both top and bottom halves, never left or right). Parallel lines often crossing one another at roughly 90 degrees are common, but not lines that cross diagonally. Circles can be stretched, as can half-circles, but usually horizontally or vertically, not diagonally. The perimeter line of these motifs is greatly respected: many internal divisions may be added but these will not cross the perimeter. Alternatively, lines may radiate outward from the motif (usually in regular patterns, either all around or in parallel groups from top or bottom) but these lines will not cross into the interior.

This kind of Geometric-tradition rock art, both painted and engraved, is found spread across most of Central Africa. Since this art is composed of simple geometric designs, it is likely that unrelated art traditions in other areas will contain some common images, such as the circle; but what characterises the Geometric tradition is its overall composition of more than 90 per cent geometric forms. Importantly, some simple geometric shapes are not used; they include spirals, triangles, zigzag lines, and diamonds.

Links with other areas are therefore not made on the basis of a few similarities in use of form, but on the specific repertoire of geometric shapes. Those areas that can be linked within the Geometric rock art zone are northern Mozambique, Angola, the Katanga region of the Democratic Republic of Congo, southern and western Tanzania, and the area around Lake Victoria. North of this the rock art changes to the manners of depiction, conventions and subjects of Saharan rock art. Saharan rock art is mostly naturalistic, with a complex series of human and animal depictions.

Saharan rock art has been extensively recorded and sequenced but researchers have made little progress as yet in revealing its meanings. Central African research has been more productive. There is now strong evidence of links between the later Central African Geometric rock art and historically recorded groups known as BaTwa. Recent studies have gone on to argue, using historical records, oral traditions, stone tool and other archaeological evidence, that the Central African BaTwa were related physically and culturally to modern-day Pygmies. Confidence in the linkage of the BaTwa to Pygmy

Central African Geometric Tradition rock art.

Central Tanzanian rock art. Three anthropomorphic figures in red paint with the strange heads so characteristic of the tradition are depicted.

groups comes from the extent to which a whole of series of details in the placement and content of BaTwa Geometric-tradition art can be explained by reference to known Pygmy traditions and practices.

This argument has important implications for our understanding of the peopling of Central Africa. Given that the older Geometric-tradition rock art demonstrably predates the Bantu-speaker habitation of the region, the huge swathe of Geometric rock art implies a massive area of Pygmy occupation in the not so distant past. Less than 3 000 years ago, we may have had a zone of Pygmy occupation that was at least as big as, if not bigger than, that of the San in southern Africa at that time. Following the rock art evidence, the zone reached from the coast of Angola in the west to the southern coast of Tanzania in the east and the Zambezi in the south to Lake Victoria in the north.

This is a bold claim that awaits further investigation. At present one can simply conclude that it is the explanation that best fits with the available archaeological and anthropological evidence. It is also a model eminently open to testing: mitochondrial DNA testing among modern populations, particularly in those areas where BaTwa groups are known to have survived until just a century or two ago, should be able to provide a decisive answer.

Even if the closeness of the genetic link between the former Central African hunter-gatherers and the modern Pygmies requires further investigation, the matter of cultural affiliation seems beyond question. Central African hunter-gatherer rock art provides direct evidence of a huge area in which a particular set of cultural practices held sway prior to the coming of Bantu speakers. These cultural practices were fundamentally different from those of both Bantu speakers and the San.

Whatever complexities and arguments surround the genetic evidence, the rock art evidence fundamentally undermines the position of those who try to argue that the Pygmies are recent ances- tors of Bantu speakers who have chanced to become small due to dietary and other deficiencies. This cannot be the case. The rock arts of the two groups could scarcely have been more divergent at their time of contact. I therefore concur with those researchers who have long held the view that the Pygmies are the descendants of the ancient indigenous inhabitants of Central Africa. In close keeping with this position, the Pygmy–BaTwa rock art tradition appears to have a history that is at least as long as its southern African San counterpart, and only came to an end a few centuries ago.

Central Tanzanian rock art

The final sub-Saharan hunter-gatherer art zone occupies a small section of central Tanzania centred on Kondoa district. It is a localised tradition comprising brush-painted animal and human subjects in a varied and stylised manner that stands apart from the finger-painted Geometric rock art dominating all other parts of Central Africa. The southern boundary of this art follows the southern limits of Kondoa and Singida districts, and the northern boundary is Lake Eyasi. With a maximum radius of 200 kilo- metres, this art zone is by far the most regionally confined of all African hunter-gatherer rock arts.

The art contains depictions of a wide variety of animals including most of the large mammals such as giraffe, eland, kudu, lion, elephant and rhino as well as a few birds and reptiles. It is painted in an unusually varied array of styles ranging from outline, through linear, dotted and gridded fills to partially and fully filled forms. Humans are depicted in the same ways in a range of standing, bending and 'floating' postures, sometimes with bows, sometimes wearing long capes, and often with large and bizarre head forms that appear to reflect the wearing of headdresses. A few humans are painted with animal heads.

human remains appear to be dominated by the most robust parts such as mandibular and maxillary fragments, often with teeth, isolated teeth and some cranial and long bone shaft fragments.

A few more human bones came from Hilary Deacon's excavations. These human remains are, by all accounts, very variable in size and robustness, not all of this associated with the sexual distinction between supposed males and females. All are modern in the sense of falling within the range of modern African skeletal samples, though some only just so. The human remains come from a variety of layers from MSA1 and MSA2, from about 110 000 years ago to about 90 000 years ago, with fewer from higher up the profile. One fragment, a partial temporal bone, has a set of cut-marks that are similar to those found on the bones of other animals. Tim White and Hilary Deacon have both argued that this is evidence of ritual or (less likely) nutritional cannibalism, a practice they both view as distinctly modern. We should note here that cannibalism has long been argued for the Neanderthalers of Europe, though not without controversy.

Hilary Deacon's excavations at Klasies River have substantially clarified the stratigraphy and dating, while allowing him to develop some of his own specific ideas about MSA behaviour. It should be said that the general stratigraphic sequence of MSA1 to 4, with the Howiesons Poort between the MSA2 and MSA3, has survived closer scrutiny, though there is the suggestion, welcome I believe, that the terms MSA1 and MSA2 be replaced by more local names, Klasies River and Mossel Bay facies. This kind of nomenclature implies that assemblage types may have only local currency. So far both MSA3 and MSA4 are represented by fairly small samples.

More significantly, Deacon noted that the composition of many of the layers was dominated by burnt or humified (turned to humus) plant material, difficult to identify with precision but arguably plant food residue. This seemed very like the humified bedding and underground plant food waste he had found repeatedly in LSA sites from the Eastern Cape, and was taken to imply a continuity of food-gathering strategies. In fact Deacon argued that the integration of shellfish and the underground storage organs of bulbs (geophytes), both presumably by women gatherers, further supported his idea that MSA practices at Klasies River reflected the existence of modern foraging strategies in the Cape. The processing and consumption of these foods around clearly recognisable fireplaces reminded him strongly of the hearth-oriented domestic behaviour of San women. For him, the MSA people at Klasies River were modern in both anatomy and behaviour.

Sara Wurz, working with both Wymer and Singer's and Deacon's assemblages, has greatly clarified the technology of stone-toolmaking through this crucial sequence. She has provided quantitative accounts of the differences between MSA1, MSA2 and Howiesons Poort production of blanks (flakes which can later be shaped into tools) and shown that some techniques come and go through time. Blade production, for example, characterises both the MSA1 and the Howiesons Poort assemblages, though silcrete is more commonly used in the latter. The platform characteristics of some of these blades match the details on experimentally produced ones using soft hammer, but not those that are punch struck. MSA2, by contrast, is oriented to the production of triangular flakes from prepared cores, mostly not of the Levallois type favoured in the European and the Near Eastern MP. (In the Levallois technique, the core is prepared in a rounded form by removing flakes at the edges. Flakes are then struck from the rounded edge towards the centre.)

Moving west, the excavations at Pinnacle Point near Mossel Bay by Curtis Marean, Peter Nilssen and a large group of their colleagues seem likely eventually to surpass the importance of the Klasies

Sequencing the stylistic variations within the traditions has proved difficult. There are too many conflicting overlays when one collects together the evidence from a large number of sites. It now appears that variety in manner of depiction is one of the characteristics of this art tradition.

The distribution of this art closely matches the historically known distribution of the only two click-speaking groups in East Africa: the Hadzabe and the Sandawe. An enduring link between the rock art and some Sandawe groups was demonstrated in the 1950s when a colonial postmaster observed a Sandawe man making a rock painting.

As with the other two sub-Saharan hunter-gatherer rock arts, it appears that Central Tanzanian art was part of traditional religious practice. Researchers have connected some of the art with hunting magic and some with an ecstatic cult called *simbó*. In *simbó*, dancers use vigorous movement and hallucinogenic beer to attain an ecstatic state. In this state the Sandawe say that people become animals such as lions. The many bizarre human-head forms, the floating trance postures and the depiction of therianthropes (animal-people) demonstrate that much of Central Tanzanian rock art is linked to this ritual experience of altered states of consciousness.

The interest of Hadzabe and Sandawe rock art here is in its broader implications. This art forms an island within the Central African Geometric zone and yet it shows many signs of being a very ancient island that has maintained its integrity in the face of long-term external interactions. This fits well with both the genetic and linguistic characteristics of the painting population.

There has been much debate on the relationship between the click languages spoken by the Hadzabe and Sandawe and those spoken by the southern African San, but recent studies have tended to emphasise extreme distance. Equally, recent genetic evidence has found the Hadzabe and Sandawe and the southern African San are the most genetically divergent of all the world populations. A group of geneticists has recently estimated that the ancestors of the San and the Hadzabe separated between 160 000 and 70 000 years ago. As they note, this period places the most recent shared ancestry of these two populations at the point of the earliest divergence among extant human populations. Importantly, it also places their separation prior to human expansion out of Africa.

If these truly are two of the most divergent populations on earth, then the fact that they are the only two to speak ancient click languages is suggestive of the nature of the first languages. One is tempted to wonder similarly about the many shared traits in the two separated rock arts. It seems that some groups, presumably ones ancestral to modern Pygmies, have divided these populations for tens of millennia. This means that, if the shared traits in San and Hadzabe—Sandawe rock art, drawing upon ecstatic dances and visualising their experiences in terms of human—animal transformations, show historical continuity rather than common responses to common neuropsychological stimuli, then the origins of art lie much earlier than we have realised up until now. There are rather too many 'ifs' to have confidence in this intriguing idea, but it illustrates the enormous potential of linking the research endeavours and findings of archaeology and genetics.

River finds, if only because of the extraordinary care and attention that is going into the recovery and analysis of material remains, including faunal and artefactual assemblages. There are several large caves and rock shelters in the cliffs near Pinnacle Point, a few kilometres west of the famous but poorly described Cape St Blaize Cave, type site of the Mossel Bay Variation of John Goodwin.

Here again onshore sand accumulation is associated with the living floors. Luminescence dating distinguishes between these periods of habitation and gives us their chronological sequence. Although little has yet been published, there appear to be both Howiesons Poort and Stillbay assemblages stratified within the deposits of these caves, indicated by shells and interposed between MSA assemblages without the characteristic segments or bifacially worked points. It is too early to say much more about

The complex stratigraphy at Diepkloof Rock Shelter.

NEIL RUSCH

this research programme, except that results are eagerly awaited.

Further west, the exciting results of excavations at Blombos Cave by Christopher Henshilwood are well known, and have supported some significant comments about the behavioural modernity of MSA people. The views of Henshilwood and his colleagues are diametrically opposed to those of Richard Klein. Blombos Cave was, until excavation, a rather unobtrusive, apparently unexceptional small cave opening about 40 metres up in the cliffside, facing down onto a rocky bay. The excavations have shown that the shallow LSA deposits, all less than 2000 years old, are lying on top of an aeolian (wind-blown) sand that is part of a massive onshore dune formation which once completely blocked the cave. Remnants of this dune body still survive outside the cave nearer the shore, and have been securely dated by single-grain optically stimulated luminescence to about 70 000 years.

It now appears that at the lowering of sea level with the onset of the last ice advance, the beginning of Marine Isotope Stage 4, strong southerly winds blew a considerable amount of shelly sand onshore. Underneath this sand in the cave is a deep series of shelly middens with clearly MSA stone tools and some other quite remarkable artefacts and food waste. The sand helped preserve the organic remains in the MSA and provide an important sterile horizon between MSA and LSA. Only recently, when higher sea levels caused erosion of the outside sand dune, was it possible for LSA people to enter and live in the site.

The lowermost excavated MSA layers in Blombos Cave are not yet published but are thought to be about 110 000 years old, not unlike the age of the MSA1 at Klasies River. Quite unlike Klasies River, however, is the fact that most of the upper MSA assemblages are distinctively Stillbay in character. Blombos Cave is, of course, only a few kilometres from Still Bay itself. All the layers so far excavated are shelly, though the undescribed deepest layers are more shell-rich than the already labelled Stillbay ones above. Immediately below the sterile dune sand there are Stillbay bifacial points associated with the bone tools, engraved ochre fragments, and pierced *Nassarius kraussianus* beads described above, all securely dated to more than 70 000 years old. A point of considerable debate is why the Klasies River sites and Blombos Cave have such different contents, though the uniqueness of each depositional repository is a feature reinforced by every new excavation. Most of us assume, however, that underlying these uniquenesses is a common cultural stratigraphy, albeit one variously reflected from place to place.

Several archaeologists have noted that large samples of bifacial points are quite rare, and often occur in small sites such as Blombos Cave rather than large sites such as Klasies River. Hilary and Janette Deacon speculate that the former may have been craft production sites where artefacts were produced for show rather than for use. Other sites do have these bifacial points, but very few of them. If this is right, they argue, then the extremely finely made, and arguably far more symmetrical than necessary, Stillbay points may have been exchanged from group to group in much the same way that recent San hunter-gatherers exchanged arrows and other artefacts. This they regard as further evidence that MSA people were 'modern in both mind and body'.

Die Kelders is another cave that has been excavated more than once. In the early 1970s the late Frank Schweitzer, working from the (then) South African Museum, excavated a substantial part of the LSA and a small part of the underlying MSA deposit in this spectacular coastal cave near Gansbaai in the south-western Cape. Some 25 years later Richard Klein, Fred Grine, Graham Avery and Curtis Marean re-excavated at Die Kelders and removed a larger sample of MSA material.

Between the LSA shell middens, all of which dated to less than 2000 years, and the MSA is another sterile sand body, blown into the cave at some earlier time of lowered sea level. MSA layers are draped over a series of very large boulders near bedrock, indicating that a good deal of compaction and slumping have occurred since deposition. Although Die Kelders is located at the high tide level, there are few really shelly deposits in the MSA sequence. Small pockets of shell do, however, imply that shell was originally more common. As there are the remains of seals among the animal bones, clearly the cave was fairly close to the shore during the MSA occupations. There is nothing resembling a Stillbay assemblage and only the barest trace of Howiesons Poort, in the form of a shift toward blade production and a slightly higher interest in fine-grained rocks by the toolmakers, at some point in the MSA sequence. Otherwise, the most characteristic tool forms are notches and the fine tooth-like serrations called denticulates. The MSA is not well dated but appears to lie between about 80 000 and 50 000 years ago.

The Kelders animal bone assemblages were among the first MSA faunal remains to become available as tests of Klein's interpretations of the Klasies River observations. His analyses of the bones confirmed, in his view, the idea that MSA people hunted, fished, fowled and gathered in ways quite different from the later LSA people. Because all fragmentary hominin remains from both Klasies River and Die Kelders are modern, this has led to Klein's position of arguing for anatomical modernity well before behavioural modernity. He detects no real evidence of 'symbolically mediated behaviour' much before the appearance of Cro-Magnon people in Europe. For him, an intriguing question is why it took modern people 50 000 years to start to show signs of the innovative behaviour he associates with later moderns.

Finally, in this survey of south coast sites, it is worth mentioning Peers Cave, the largest cave on the Cape Peninsula, and one with a particularly chequered history. First excavated in the 1920s by the father and son team of Victor and Bertie Peers, it was subsequently dug by Keith Jolly in the 1940s and then Barbara Anthony in the 1960s. Unfortunately none of these excavations has been properly reported and there appears to be little left to examine. Thomas Volman and Royden Yates revisited the site in 2003 and thought they had successfully found some undisturbed MSA deposit, part of which they excavated. Though not an ideal circumstance, Volman and Yates reported the extremely important observation that, as noted by earlier excavators, both Howiesons Poort and Stillbay assemblages are present in this site, with the Stillbay lower and thus earlier than the Howiesons Poort. This has been the first such stratified observation, because, as will have become clear here, Blombos Cave has Stillbay but no Howiesons Poort and Klasies River has Howiesons Poort but no Stillbay. Boomplaas has reportedly Howiesons Poort but no Stillbay, and Die Kelders may have neither.

Cape interior

In the arid interior of the Cape there are very few substantial caves that might have survived since MSA times. This makes it quite difficult to compare the record from here with those of coastal regions where caves are far more common. Garth Sampson's research in the tributaries of the Orange River, however, adds some important details to the MSA distribution pattern. He had worked in the middle reaches of the Orange River Valley in the late 1960s as part of a rescue project ahead of the construction of some very large dams and was impressed by the sheer quantity of surface scatters of material of all ages. With research funding from the US National Science Foundation, he initiated a massive foot survey of archaeological remains in the Seacow Valley, a major tributary of the Orange.

Although he found many LSA and ESA sites, it is the MSA that is of interest here. Significantly, of more than a thousand recorded MSA sites, none seemed to be Stillbay or Howiesons Poort. He called the majority of them Orangian, though they remain undated. His systematic searches confirmed what had been apparent from more selective investigations elsewhere in the central interior of the country, that there are many MSA occurrences, but few of them have the distinctive set of (claimed precocious) characteristics that are relatively common along the south and west coasts. It is harder to assess whether the ochre, bead and worked bone associations are absent there too, but they are certainly rare.

Wonderwerk is a single, very large cave on the fringes of the Kalahari in the extreme northern Cape. Excavated extensively by Peter Beaumont, it is one of the few cave sites, Montagu Cave and Cave of Hearths being the others, to preserve material back as far as the ESA. Another occurrence of relevance in the central interior is the deep sinkhole sequence from Kathu Pan, where Beaumont has described a small assemblage of about a

Finely incised geometric pattern on stone from Wonderwerk Cave, Northern Cape, South Africa.

The archaeological excavations at Wonderwerk Cave.

hundred pieces as Howiesons Poort. From these observations little can be said except that Howiesons Poort or Stillbay assemblages form a minuscule fraction of the abundant MSA in the interior. It is hard to avoid the implication that the distributions of these assemblage types were focused on the coastal mountains and associated sandy plains. More of this later.

Cape west coast

The coastal topography of the west, Atlantic Ocean coastline of South Africa is much more subdued than that of the south, Indian Ocean side, with far fewer bluffs and cliffs. As a consequence, caves are much less common near the present shoreline. The research history of this coast has also, perhaps as a result of this, tended to emphasise site surveys and landscape studies rather than focus on the excavation of deep sites. For these reasons some different

aspects of MSA behaviour have surfaced here, notably the relevance of seafood in the history of hominin practices.

Ysterfontein, Sea Harvest, the Hoedjiespunt sites and Boegoeberg are all residual shelters, surviving rear fragments of once larger cavities formed at the interface between underlying diorite or granite bedrock and overlying shelly aeolian sands eroded at the coastal margin. What seems to have happened is that sands have blown over uneven bedrock platforms and subsequently, with repetitive plant colonisation and pedogenesis, partly cemented into thick shelves or carapaces of calcrete. Between pillars of diorite or granite the lower, uncemented sands have eroded out leaving a series of small shelters suitable for use by MSA coastal people, and just as often hyenas. Some of these shelters filled up with shell-midden material and very much later were almost completely destroyed by harbour construction,

Sieving for lithic tools and other archaeological remains outside Blombos Cave.

road-building or mining operations. Shelly occupation deposits tucked in the back of the shelters have survived. All sites with bone, whether archaeological or palaeontological, were intrusions long after the original deposition and subsequent cementation of sediment.

The stone tools throughout the infills at these sites are hard to characterise, though the faceted platforms, flake points and prepared cores are obviously MSA. Substantially made from silcrete and quartz, the most distinctive artefact types are notched and denticulated pieces of variable form. There are no obvious hints at either a Howiesons Poort or a Stillbay assemblage in any of these sites, and no clear typological clue as to where in the MSA cultural sequence this depositional history belongs. Such a history on the west coast is, in any case, poorly envisaged as yet. It would not be surprising, from the uniformity of these stone tools as well as the relatively constant stratigraphic placement of the cavities occupied, if they were all substantially contemporary with

one another, and perhaps with Die Kelders. The assemblages from Diepkloof, described below, may hint that these sites all predate the Stillbay, but we cannot be sure of this yet.

These coastal MSA assemblages have abundant ochre, much of it clearly striated and bevelled from use, and very large quantities of ostrich eggshell, all fragmentary and none, it seems, used as water flasks or intentionally marked. Human skeletal remains are very rare in these west coast MSA shell middens, but the fragments from Sea Harvest have been described as modern. The apparently archaic fragments from Hoedjiespunt are associated with a hyena lair and are estimated to be about 280 000 years old, much older than any MSA shell midden thus far identified. Compared with the huge volumes removed from Klasies River, these other sites including Ysterfontein and Hoedjiespunt reflect only minuscule excavations, implying that the density of hominin remains is probably not dissimilar between the coasts. None are burials.

Although sediment samples for single-grain, optically stimulated luminescence dating have been taken from Ysterfontein, there are no results as yet. Previously reported ams (accelerated mass spectrometry) radiocarbon dates on ostrich eggshell fragments from Ysterfontein, Sea Harvest and Boegoeberg are certainly minimum dates, indicating ages of more than 50 000 years. Thermoluminescence and electron spin resonance age estimates for Hoedjiespunt suggest that these shell middens may be as much as 110 000 years old. From what we know of LSA site locations, these MSA shell middens are not likely to have been more than a few hundred metres from the contemporary shore, probably a lot less. If the age of the Stillbay is correctly assessed as about 75 000 years, sometime in Marine Isotope Stage 4, then these MSA visits to the shore were probably made during one or other substages of MIS 5, arguably the warmer episodes of 5a, 5c or 5e, when sea level approached or even surpassed the present level. An age of 80 000 to 115 000 years would be consistent with this.

The significance of these and many other recorded (but as yet briefly sampled or unexcavated) sites along the Atlantic coast lies in the demonstration that shellfish-gathering was common along this coast during the MSA as it was at Klasies River and elsewhere. The ephemeral nature of the west coast sites and the lack of substantial midden build-up in any one place underline Hilary Deacon's point about the brief, intermittent and occasional nature of site visits along the coasts at this time. The shelly horizons at all these sites are not so different from the briefly occupied scatters at Dunefield Midden and elsewhere in the late Holocene. I agree with Deacon that these middens are likely to reflect brief visits by people who mostly lived somewhere else. This implies a level of resource integration that recalls the LSA, though we do not as yet have reason to suppose the visits were seasonally scheduled. I return to the implications of regular shellfish-gathering later.

Diepkloof Rock Shelter, about 17 kilometres upstream from the mouth of the Verlorenvlei, is easily the most significant MSA site in the Western Cape. A very large overhang about 45 metres up from the fresh water of this coastal lake, the site has up to 4 metres of extremely well-stratified deposit, almost all of it MSA. A shallow veneer of LSA lies at the surface, apparently separated by some 40 000 years or more from the underlying occupations.

After several years of careful excavation, we now know the sequence of artefact manufacture and associated events at Diepkloof. The uppermost wedge of MSA deposits is characterised by unifacial points made from silcrete or quartz. The assemblages as a whole have about equal proportions of these stone raw materials. From the cores, the platforms, the dorsal scarring and the finished pieces it is obvious that triangular flakes were the preferred blank forms. Below this is a deep sequence of layers containing large, backed segments of the kind always considered Howiesons Poort.

What is interesting here, though, is that in the upper part of this Howiesons Poort there are consistently large numbers of intentionally marked ostrich eggshell fragments, as mentioned above. These do not extend down as far as the lowermost segments. The Howiesons Poort layers are dominated by silcrete and show some marked differences from the unifacial point layers above. With the segments there is abundant evidence for soft-hammer blade production, easily visible on the platform details, from the cores, and in the standardised blade dimensions. Many are ribbon-like blades, and some are technically bladelets. There are also burins. In short, these assemblages from Diepkloof closely resemble the type collection from the Howiesons Poort rock shelter. As at Klasies River, the Howiesons Poort is not the final MSA.

Below the lowest backed segment there are several excavated layers with nothing particularly diagnostic, though plenty of stone and bone. The notched and denticulated forms here may be a clue to the relative position of the coastal samples, which all have these kinds of retouched pieces too. Below this again, there are several layers, amounting to about half a metre of deposit, in which bifacially flaked leaf-shaped points are regularly found. Some are broken, some are whole, some are mere tips, and a few appear to be rough-outs. These are not obviously made from blades or flakes, and the preferred raw material through-out these layers is quartzite. The points are identical in form and manufacture to those from Blombos Cave, and, indeed the original Stillbay surface collection.

There is not a single layer that has produced any two of the diagnostic unifacial points, backed segments or bifacial points. This has surprised us. Below the lowest bifacial point there has been another surprise. Underneath a few excavated layers with no particularly diagnostic artefacts, the stone tool assemblages are again dominated by blade production and a strong preference for silcrete. We are not yet sure what this means, but

it might hint that the superimposition of these supposedly diagnostic artefacts is not simple and may include reversals of decisions about raw material and about blank production by the toolmakers.

Hollow Rock Shelter was found during searches for rock paintings in the rocky terrain east of the Pakhuis Pass in the northern Cederberg. It is a remarkable site, located underneath a very large rock that is perched on three points, hence its name. The deposit is shallow, perhaps a quarter of a metre at most, and has no organic preserva-tion. Why the fuss? you may ask. Simply because Hollow Rock Shelter has what appears to be a completely preserved assemblage in which the prime purpose seems to have been the production of bifacially flaked leaf-shaped points, lots of them. Although only partly analysed, this assem-blage clearly has the cores, the blanks, the shaping flakes and the finished pieces, in a range of raw materials including silcrete, several kinds of

Ostrich eggshell work, such as necklaces, headbands (below) and decorated shells (opposite page), is a common feature of the Later Stone Age and historical times. Such work appears to have originated during the Middle Stone Age period.

quartzite, and hornfels, to define the Stillbay in the Western Cape. Along with Dale Rose Parlour and Tunnel Cave on the Cape Peninsula and Blombos Cave in the southern Cape, this observation has given rise to the idea that frequent bifacial-point manufacture may preferentially take place in very small shelters. The distribution suggests that bifacial point manufacture does in fact not only take place in small shelters, from the wide spread of bifacial points across the landscape, including hilltop saddles, deflated sandy dunes and ledges in front of painted rock shelters.

Apollo XI is the name given by Eric Wendt to a shelter he was excavating in the Huns Mountains of southern Namibia when astronauts landed on the moon in 1969. He excavated only a narrow trench through these interesting deposits, but enough to expose a long MSA and LSA stack of layers. Among many other interesting finds, not least of them the painted slabs that are apparently 25 000 years old, Wendt noted that there was a clearly Howiesons Poort assemblage sandwiched between two MSA assemblages. The Howiesons Poort was too old to be dated by conventional radiocarbon dating and typologically and technologically resembled those from Klasies River and Howiesons Poort shelter. Characteristic are the ribbon-like blades and some burins. Wendt also found fragments of ostrich eggshell flasks in the Howiesons Poort layers.

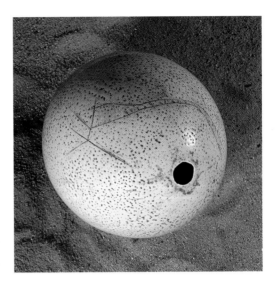

North-eastern interior

In the north-eastern parts of South Africa, Border Cave excavated by Peter Beaumont, Umhlatuzana excavated by Jonathan Kaplan, several Lesotho sites excavated by Pat Carter, and Sibudu currently being excavated by Lyn Wadley, all have assemblages with backed segments, and some of them have bifacially flaked points of various kinds as well. My impression is that this region reflects a different cultural history from that of the southern and western coasts. While the Howiesons Poort assemblages from Lesotho, Border Cave and Sibudu certainly conform to the Howiesons Poort pattern from further south, having soft-hammer-struck blades and large, backed pieces including segments and trapezes, there is some doubt as to whether the assemblages with bifacial points should be called Stillbay. If we restrict the definition of a Stillbay point to ones that are lenticular in shape, like a biconvex lens, then those from the north-eastern interior are something else. At the Cave of Hearths Revil Mason described round-based bifacially flaked points (hemilemniscates, in his words), and Beaumont, Kaplan and Wadley have hollow-based bifacials from their sites. Not only this, but the stratigraphic separation between the backed segments and the bifacials is not maintained at Umhlatuzana, nor perhaps at Sibudu. There are no bifacial points in any of the Lesotho sequences.

It may be worth reminding ourselves that John Goodwin thought that the different distributions of flakable raw materials had played a great part in defining the Industries and Variations he recognised in 1929. The MSA assemblages of the Cape Fold Region are dominated by silcretes and fine-grained quartzites, but these are replaced in the interior by hornfels and in the north-east by a wide range of basement rocks. It is clear that the Howiesons Poort technical characteristics seem to translate from silcrete into other raw materials not found in the south and west, whereas the shapes of bifacially worked points seem to change with the availabilities of different rock types. Of course, it may not have been the rock types but some associated environmental or social boundary that has generated the apparent distinctions in point choice. It is also clear from early accounts that excavators and collectors expected to find segments and bifacial points together, and this is sometimes the case even today.

Despite these uncertainties, which will be resolved by more excavations, shared analytical approaches and improved chronologies, there are a few generalisations that we can confidently make. Assemblages with either large, backed segments or one or other kind of bifacial points are mostly distributed around the topographically varied landscapes within 200 kilometres of the present shoreline, often much closer. Since some of these are likely to date from periods of lowered sea level, we may assume that the now-drowned continental shelves also have assemblages of these sorts. We may even wonder whether the focal areas occupied by Howiesons Poort and Stillbay groups weren't centred on the coast and accessible interiors. Certainly, where organic preservation is good, marine foods appear to have been a regular association of these characteristic artefacts. Almost all of these occurrences are in caves or rock shelters. Finally we can be sure that the appearance of bifacial points, apparently first, then large, backed segments later, was relatively late in the MSA – that is, if the presumed beginnings of the MSA really do lie around 250 000 years ago in southern as well as eastern Africa.

Models and explanations

Now that both the European and the African archaeological records are reasonably accurately dated, we can return to the issue of innovative toolmaking and migrationist narratives and review the possible meanings of the Howiesons Poort and Stillbay assemblage types. The burin, it seems, is now on the other foot. Whereas a few burins and an interest in blade production at 12 000 years ago in South Africa were at best unexceptional or at worst antiquarian, at 65 000 years ago they are groundbreaking and ahead of their time here and elsewhere.

Most narratives currently on offer identify such innovations, relate them to an increasing intelligence, and argue that some kind of growth in nonverbal symbolic capacity underpins ecological success and demographic expansion. Just about everyone agrees that confidence in new dating methods and dramatic evidence from genetics have made 'the origins of modern people' one of the big questions of palaeoanthropology. The narratives differ quite markedly, however, in the timing of and stimulus for the innovative experiments.

Richard Klein's version is widely quoted, in large part because it is clearly and testably presented by him. Inspired by his longstanding interest in the fate of the Neanderthalers, he has argued that anatomically modern people were able to expand out of Africa and replace existing archaic populations only after about 50 000 years ago. The spark for this advance must, he believes, have been some neurological mutation, perhaps connected with the development of complex language, which facilitated a suite of advantageous behaviours. Otherwise, he asks, why did modern people not occupy the world at 100 000 or more years ago? His scheme only works if there are no signs of innovative behaviour until shortly before the intrusion into Europe, which might explain his doubting many of the early signs in the African MSA. The penetration of people into Australia seems another indication that the capacity to innovate had begun well before 60 000 years ago. The beads from Blombos, the marked ostrich eggshell from Diepkloof and, if they are really that old, the harpoons from Katanda are mortal blows to this picture of recent

Bifacially worked Stillbay points from the Middle Stone Age.
BLOMBOS CAVE PROJECT

modern human behavioural origins.

Sally McBrearty and Alison Brooks have a version that demands a much longer timescale. Their position is that the traits often listed as reflecting modern, or we might now say 'symbolically mediated', behaviour did not arise at one time or in one place. Rather, they suggest, these linked behaviours coalesced as a set through the course of the MSA, beginning as early as 300 000 years ago. For them there was no revolution, merely an evolution toward the kinds of practices we see commonly among recent hunter-gatherers.

The idea of a human revolution is a Eurocentric notion strongly influenced by the punctuation experienced in that continent with the abrupt replacement of Neanderthalers by Cro-Magnon modern people. Ironically, though they claim not to favour a trait-list approach, their evidence for a long, slow evolutionary process is codified in a list of 'behavioural innovations of the Middle Stone Age'. The chart attempts to demonstrate that many such innovations originate far beyond the later MSA, earlier perhaps than the appearance of our own species, *Homo sapiens*.

This bold and perhaps justified attempt to decouple the anatomical and the behavioural relies on a very particular reading of the material

evidence. The claim, for example, that 'blades', 'points', 'pigment processing' and 'grindstones' all originate before 250 000 years ago and persist continuously since then, is a poor fit with the South African record. A major problem is that MSA assemblages of any sort that are more than 120 000 years old are very hard to find, so that any continuity has to be assumed, not demonstrated. Moreover, grindstones are, in my experience, extremely rare, even nonexistent in MSA contexts, certainly by comparison with LSA contexts, where they are quite common. As for points, blades and pigment processing, it is misleading I think to suggest any continuity of such items or practices through the MSA.

The problem is one of conceptualisation. A chart such as McBrearty and Brooks's completely minimises the problems of variable definitions or the confusions created by objects incorrectly provenanced. Are the blades of 280 000 years ago really the blades of 20 000 years ago? What about the documented coming and going of flake and blade blank production through the Klasies River sequence? The claimed continuity is as much a product of their methodology as it is of the record. It reminds me of the conundrum: Is the glass half full or half empty? Obviously there is some continuity and some change in the cultural record of the last 250 000 years. McBrearty and Brooks see continuity and the accumulation of difference, Klein sees relative stagnation followed by abrupt change.

Hilary Deacon is largely supportive of the McBrearty and Brooks model, though for quite different reasons. Also rejecting a trait list, especially a Eurocentric one, he builds a case that MSA people well before 50 000 years ago were engaging in practices still characteristic of San hunter-gatherers today. Strongly influenced by his experience of Holocene excavations in the Eastern Cape, he was convinced that many of the ecological and social practices of this time were already visible in the lowermost layers at Klasies River. As detailed earlier, these included

The stratigraphy at Ysterfontein.

the integration of coastal shellfish and inland geophytes into coherent, integrated subsistence patterns; the exchange systems that allowed raw materials or other goods to be passed between groups; the attention to standardisation of stone tools that allowed them to operate stylistically as well as functionally; and the domestic arrangements of hearths and food-processing spaces long noted among the San. The trappings and details of MSA assemblages might be different, he thought, but the minds behind the artefacts were distinctly modern.

An interesting question is what the systems were like before the time of the MSA1 at Klasies River. None of the practices listed above can be shown to have existed at 150 000 years ago, let alone any earlier. Of course, as we all know from experience, this might simply be a lack of appropriate evidence. It is crucial that we recognise that claims for MSA practices to be the earliest depend on showing that ESA people were not doing those things even earlier. The assumption from occasional traces that they were, lies at the root of the McBrearty and Brooks position. Perhaps this is why Deacon is supportive of their case. The same can probably be said for the positions of Henshilwood, D'Errico, Marean and their colleagues. Rejecting the short chronology of Klein, as excavators of some of the contrary evidence they appear to leave open the possibility that patterns recorded from 90 000 years ago will eventually be shown to originate some 290 000 years ago. Perhaps.

Lyn Wadley has been at pains to define 'symbolically mediated' in a way that is useful as a framework for dealing with our archaeological record. This has led her to contest some of the arguments in favour of the necessarily symbolic implications of ochre assemblages. Beads and the symbolic use of space are, she feels, much more useful indicators of the behaviours we would expect to find among recent hunter-gatherers. My impression is she has an open mind about the evidence for symbolic mediation in the earlier half of the MSA. Sibudu Cave, like several others, will show us whether there is something unique about the later part of the MSA.

I agree with most commentators that we should eschew a trait list, especially one derived from the specifics of Europe; we should disentangle the package and investigate strands separately before interpreting the entanglement; we should not automatically expect the anatomical to match the behavioural; and we should look particularly at the integration of brain development, technological innovation and language. There are a few specific points I would raise that do not appear to be high on the priority lists of my colleagues. In particular, I wonder whether the appearance of the Stillbay and Howiesons Poort assemblages with clear symbolic associations, after 200 000 years of unremarkable MSA, is not a key event in the human career. I offer here a few comments on what we might expect to learn from a more extensive, carefully excavated material record.

Is there, for example, any other implication to be drawn from the remarkably shell-midden context of these obviously anatomically modern fossil remains and arguably precocious artefactual innovations? There are two interesting ideas here, apart from the rather negative, or neutral, view that there is nothing to explain. The first of these, argued by Christopher Henshilwood and Curtis Marean, is that the shift toward more extensive use of shellfish is simply an issue of diet breadth, an intensification of resources used due, perhaps, to an increase in population pressure. The second is that shellfish-gathering, along with the exploitation of other marine foods, provided the nutritional basis for the expansion of brain tissue characteristic of our own species, *Homo sapiens*. Although these seem to offer

competing opinions about the role of shellfish-gathering and reasons for the appearance of shell middens, they may not in fact be mutually exclusive. First the former.

Henshilwood and Marean, responding primarily to the idea that modern human behaviour appeared quite suddenly about 50 000 years ago and included a series of new subsistence practices such as shellfish-gathering, invoke behavioural ecology theory. They suggest that shifts toward fishing, fowling, shellfish-gathering and even toward greater attention to more dangerous prey might reflect not intellectual advances but merely resource intensification brought about by changes in the predation strategies of MSA people. Increased population pressure, changes in the ranking of resources brought about by some technological innovation, or changes in the availability of high-ranked resources due to increased competition might have persuaded hunter-gatherers to alter and broaden their prey choices. The problem here is obviously one of testability. What independent measures do we have of increases or changes of this sort? None, it seems, as yet. The appeal to theory, attractive as it is to some, is of no help unless we can generate refutable test implications visible in the archaeological record. Here I betray my Popperian leanings.

If we assume that the proclaimed modern skeletal fragments from MSA sites mean that the hominins were fully encephalised human beings with a brain weight to body weight ratio characteristic of our species, then another scenario presents itself. Others have argued that investment in such a relatively large brain is expensive and requires an assured supply of appropriate nutrients. In my view, not shared by all, the most critical nutrient is the long-chain polyunsaturated fatty acid (LCPUFA) called DHA (docosahexaenoic acid), which is deployed on all the synaptic junctions of the brain and all the retinal receptors of the eye.

This critical component is in short supply in terrestrial ecosystems but is superabundant in the fatty tissues of all marine organisms, including shellfish. An adequate supply of DHA along with other, more easily obtained LCPUFAs is particularly critical for the growing foetus and neonate at the time of the most dramatic brain growth. The key question is then: How do mothers, pregnant and breastfeeding, access these supplies? I have suggested before that gathering shellfish and other marine wash-ups along the shore is a far more likely source than hoping for a share of the brains of recently killed hunted prey. Brains go rancid quickly; shellfish are a living accessible store of the appropriate nutrients. We know ethnographically that women do scour the shore for such edible resources.

These issues highlight a recurrent thread through the debate about the appearance and spread of modern people. What is the most persuasive set of linkages between components of the record, such as larger brains, language, shellfish-gathering, symbolic artefact manufacture, geographic range extension, population size increase? My view is that shellfish-gathering is, as Henshilwood and Marean argue, a poor choice for a modern behaviour trait list. More likely it precedes and enables the growth of larger, more complex brains, which in turn may have enabled new social and symbolic practices to emerge and flourish. The key will be to establish a secure chronological framework in which changes in these various components can be monitored, systematically compared, duplicated in a number of sites, and then assembled into persuasive narratives. I am not convinced that the theory-driven scenario-building guarantees any greater chance of historical accuracy.

Africa, of course, was a very different place for most of the MSA. During Marine Isotope Stages 4, 6 and 8, which we need to remember make up most of MSA times, expansion of the Saharan and Kalaharian dry belts squeezed the continent into three pieces, with very little interchange possible between Mediterranean, Equatorial and Cape Africas. These scenarios are critical for the enabling and prevention of genetic exchanges, but no less so for the spread of ideas, innovations and people. The 'waves' of modern people needed to negotiate some pretty difficult bottlenecks of a physical as well as genetic kind.

The mountain folds of the Cape at these times offered a range of topographic and resource landscapes within exploitable distance of the coasts, and appear to have been the heartland of Khoesan development. There are a number of intriguing parallels between cultural and natural boundaries that may have played some part in the story of our species. The Cape Fold Belt mountain ranges, the winter rainfall system, the fynbos vegetation, and the homeland of San hunter-gatherers combine to make the extreme south of the continent a very special place. Add to this the observation that the oldest mtDNA lineages and possibly the oldest, certainly one of the most distinctive, language families also hail from this Cape.

John Goodwin has the last word

The Howiesons Poort and Stillbay assemblage types are, as Goodwin and his contemporaries thought, remarkable. Whereas well over 99 per cent of all MSA artefacts are found in the open, well over 99 per cent of all Howiesons Poort and Stillbay artefacts have been found in caves. The ways in which they differ from conventional MSA assemblages are precocious in that they reflect practices that later became widespread, successful and lasting. Beads and other ornaments, decorated objects, images of geometric or naturalistic designs, storage facilities and complex integrations of subsistence choices are characteristic of all recent and Holocene hunter-gatherers.

The Howiesons Poort and Stillbay were, indeed, intermediate in form but proved to be powerful indicators of the nonlinear trajectory of behavioural evolution. They did not, apparently, lead on directly to LSA assemblages. The most interesting issue, not envisaged by Goodwin, may yet turn out to be the explanation of the post-Howiesons Poort MSA in southern Africa. Why were such supposedly advantageous practices abandoned?

John Goodwin had a strong literary bent. If he were writing the story of modern people, he might feel he has Chapter 1 pretty well sketched out. Innovative people on the southern coasts of Africa develop some useful practices for surviving in an arid landscape. Many of these practices depend on elaborate nonverbal communication. They find they can compete successfully with northern neighbours, populations expand, and as climates change they can extend their range into hitherto difficult terrain.

Goodwin the author also has some clear thoughts about the ending of his story. In Chapter 8 innovative people successfully replace their European competitors in a drama that includes tragic quarrelling, racist taunts and brutal revenge. But what happened in between, both chronologically and geographically? The language of migration and diffusion remains largely metaphorical until the evidence accrues. At least twenty thousand years separate Chapters 1 and 8, a thousand generations, six thousand kilometres. This is no Jean Auel narrative of a fictitious Ayla.

Ironically, our chronologies deal in millennia while our artefacts were made in hours. Our models generalise to groups while our beads were made by individuals. Our metaphors speak of processes that take generations while our observations point to shifts that may never have been noticeable. We are not writing a novel, or even an epic, but a history. The incoming results from Sibudu, from the caves at Pinnacle Point, from Blombos, Ysterfontein and Diepkloof are the details we need to help Goodwin finish his story. 'We are the scatterlings of Africa, both you and I.'

Ongoing excavation at cave sites throughout southern Africa will continue to yield exciting discoveries, especially in the Middle Stone Age period, that shed new light on Africa's creative past. SCHOOL OF GEOGRAPHY, ARCHAEOLOGY AND ENVIRONMENTAL SCIENCE, WITS UNIVERSITY

Rediscovering
Africa

San fine-line rock painting from the Origins Centre, depicting Boer settlers.

Rediscovering Africa

PETER MITCHELL

The African context for southern Africa's recent past

Africa has never needed rediscovering; hominids have occupied it for as long as the human lineage has existed. Indeed, it was Africans and their descendants who discovered the rest of the world, first as *Homo ergaster* and then (perhaps) *Homo heidelbergensis*; and later as at least two migratory pulses of anatomically modern people (*Homo sapiens sapiens*) worked their way across the southern end of the Red Sea and the Sinai Peninsula to enter Eurasia.

Some textbooks and university courses still emphasise Africa as the common birthplace of humanity only to exclude the continent from subsequent historical narratives about the development of food production, new technologies,

San engraving of a feline, Origins Centre.

urban communities, states and empires, and intercontinental networks of trade and commerce. Here the term 'rediscovery' does have merit after all. It requires us to overcome these biases in order to situate Africa's past within a broader comparative context and fruitfully explore the ways in which African communities were connected with societies elsewhere in the world.

These connections save us from marginalising Africa's past within the broader narrative of human history, but they also risk reinforcing the way that narrative has usually been recounted, as a simple developmental sequence from hunting and gathering through the acquisition of herding, cultivation and metallurgy to the constitution of towns and states. While that story is partly true, southern African archaeology, like the archaeology of the rest of the continent, also challenges some of the old assumptions. For example, far from pastoralism being a secondary development of cereal cultivation and inextricably linked to it through systems of tribute or exchange, as is generally argued for the Middle East, the African evidence shows how societies committed to herding could flourish independently of farming.

Not only that, but there is reason to think that the herding of cattle developed earlier in Africa than anywhere else. Moreover, herders in southern Africa in particular lived side by side for centuries with hunter-gatherers, farmers, the citizens of large kingdoms and, latterly, European settlers. Probably nowhere else in the world can boast of such a fascinating combination of histories, nor of such a rich mix of archaeological, historical, linguistic and genetic resources ready to investigate them.

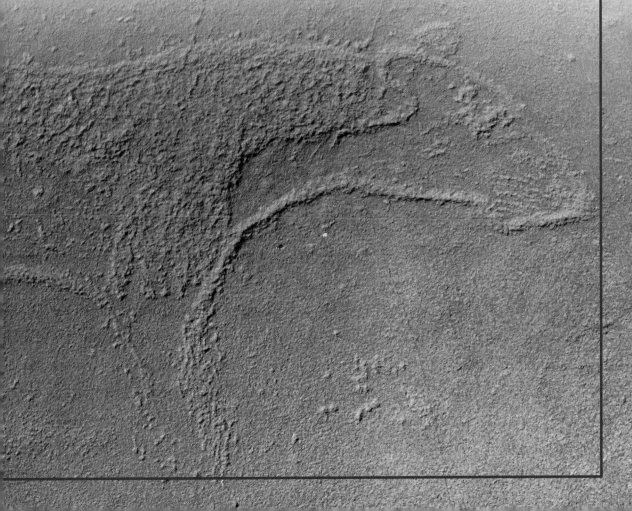

San trance dancer.

This essay covers a period which runs from the introduction of domestic livestock into southern Africa a little over 2000 BP, through the region's subsequent settlement by farming communities, to the emergence of complex hierarchical political structures linked to trading systems that spanned the Indian Ocean. Drawn into those systems and responsible for their utter transformation came European merchants, and it was as a result of that process that European colonisation of parts of southern Africa got under way, bringing with it still further changes for the subcontinent's inhabitants.

Through all the changes, hunter-gatherer peoples have been an enduring presence. Their numbers and physical areas have definitely dwindled from 2000 BP, but their history has been quite different from the story of inevitable assimilation, retreat and disappearance propagated by some popular writers or apartheid's official apologists. Instead, as I shall show, they have been active in all aspects of southern Africa's history over the past two millennia. Before discussing that history, however, it may be helpful

to sketch in the later prehistory of the more northerly parts of Africa, by way of background.

Across the world people responded in different ways to the challenges and opportunities created by the massive climatic and environmental changes that marked the ending of the last Ice Age. Some communities had to relocate in the face of rising sea levels or found themselves able to exploit previously uninhabitable or marginal regions. Some took advantage of abundant new resources to establish larger, more settled encampments whereas others suffered, finding it difficult even to maintain earlier ways of life. Many intensified the collection of plant foods or other gatherable, storable resources, such as fish. In some cases, this intensified exploitation of species ultimately led to their selective breeding under close human control – in a word, domestication.

The result, in very broad terms, was a slow but increasingly widespread and permanent shift from a broad-based economy exploiting a wide range of plants and animals to one focused on a much narrower set of resources. Since, however, those domesticated plants and animals typically provided high yields, demanded more labour, and (where cultivation was taken up) also facilitated permanent settlement in one place, another consequence was gradual but substantial population growth.

As that growth interacted over several millennia with changing ecological conditions, new technologies and new forms of social and political organisation, the eventual result was the expansion of food-producing societies and economies over larger and larger areas of the African continent. For example, some of the first people to recolonise the eastern Sahara as rain returned there after the Ice Age may have tamed wild cattle as a source of meat, blood, milk and transport. This hypothesis is still hotly debated by archaeologists, but there is no doubt that by 7800 BP not only cattle but also sheep and goats were present in domesticated form in north-east Africa, the latter two species having been introduced from the Near East.

The evidence of excavations and rock art shows that a way of life combining pastoralism with fishing, hunting, and the gathering of wild cereals spread across what is now the Sahara over the next 3000 years. Pottery, which was invented by early Saharan hunter-gatherer-fishers almost 10 000 BP, played a crucial role in the exploitation of all these resources: pots were used to store and cook them, and to collect and hold water and milk.

Repeated oscillations between wetter and drier conditions contributed to the expansion and relocation of pastoralist groups through the Sahara, but by 5200 BP the climate turned markedly more arid, forcing many of them south into areas that now became free of sleeping sickness and other livestock diseases for the first time. It is from about this period that we see the first signs of domestic livestock being kept in what is now the Sahel region of West Africa and in northern Kenya.

Whether any of these early pastoralists were also domesticating grains is a moot point. We have hard evidence that pearl millet, one of the most widespread African grains, differs diagnostically in shape and size from its wild form about 3700 BP. It may have been domesticated not long before, probably in the southern Sahara and as a way of contending with increasingly harsh conditions there. Sorghum, another widely grown cereal, cannot be traced back as far in Africa, although we know that people had been using it intensively for many thousands of years. If they also grew it, they presumably harvested it in ways that did not select for the physical changes that characterise modern domesticated varieties, leaving us with the impression that it was still being gathered, not cultivated.

The fact that domesticated forms of sorghum and millet are known from India and Pakistan before they are known in Africa hints at this, and at a longer history. Intriguingly, it also suggests links between the two continents 4000 or more years ago, a topic scarcely investigated yet. Links are indicated again by finds of Indian pottery in cave sites on Mafia Island, off the coast of Tanzania, dating to around 2500 BP, approximately the same age as evidence for the cultivation of bananas – a plant with Indonesian origins – in the West African state of Cameroon. Clearly, there is much to learn about Africa's long-distance connections at this early period.

The combination of sorghum and pearl millet with livestock-keeping proved a powerful one and, in outline, was the subsistence strategy pursued by most people in southern Africa at the time of the first Portuguese voyages round the Cape. But it is far from being the only farming system developed in Africa. As well as the combination of cattle, sheep and goats with wheat, barley and legumes that spread from the Middle East across North Africa and along the lower Nile Valley, these same resources were combined, in ways of which we remain ignorant, with wholly indigenous food plants in the highlands of Ethiopia. To their south, the banana-like enset plant and finger millet, another cereal, were brought under cultivation, while in the forest–savannah edge of West Africa yams and oil palm formed the basis for another farming complex from perhaps as early as 3500 BP.

Hunting and gathering remained a viable way of life in many regions, and wild plants and animals continued to be exploited even by farmers and herders, but food production had taken substantial hold across most of Africa north of the equator by 3000 BP. Its introduction further south, beginning with the rain forests of the Congo Basin and west Central Africa, seems to have been heavily bound up with the expansion of people speaking Bantu languages.

In brief, linguists agree in placing the origins of the Bantu-speaking family along the Nigerian–Cameroon border and broadly distinguish between Western and Eastern Bantu languages. Reconstructions of their early forms suggest that speakers of what is termed Proto-Western Bantu hunted, fished, kept goats, and grew yams and oil palm, initially without knowledge of iron. This fits archaeological evidence dating back to the third millennium BP from sites in Cameroon, Gabon and Congo-Brazzaville; but beyond about 10 degrees south, increasing aridity probably limited those economies.

Because Angola's Western Bantu languages use terms for cattle-keeping and cereal agriculture derived from Eastern Bantu sources, it is likely that cereals and cattle were a secondary introduction there from the east. Another linguistic trace shows that speakers of early forms of Eastern Bantu apparently moved eastward from Cameroon along the northern edge of the equatorial forests to end up around the Great Lakes of East Africa. There, so linguistic data tell us, they acquired cattle, sheep and cereals, presumably from communities living there already, though we have no archaeological evidence yet for who those cultivators may have been.

What we do have is good evidence for iron-smelting and for the manufacture of distinctive kinds of pottery, which archaeologists collectively term Chifumbaze. The origins of iron production in sub-Saharan Africa remain deeply obscure (was it independently invented or brought from

North Africa or Asia by one or more routes?). However, the association between a farming economy that combined cereals and legumes with livestock, and pottery and the making and use of iron tools and weapons proved an enduring one that ultimately spread as far south as the East London area of South Africa. With it, though not in a single move, came the languages and cultures that characterise southern Africa's Bantu-speaking peoples today. In the subcontinent's more arid western half, livestock and pottery reached even further, to Africa's southernmost tip.

I now turn to discuss southern Africa's recent past in more detail.

Taking stock: herders and hunter-gatherers

When Europeans first voyaged round the coast of southern Africa they noted the presence in Namibia and along South Africa's western and south-western shores of people rich in sheep and cattle, animals that they avidly sought to acquire through trade or theft. These people spoke click languages belonging to the Khoesan language family and, at least in the Cape, called themselves by terms that modern archaeologists gloss as Khoekhoen, meaning 'men of men'. Neither sheep nor cattle – nor for that matter the goats they kept or the dogs that helped them to hunt and herd – are native to southern Africa, so how and when did they arrive there? And do their exotic origins imply that the Khoekhoen too came to southernmost Africa from elsewhere?

These questions, which scholars have pursued for some 300 years, can now be tackled – if not fully resolved – with archaeological evidence, much of it quite new. One aid is accelerator mass spectrometry (AMS) radiocarbon dating, which enables scientists to measure directly how much radiocarbon is present in a sample. The vital point here is that the sample size can be much smaller than with the old type of radiocarbon dating, to fix the age even of individual teeth or seeds. By dating the teeth and bones of sheep and cattle from archaeological deposits, we have begun to pinpoint when these animals were introduced to southern Africa.

The bones of two sheep from Blombos Cave in the Western Cape have been directly dated to at least 1900 BP, with a third from Spoegrivier in Namaqualand dated to a century earlier. There can be no doubt, then, that domesticated sheep were present in southernmost Africa some 2000 BP, a date that necessarily implies their still older presence further north (since they had come into Africa from the Middle East). For the moment this is well confirmed at the open-air site of Toteng 1 in northern Botswana, where both sheep and cattle bones are directly dated to more than 2100 BP, the oldest examples yet known in southern Africa.

To account for their presence there at this time we might postulate a movement of stone-tool-using pastoralists from East Africa, where such groups were present by at least 3000 BP. If this is right, then they still remain frustratingly invisible to archaeologists working south of the Serengeti, though some linguistic reconstructions and a few similarities in pottery do hint at connections between East African and southern African herders. Alternatively, perhaps Bantu-speaking iron-using communities were the donor community for these animals arriving in southern Africa: a couple of radiocarbon dates from sites in western Zambia suggest this, but we need more detailed evidence to be sure.

Recently researchers have realised the importance of considering how the presence of animal diseases can influence the ease with which animals can be kept in a particular area and how people can take steps to guard their herds from such perils. We should not forget that, once past the wooded savannahs of south Central Africa, sheep at least would have entered semi-arid areas that would have been disease-free and ecologically not unlike those in which their wild Middle Eastern ancestors had once roamed.

Pottery is present at all three of the sites I have mentioned and it seems likely that it was introduced to southern Africa about the same time as sheep, even if the two do not always occur together. Interestingly, this early pottery is quite diverse, with spouted, incised forms known from the important Kasteelberg complex of sites near Vredenburg; ripple-rim ware found in both central Namibia and Limpopo Province; and the enigmatic Bambata ware present in mostly rock-shelter situations in Botswana, Zimbabwe and northernmost South Africa. It is difficult to be sure what conclusions we should draw from this diversity, except that it points to a potentially complex pattern of movements and contacts across a very broad region.

The work of linguists offers an additional perspective on what was taking place. Their research suggests that the Khoe language spoken by the Khoekhoen encountered by Europeans at the Cape, contemporary Nama speakers and a few other groups forms part of a broader Tshu-Khwe family. The divergence of Khoe from this family seems to have taken place in northern Botswana some 2000 years ago, precisely the time and place for which we now have early evidence of domesticated sheep and cattle. Other Tshu-Khwe languages, of which four groups can be distinguished, are found across the Kalahari and its margins. Their broad distribution suggests that whatever brought about the expansion of Khoe was only one component of a wider dispersal of Tshu-Khwe speakers. The increased number of Stone Age archaeological sites across much of Botswana within the last 2000 years may reflect this dispersal, which probably involved groups both with and without sheep. In recent times, many Khoe speakers, including the Nharo and G/wi San, have lived by hunting and gathering rather than herding.

Were Khoe speakers themselves responsible for the initial spread of sheep across southern Africa? The correlation that can be made between a northern origin for the animals (and the technological know-how needed for the ceramics often found with them) and a northern origin for

Khoe as a language is certainly an appealing one.

It has recently been reinforced from another angle, that of rock art: Ben Smith and Sven Ouzman have argued in favour of associating the Khoekhoen with South Africa's Geometric rock engravings. The distribution of this art, they say, suggests that the Khoekhoen moved south-east from northern Botswana into Limpopo Province and then spread south-west across the South African interior, ultimately reaching the Cape. But it is difficult to interpret the distribution of the art in strictly historical terms: we lack firm dates for most of it, and it occurs in some areas where Khoekhoen seem never to have lived but is absent from others where they certainly did.

The distribution of the few relevant radio-carbon dates that we possess seems rather to argue for a rapid, southward diffusion of sheep and pottery through Namibia and into the Cape. This may have been parallel to, but was probably not dependent on, another expansion of sheep-keeping into the Limpopo Valley, an area where rock paintings of sheep are well known. Sherds of Bambata pottery similar to that recovered from Toteng 1 are known as far south as the Waterberg and Magaliesberg, but are too rare for us to know yet whether they were being made locally or exchanged over some distance, let alone whether sheep were also present so far south.

The southward movement of sheep may not, however, have been through migration. Karim Sadr and others have developed another scenario, based in part on their fieldwork at Kasteelberg in South Africa. Sadr notes a series of changes in the cultural sequence there around 1100 BP that he links to the first appearance of pottery made with lugs, a style strongly associated with Khoe speakers in recent centuries. For him, this means that the people who kept sheep in the Cape before this date cannot have been Khoekhoen. He suggests instead that they were

Alpha to Omega

Language origins and demise

Nigel Crawhall

When I am no longer here, and I die, I want it to be known in my language that this was our land.
– Anna Kassie, N/u speaker, Northern Cape

Have you ever wondered what the first word was? Or what the last one will be? In the next ten to fifteen years we can expect that the last word of N/u will be spoken in South Africa. N/u is the last language of the !Ui branch of the !Ui-Taa language family, once the only language family used from one end of South Africa to the other. There were only eleven speakers of N/u still alive in 2005. It is conceivable that it will be Anna Kassie who has the last word on this matter, as the youngest speaker at 69 years of age.

N/u is a click language. A click is a consonant formed by pulling the tongue back from different parts of the mouth, creating distinctive, very short sharp sounds. There are five basic clicks in the !Ui-Taa languages, which can modified by voicing, aspiration, nasalisation and so forth. Three of these clicks were absorbed into Nguni languages in South Africa, hence they are found today in Zulu, Xhosa, Ndebele and Swati. However, many of the original click languages have disappeared. In South Africa /Xam, //Kū//e, Seroa, //Xegwi, ≠Unkwe, !Gã!ne, /Uingkekwe, 'Khuai, /ʼAuo, /Haasi, ≠Aro, !Audjen and //Kxʼau are all extinct. We do not even have examples of words from the last three. Almost all of these !Ui-Taa languages went extinct within the last century and N/u will no doubt follow suit.

According to UNESCO there are over six thousand languages on earth today. Over half of them will die out in the next twenty years due to many factors, notably economic marginalisation of indigenous peoples and the effects of globalisation. United Nations agencies and various scientific research initiatives have shared concerns about the implications of the rapid demise of many of the world's lesser-known languages.

First and foremost there is a grave threat to our planet's knowledge base, including philosophical, spiritual and epistemological diversity. Whereas some people may welcome having fewer languages as a step to greater world communication, the truth is more like burning down the multiple libraries of Alexandria and replacing them with a tabloid. A small fraction of the world's current knowledge has been recorded in English. For example, we know that there is a close correlation between biological diversity and human language diversity. Indigenous people's cultures and languages are rich in detail of ecological and biological information and particular skills developed over millennia.

One of the more startling considerations is that geneticists are able to work with language data to construct models of human population diffusion across the planet, and more recently they have cast light on the very origins of modern human speech. The death of so many under- or undocumented languages further threatens our ability to understand human prehistory.

Kalahari perspective

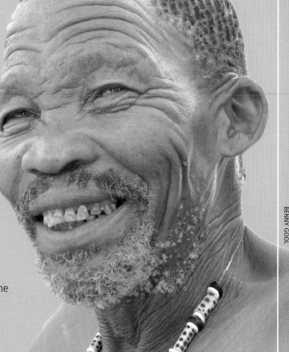

Dawid Kruiper, one of the last N/u speakers.

In 1997, working as a linguist with the South African San Institute, I met Mrs Elsie Vaalbooi, a speaker of the N/u language (also called ≠Khomani in the literature). According to an expert linguist, Anthony Traill, N/u should have died more than thirty years earlier. With community help our research team was eventually able to identify 28 full and partial speakers of N/u. Most of them were elderly and living in poverty, dying of preventable diseases such as tuberculosis.

Research with the N/u speakers allowed us to glimpse a language that had probably evolved in relative isolation from other African languages and which had been frozen in time by its rapid demise in the 1940s. Most non-experts think of click languages as either a single language or at least from a one-language family. In fact there are three major language families within the Khoesan language stock, as well as several isolated varieties. Research by Bonny Sands in 1998 demonstrated that the East African click languages, notably Hadzane, could not be said to be related to the Khoesan stock in southern Africa. Sands looked at aspects of terminology, grammatical forms and sound correspondence. Her work showed that Hadzane shared its click inventory with the southern African Khoesan languages, but there was not conclusive evidence that the languages were related to one another.

BENNY GOOL

Typical Khoe pot on display in the Origins Centre. DAVID PEARCE

indigenous hunter-gatherers who, for prestige or economic security, acquired sheep and ceramics through exchange with others. Animals and ideas thus passed southward from where they had first been acquired in northern Botswana through networks of connection rather than migrations.

The archaeological record of several coastal areas of the Western and Eastern Cape does indeed point to the emergence of more sedentary, economically specialised groups in the centuries immediately before the arrival of sheep, and it is possible that this created a suitably receptive social environment for them to become an attractive resource. Kazunobu Ikeya's study of contemporary San groups in central Botswana shows that herding a few animals can be compatible with maintaining the egalitarian, sharing-oriented social relations that characterise modern Kalahari hunter-gatherers.

Inspired by Morris Swadesh, Sands used the comparative method to assess the genealogical relationship between Hadzane and examples of southern African Khoesan languages. In the Swadesh method, a core list of 100 words is collected in the languages that need to be compared. Allowing for sound shifts (systematic changes of vowels or consonants), the researcher can identify how many of the 100 terms are the same in the two languages. This then generates a percentage of 'cognates'. Using a time calibration derived from European history, Swadesh then associated each percentage with a certain number of years, up to 25 500 years. So, for example, if two languages have only one word in common, that means they separated from each other around 23 000 BP. The technique is referred to as 'glottochronology'.

Many linguists today are sceptical about Swadesh's glottochronology. The external calibration for the method was based on European history and cannot necessarily be applied to other language families. Even the proponents of glottochronology do not believe it can make statistical sense beyond 6000 to 10 000 BP. The glottochronology method gives us some idea of relative time depths but it is a blunt tool for examining issues of remote prehistory.

Despite the limitations of glottochronology I applied it to the case of !Ui-Taa languages. I was trying to understand how long the !Ui-Taa-speaking people had been spreading out across the region and whether this information would link up with other data such as rock art dating. Accordingly, the Swadesh scale indicates a time depth between N/u and !Xóõ (!Xóõ being from the Taa branch of the family) of over 2500 years. We need to take this date as an approximation, but it gives us an idea of the prehistory of this particular language family as a relatively recent expansion out of the Free State or southern Cape.

The margin of error for each stage is great, particularly due to the tremendously complex phonologies of Khoesan languages and the weak quality of early transcriptions. For example, *!u*

(*Acacia erioloba*) and *!'u* (two) may sound almost identical, but they have nothing etymologically to do with one another, yet *!ui* (human) and *!u* (human) are in fact variations of one another and are hence cognate between languages.

Christopher Ehret is one of the linguists who are keen on a literal application of the glottochronological method and attempts to tie it in with other historical or archaeological evidence. Where Ehret applies this to recent history (for which we have external calibration), such as with Bantu languages, the results are interesting. Where he has applied it to greater time depths, there is some concern about the conclusions. Ehret uses glottochronology and evidence of a shift in lithic complexes (with the change of stone tool kit types from Albany to Wilton) to posit that the genesis of the diffusion of the three major families of the Khoesan language stock would have taken place about 8000 BP. As Ehret's theory links the alleged language diffusion with the emergence of the Wilton complex, it implies in turn a human or cultural penetration from East Africa into southern Africa at about 10 000 BP. Ehret argues in favour of seeing these events as a migration from east to south of the current Khoesan-speaking peoples.

Genetics and prehistory

Geneticists have been using language as a way to trace the progressive populating of the earth. Some, particularly those associated with Professor Luigi Luca Cavalli-Sforza from Stanford University, have been using language diversity as a clue to study how modern *Homo sapiens* diffused out across Africa and then across the planet.

Recent dramatic technical advances in DNA research and computer capacity have allowed geneticists to get closer to understanding where and how human languages originated, as well as create maps of the populating of the planet. In South Africa, Professor Wilmot James and the Human Sciences Research Council have been stimulating interdisciplinary dialogue about the African Human Genome Initiative (see http://www.sanbi.ac.za/mrc/research_workshop.html).

Two recent scientific discoveries in genetics have fuelled resurgence in discussions on the origin of human languages. In 2002 a team of geneticists led by C.S.L. Lai identified the FOXP2 gene as playing an important organisational role in speech formation and motor co-ordination. The FOXP2 research raised some important new considerations on the timing of the emergence of speech capacity.

In a separate endeavour, a team of Stanford University researchers headed by Alec Knight was able to identify a gene signature amongst Hadzabe hunter-gatherers in northern Tanzania which identified them as descendants of the second-oldest modern human gene type on the planet. The fact that the Hadzabe speak with clicks in their language, as do speakers of the Khoe and San languages in southern Africa, raised issues of time depth in the emergence of modern human speech. Both genetic breakthroughs help us pinpoint the start of modern human speech, and the results are surprising.

Following Charles Darwin's lead, Cavalli-Sforza has argued that linguistic diversity on the planet is closely related to human genetic diversity. As peoples migrated across and out of Africa their language systems constantly mutated, in a manner not too dissimilar to their physical genes. In his book *Genes, Peoples and Languages*, Cavalli-Sforza sets out the evidence that human migration patterns are expressed in the linguistic diffusion that we see in current-day populations. There are some examples where it is quite possible to use language as a co-factor in tracing prehistoric movements of peoples. The expansion of the Polynesian languages across the Pacific and the expansion of Bantu languages across Africa are two robust examples.

The site of Kasteelberg.

SCHOOL OF GEOGRAPHY, ARCHAEOLOGY AND ENVIRONMENTAL SCIENCE, WITS UNIVERSITY

However, whether these modern observations – with their admittedly shallow time depth – provide a suitable analogy for the more distant past is another question. Furthermore, the few animals for which we find evidence in the archaeological record necessarily imply the existence of much larger live herds and substantial technical knowledge on how to care for them. For Andy Smith, who pioneered excavations at Kasteelberg, these points are telling evidence in favour of sheep having been introduced to the Cape by a migratory movement of Khoekhoen, the model that Sadr's analyses lead him to reject.

Thus far, we have looked at debates surrounding the introduction of sheep and pottery to southern Africa, and particularly to the Cape. This reflects the emphasis of much recent archaeological discussion, but is, of course, merely one aspect of a more complex reality. European observers noted that, as well as sheep, the Khoekhoen also possessed extensive herds of cattle, and it seems likely that these animals were introduced to the Cape substantially later (1100 years ago or less?), and perhaps from Bantu speakers living further to the east. Moreover, the growth of the hierarchical, combative tribal groupings encountered by the first Dutch settlers at the Cape may have been encouraged not only by the availability of cattle, but also by competition for access to the metal and tobacco that Europeans introduced after 1488. If so, then some of the key features of Cape Khoekhoe society that European travellers noted may have developed not long before they wrote them down.

Much of what we know about the Cape Khoekhoen comes from the single site complex at Kasteelberg that I have already mentioned. Presumably many other sites of herders were lost to intensive agriculture and urbanisation. Kasteelberg itself was frequently occupied because of its prominent position in the landscape, the shelter it gave from the wind, and its proximity to the rich seal and shellfish resources of the Atlantic coast; at least some of the pottery found there was probably used to render seal oil, which may have been mixed with red ochre before being used as a cosmetic. By about 500 BP, when we must imagine a large herder population there, it is unclear whether separate hunter-gatherer sites can still be distinguished.

In his analysis of the Cape's later prehistory, Smith emphasises differences in material culture to the

Another good example is the study of the origins of the Roma (gypsies). Lyle Campbell notes that most of what we know about the history of these people comes from the study of their language, Romani. The migration of the Roma people is dated according to loan words that entered (or did not enter) their languages as they moved from India through Asia Minor into Europe. As there are no Arabic loan words in European Romani, scholars infer that the gypsies left Iran before the Muslim conquest 1100 years ago. Centuries of migration can be traced using this method.

Hadzabe breakthrough

Did people or languages move between East and southern Africa? The speculation on the time depth and details of the contact between East Africa and southern Africa could have gone on indefinitely with no real resolution. The truth is that linguists do not have enough evidence to argue a particular version of this remote prehistory. The points argued by Sands make it hard to accept some of the assumptions found in Ehret and other writers about the interrelatedness of click languages. Then in 2003 Alec Knight and his collaborators published their paper on Hadza genetics; both the mitochondrial DNA (from the mother's line) and Y-chromosome (from the father's) showed a very deep split from the Khoesan root – as great as between any two African populations.

This means that the San, who have the underlying gene type of all modern humans, are more different from the Hadzabe than they are from anyone else in Africa. This suggests that the Hadzabe must have separated off from the San (and survived as genetically distinct) before any other peoples. According to Knight and Mountain, the likely time-depth separation, based on several sources of data, is in the order of 90 000 to 40 000 BP.

The implications of the findings are startling. First, we have some sense of the time-depth separation between East African peoples and southern African peoples. Secondly, we have evidence that the descendants of the two earliest genetic stocks in Africa use click languages today. The team at Stanford is looking at new data that will highlight a link between the Hadzabe, the Khoesan peoples, and the other group of click-language speakers, the Sandawe of Tanzania.

Knight's team consider the possibility that around 60 000 BP clicks were widespread and were filtered out with the evolution of newer languages. Today we see the remnants: Hadzane, Sandawe, trace clicks in Dahalo, and the three families that make up the Khoesan stock (Ju, Khoe and !Ui-Taa). If true, this strongly suggests that clicks were a feature of early modern human speech. We now have circumstantial evidence about language in a time period we never imagined possible.

FOXP2

Another genetic breakthrough, unrelated to the African genome research, also casts light on the prehistory of human languages: the discovery of the functions of FOXP2.

In 2001 Lai and her team published their report on the FOXP2 gene that was apparently responsible for ordering elements of our speech capacity. Some of the media leapt to the conclusion that FOXP2 was 'the language gene'. In fact FOXP2 – a forkhead or winged helix protein, the second one identified in the P subfamily of FOX genes – organises a number of functions in our body including aspects of how our heart works, and motor control related to speech, as well as how our brain comprehends and produces speech.

In 2002 a German team of researchers led by Wolfgang Enard published another paper on FOXP2, advancing the evidence that this particular mutation in humans is perhaps critical to the emergence of modern human speech capacity. Enard and his team estimate that the mutations in the FOXP2 occurred between 100 000 and 10 000 BP.

point of creating two (almost wholly opposed) categories of hunter-gatherer and herder sites; Carmel Schrire and others suggest that all the region's inhabitants formed a single socio-economic community. The debate is by no means wholly resolved, and needs to be considered in a broader geographical context that takes account of information from other areas, such as the southern Cape, the Richtersveld and the lower Gariep (where a similar opposition between two sets of lithic and ceramic assemblages has been identified).

Enough historical data do exist, however, to indicate that the first European observers to travel through the Western Cape encountered people (Soaqua) who differed from Khoekhoe herders in lifestyle and language; people whom we would term hunter-gatherers. These people probably occupied many of the small rock shelters in broken terrain in the Cederberg that have a distinctive spatial pattern of a central hearth surrounded by areas of grass bedding. Excellent preservation conditions at many of these sites document a subsistence economy remarkably similar to that attributed by the early Dutch settlers to the Soaqua, one grounded in underground plant foods, small antelope, tortoise and dassie.

The same preservation conditions have also allowed the recovery of artefacts made from wood, cordage, leather and other fragile materials that are only rarely found elsewhere. Much closer to the coast, the open-air site of Dunefield Midden provides other openings on to the past, although whether its inhabitants were herders or hunter-gatherers remains in question. Extensively excavated and almost wholly comprising a single occupation dated around 650 BP, it offers unparalleled opportunities for examining how people organised their use of space in preparing and consuming food, as well as in making a range of artefacts.

Place-name evidence and finds of pottery with lugs show that at one time the Khoekhoen

Terrence Deacon notes that palaeontologists have identified changes in the hominid brain size at the time of *Homo habilis* as being the first sign of language capacity in our ancestors. We thus have a likely starting point in terms of evolutionary predisposition amongst *Homo* ancestors; however, it is a big gap between 2 million BP and the impact of FOXP2 mutation around 200 000 BP.

Part of the problem in setting dates about the genes and the emergence of modern languages is that the capacity for human speech is related to several special features including the extra depth of our larynx, the nerve density and flexibility of our tongue, the ability to use the cavity of our mouth to make sounds at the front and the back, and so forth. Richard Kay and his colleagues demonstrate that, as far as the hypoglossal canal is concerned, the basic anatomy for speech would have been available prior to 300 000 BP, substantially before the FOXP2 mutation.

Deacon notes that the laryngeal changes which allowed for vocalisation, an essential component in the production of vowels and voiced consonants, were a relatively recent phenomenon in our anatomical changes. We humans are unique in having a larynx set deeply in our throat. It allows us to produce a wide range of sounds not available to other primates.

The depth of the larynx and our capacity for vocalisation might be clues to the puzzle about the antiquity of clicks. Clicks do not require a voice box. It is possible to make a range of distinct and intelligible sounds using only the tongue moving off the palate, alveolar ridge and the back of the teeth, as well as the bilabial click.

According to Kenneth Clarke, FOXP2 may have been responsible for the great leap forward. He suggests that if we assume that certain bodily changes – such as the placement of the larynx and the expansion of the nerve network controlling the chest – were already completed by 70 000 BP, then the key mutation of the FOXP2 might have served as the missing link for the production of human speech.

Seventy thousand years ago happens to be another significant date. It is the estimated age of the carved ochre baton found at Blombos Cave in South Africa. The Blombos carving is the earliest evidence of human cultural expression. Archaeologists tend to like the idea that speaking humans are 'cultural' humans, and would have been evolving symbolic and artistic expressions. Still, we would wait until 35 000 BP before the widespread start of rock art in several places on the planet.

At the other end of the spectrum, languages such as !Xun or N/u have over 140 distinct sounds (the outer limit of human auditory capacity), and yet most words are only a single syllable long, and meaning is produced by order rather than inflection.

FOXP2 cannot explain the full story of the evolution of the human brain and our capacity for language. However, it may well be a critically important step on that journey. Did FOXP2 mean we developed language capacity rapidly and by accident? Wolfgang Enard argues that the mutation of FOXP2 was possibly accidental but it still had to be harnessed by our ancestors. Owing to FOXP2 not being in itself an evolutionary progression, there were probably closely related hominids with and without the variation, but ultimately the FOXP2 equipped *Homo sapiens* and we thrived.

We can safely assume that development of modern human speech is a combination of evolutionary processes that we see throughout the animal kingdom. As Deacon demonstrates, there is a long history to the development of our brain and our capacity for speech. FOXP2 opens up the possibility of a random warp in the human gene reproduction that survived and eventually became centrally important in pushing humans to the front of the food chain – it was an unpredictable great leap forward in the evolutionary process.

Conclusion

The Hadza–San circumstantial evidence that clicks could reach back 100 000 years may be hinting that they have a much deeper ancestry, one that precedes the full formation of the voice box. Conceivably, clicks may have been around since the time of *Homo erectus*. The great leap forward may have been the role of the mutating FOXP2 gene in reshaping the soft tissue components necessary for the full capacity of speech as we know it today.

From language birth to language death, the southern African !Ui-Taa language family has some important information for the rest of the world. Are there sounds and words in N/u that have been around for 500 000 years? Perhaps we will never know. The loss of these languages poses a great threat to the wellbeing of the peoples involved and to the collective knowledge base of humanity.

It is important to understand that languages are not dying out from any 'natural' process. The underlying causes of language death have to do with globalisation of economies, the loss of autonomy by local peoples and the eradication of biodiversity on earth, through the actions of humans. It is through our will that we destroy our diversity, and likewise it is through will that we have the option to conserve and value both cultural and natural diversity.

One of the most important concepts that have emerged in the dialogue between the United Nations and indigenous peoples is that of 'trusteeship'. Some indigenous peoples, including speakers of N/u, emphasise that the world does not belong to humans. We are one part of the network of life on the planet, and we are here at only one point in time. It is the responsibility of this generation to be guardians of the past and the future, and to protect the harmony of life in the present. From our origins to our eventual departure, we have a responsibility to the world.

were present as far east along the Cape coast as Mpame, though they were probably later replaced there by Bantu-speaking farmers. A little further west, groups of mixed Khoekhoe and Nguni origin (the Gonaqua or Gqunukhwebe) emerged in the last millennium. They buried at least some of their dead under stone cairns, and isotopic analysis of their skeletons shows that they adopted cereal cultivation to complement herding and foraging.

Burial cairns are also common in the Upington–Kakamas area of the Northern Cape, where herders intermarried and traded with Tswana speakers further upstream, obtaining iron and specularite (a cosmetic mineral) among other resources. Much research has also been undertaken in South Africa's Seacow River Valley, where Garth Sampson has identified a sequence of ceramic styles that parallels the finds in the Western Cape, reveals the ebb and flow of herder settlement, and records the appearance of grass-tempered pottery of a kind historically associated with hunter-gatherers.

Herder archaeology has also been pursued in Namibia, most notably by John Kinahan. In the Dâures (Brandberg) massif for example, numerous stone houses and stock enclosures were built by herders during the last millennium. There, grass seeds taken from harvester ant nests were an important additional food resource, whereas in the !Khuiseb Delta near Walvis Bay seals, shellfish, beached whales and !nara melons were exploited. Excavations at sites such as ≠Khîsa-//gubus illustrate the operation of complex exchange systems that circulated valuables such as cowrie shells and metal beads, creating reciprocal social obligations and reducing the risk of subsistence failure by allowing livestock to be exchanged for other goods. Interestingly, copper beads of the kind found at ≠Khîsa-//gubus were made in central Namibia using tuyères of stone rather than clay to smelt the copper ore, a technology found nowhere else in the world. (Tuyères are tubular objects for channelling air into the furnace in order to raise the temperature high.)

Planting seeds, smelting iron: the archaeology of early farming communities

When European sailors first reached southern Africa, Bantu-speaking peoples were absent from the region's western third, which was occupied entirely by Khoesan-speaking herders and hunter-gatherers. The reason is simple: the cereals upon which Bantu-speaking farmers depended could be cultivated only in areas of summer rainfall where annual precipitation exceeded 500 mm and growing-season night-time temperatures remained above 15 degrees centigrade. Settlement of the Karoo, the Western Cape or the Lesotho highlands was not possible given this dependence on sorghum and millet; even the highveld grasslands also saw little, if any, settlement until well into the last millennium.

The archaeology of the earliest farming communities in southern Africa is therefore very much a story of people who lived in the savannah and woodland regions of the north and east of the subcontinent. Within this broad zone, excavations in Botswana's Tsodilo Hills and KwaZulu-Natal's Thukela Valley are among those that currently have most to tell us. Understanding what those excavations have produced is facilitated by the use of models derived from studying the pottery and settlement layouts of contemporary Bantu-speaking peoples. Although, as we shall see, there is good reason to think that the connections between these groups and the earliest southern African farmers are far from simple, the models which archaeologists such as Tom Huffman have developed have helped research and are widely employed. Let us sketch the models here before proceeding further.

Within southern Africa, people speaking Eastern Bantu languages (such as Sotho–Tswana or Nguni) typically organise their settlements in a way that reflects the importance of cattle as a means of storing wealth, communicating (through sacrifice) with ancestors and establishing kinship ties with others (through bridewealth, or lobola).

Houses are thus arranged around a central cattle pen into which the senior man looks down from his house at the highest point of the settlement; and within the pen, or close to it, senior men are buried, grain is stored, and court judgments are reached.

In more or less attenuated form, this pattern can still be found in many rural areas today. Archaeologically, it can be readily traced back through recent centuries where highveld Sotho groups, for example, built walls of stone rather than timber. Excavations at Kgaswe in Botswana beautifully document the pattern in the eleventh century, while still earlier sites such as Ndondon-wane in KwaZulu-Natal and Broederstroom in North-West Province confirm that this was how farmers organised their settlements between 1700 and 1000 BP. Analysis of phytoliths from dung deposits has been particularly helpful in establishing the presence of cattle even where animal bones are few (phytoliths are small silica bodies in the cell walls of plants that are often highly diagnostic of the species or genus from which they derive). We can detect the Central Cattle Pattern (CCP) at a site by seeing where the houses and animal pens are located. Other indicators include burials found within cattle enclosures, accompanied by high-status objects such as ivory ornaments.

Because of the strength of the association between the CCP and speakers of Eastern Bantu languages today, it is widely assumed that most early farming communities in southern Africa spoke variants of those languages. There is also good ethnographic evidence in southern Africa that material culture – in particular, the form and decoration of pottery – can frequently be linked to a range of linguistic identities. Hence, changes in ceramic design may parallel, and in complex ways relate to, shifts in the distinctions between dialects. Many archaeologists say that this idea enables us to plot the movement of people from one area to another; that large-scale changes in ceramic structure over a large area reflect comparably large-scale shifts of people.

With this in mind, some archaeologists working on early (and later) farming communities now group pottery styles together into successions that could represent differences of language and the movement of different groups of people. Accepting that this is so (and it is questioned by other archaeologists who dispute the claim that ceramics and language affiliation pattern so neatly), how did early farming communities settle southern Africa?

The starting point, as we saw at the start of this essay, is the recognition that iron-using farming communities whom we presume to have been speaking Bantu languages were well established in East Africa about 2500 BP. From origins within the Chifumbaze complex, some communities (known archaeologically as the Urewe Tradition) spread rapidly south along Africa's Indian Ocean coast, reaching as far as Mozambique and adjacent parts of Swaziland, Zimbabwe and South Africa some 800 years later. About a century later again, they began to settle the coastal stretch of KwaZulu-Natal and to spread westward as far as the Magaliesberg, while people belonging to a ceramically (and thus, we presume, linguistically) different branch settled in Zimbabwe, the Limpopo Valley, and eastern Botswana.

Moving into the region from another direction (perhaps Angola?), makers of Kalundu pottery spread into eastern Botswana and south-eastwards as far as KwaZulu-Natal and the Eastern Cape from about 1600 to 900 BP. All these groups seem to have organised their settlements according to the CCP and therefore probably spoke Eastern Bantu languages. In the extreme north-west of Botswana, however, villages excavated by Jim Denbow in the Tsodilo Hills have produced pottery of a completely different type that is best paralleled at sites in Congo-Kinshasa but can also be related to ceramics found in northern Namibia, an area inhabited today by speakers of Western Bantu languages. The ancestors of peoples such as the Herero and Owambo may therefore have been present in this region from at least 1500 BP.

A typical Zulu Kraal arranged in the Central Cattle Pattern.
FROM J. TYLER, "FORTY YEARS AMONG THE ZULUS", BOSTON, 1891

Although we do not yet know how their settlements were organised, they are unlikely to have used the same CCP layout as Eastern Bantu-language speakers elsewhere in southern Africa.

This, in very brief outline and without entering detailed debate, is how many archaeologists reconstruct the history of early farming settlement in southern Africa. Yet this expansion is likely to have been far from even. No doubt it involved 'leapfrogging' at times from one agriculturally suitable location to another, for example. We should also imagine it being driven by a variety of processes: not just population growth, but also fluctuations in climate, exhaustion of local resources (firewood, soil fertility and so on), political disputes, and even simple curiosity or the desire to explore new ground.

The assimilation of hunter-gatherers is also likely to have been important, and there is some skeletal evidence to suggest that intermarriage with immigrant communities did take place. Conversely, on southern Africa's western side, where farming is most marginal, the Damara of Namibia, the Kwadi of Angola and the 'River San'

of Botswana are physically Negroid but speak Khoesan languages, a combination that hints at assimilation having been a two-way process.

What can we say about the way of life of these early farming communities? For the most part, villages were located with ready access to fertile alluvial soils, sometimes in areas where cultivation is no longer possible today, implying wetter climatic conditions than now. Plant remains are rarely found, but settlement size and location, along with numerous grindstones of a kind suited to preparing sorghum and millet, leave no doubt that cultivation was the mainstay of the subsistence economy. Wild plant foods such as marula were also collected at times, and there is good evidence for people having gathered shellfish along the coasts of Mozambique and KwaZulu-Natal.

Sheep and goats are more common than cattle among the bones that archaeologists recover, but it is difficult to be sure if this represents stock-holding rather than eating patterns, and the situation is variable anyway. Indeed, where tsetse fly infestation and other diseases made it difficult for people to keep livestock, hunting buffalo, impala and other game gained importance, something evident at both Kadzi in the Zambezi Valley and at sites in Kruger National Park. One interesting question is how far the introduction of farming impacted on the southern African environment. This question has not yet been researched systematically, but faunal and charcoal remains at sites in the Thukela Basin and Transkei hint at progressive forest clearance through a time from about 1400 BP.

Traditionally, archaeologists have described farming communities in southern Africa as belonging to the Iron Age. While this term is now giving way to others that emphasise subsistence rather than technology, there is no doubt that iron agricultural tools were important in clearing and cultivating land, just as iron weapons found a use in hunting. Probably because such artefacts were only rarely lost and because scraps of iron could be repeatedly reforged and turned into other items, we have relatively little evidence of larger objects. Instead, assemblages such as those from Divuyu and Nqoma in the Tsodilo Hills consist principally of jewellery items such as bangles and beads. More widespread is evidence of iron-smelting, remains from which are found on many sites, sometimes on a scale suggesting trade. In the case of Msuluzi Confluence in KwaZulu-Natal, the site's location on the edge of the zone of agropastoralist settlement suggests that this was with hunter-gatherers further into the interior.

In recent times in southern Africa, iron-smelting did not take place inside settlements because it was widely thought that the presence of women of reproductive age might interfere with the success of the smelt, a fear developed from the similarities seen between the reduction of iron ore and the processes of procreation and birth. Locating furnaces in secluded places beyond the village or homestead was therefore the rule, although no prohibitions were attached to the subsequent forging of iron inside settlements. Interestingly, however, while several first-millennium village sites in South Africa have produced good evidence for forging, some have also yielded evidence of furnace bases or smelting debris that *may* suggest that beliefs were somewhat differently structured over a thousand years ago.

Further evidence of this comes from considering evidence that seems to relate to how people were initiated into adulthood. Most spectacularly, this takes the form of the famous ceramic heads found near Lydenburg, Mpumalanga, which were once brilliantly coloured and suitable for fixing on posts or, in some instances, wearing as headgear. Dating from the ninth and tenth centuries, they can be matched by more fragmentary examples from Ndondonwane. Some of the Lydenburg Heads appear to show patterns of dental modification that can be paralleled with the deliberate extraction of incisors and chipping of canines that characterises human remains found at Nanda in KwaZulu-Natal.

Western Bantu speakers living in northern Namibia continue to modify their teeth in comparable ways to denote adult status even today, and the combination of skeletal and material evidence suggests that this was also so in South Africa during the first millennium. Similarities between the Lydenburg and Ndondonwane heads (and the location of the latter, near the site's central cattle pen) and the initiation masks made today from grass and reeds by Venda and north-east Sotho groups also support this interpretation.

Another kind of ritual marking passage from childhood to adulthood may be indicated by finds of ceramic figurines near centrally located rubbish deposits (again, something found among Venda and Shona peoples today), and by pits containing pots with deliberately broken bases. Metaphorical links connecting women and pots are common to many southern African societies and these pit deposits may relate to female puberty rites, the bottomless pots symbolising the ability of fertile women to act as channels to the ancestors for the purpose of giving birth. Careful disposal in pits within household clusters may have been necessary to avoid witches gaining access to such supernaturally charged items, and the identification of pots with people is sustained by similarities in fabric and design motif between the masks and the pottery found at the Lydenburg Heads site.

As I have hinted, more recent farmers in South Africa did not follow these symbolic practices. Other differences (in site location, settlement size and form, the shape of grindstones, and so on) have also long been noted in KwaZulu-Natal, one of the best-studied areas. Together with the complete break in ceramic styles that is evident nearly 1000 BP, which I discuss below, this suggests that farmers of the previous millennium were in many cases not the direct cultural ancestors of the Bantu-speaking peoples living south of the Limpopo today.

One of the Lydenburg Heads.   SOUTH AFRICAN MUSEUM

We now have evidence from the site of Likoaeng in highland Lesotho that not only iron and ceramics but also sheep (and very probably cattle) were acquired by San there – so maybe hunting and gathering was combined with some livestock-keeping, as Karim Sadr envisaged in the Western Cape.

Excavated village sites in KwaZulu-Natal suggest that ostrich eggshell beads were one item that moved in the opposite direction, from forager to farmer, but it is difficult to be sure what to make of finds of stone tools or bone points in such contexts: were they made by hunter-gatherers, perhaps when temporarily or permanently settled at a farming community? Or did farmers produce them themselves, especially where iron was difficult or expensive to acquire? Probably our archaeological finds reflect only a fraction of the exchanges that were taking place: farmers are also likely to have been able to offer cereals and milk, while foragers could trade skins, meat, ochre and honey, as well as being a valuable source of additional labour. Their knowledge of the landscape will have been important too, at least to newly settling farmers, and their position as aboriginal first peoples probably accorded them additional respect.

All in all, it therefore seems likely that these relationships, probably helped by relatively equitable and close ties of exchange and perhaps strengthened by intermarriage, will have allowed hunter-gatherers to survive within the farming frontier and outside it too. Indeed, in some areas hunter-gatherer settlement may have intensified once the additional attractions of farmer-produced resources became available, while in others hunter-gatherers may have altered or expanded their exchange networks to gain access to those resources.

Learning how to make pottery may have been one of those resources, though dates from the UKhahlamba-Drakensberg suggest that this knowledge spread well ahead of farming communities themselves. Pots will have expanded the range of foods that could be eaten and probably

Farming did not expand into a vacuum, of course, any more than did the keeping of sheep discussed earlier. The interaction between the two processes remains one of the many topics of 2000–1000 BP archaeology where more research is needed, not least to help understand why there is so little firm evidence for the presence of early Khoesan herders in the summer rainfall region of southern Africa.

Another kind of interaction, between farmers and hunter-gatherers, has been more intensively studied, and the Thukela Basin and adjacent UKhahlamba-Drakensberg and Maloti mountains are one of the best areas to examine for this. Evidence of contact here takes many forms, including finds of farmer-made pottery, iron, iron ore and schist bowls in several rock shelter sites. As I have pointed out, farmers may well have produced iron to trade with hunter-gatherers.

increased nutritional gains by allowing the boiling of meat and bones, but no comprehensive assessment of the function or origins of these early hunter-gatherer ceramics has yet been undertaken.

Building hierarchies, fostering trade: the Zimbabwe Culture and other states

Early farming communities clearly maintained wide-ranging contacts among themselves, as well as with their hunter-gatherer neighbours, and archaeology shows that commodities like iron, copper and salt were traded over distances of up to 200 kilometres. Beginning perhaps as soon as 1500 BP, Middle Eastern merchants started to visit the eastern coast of southern Africa. Finds of southern Arabian pottery of this age have been made at Chibuene in southern Mozambique and by the ninth century occasional glass beads turn up in South Africa (in KwaZulu-Natal, Mpumalanga, and Limpopo Province) and Zimbabwe. None of this need imply more than occasional trading activity, but during the tenth century these contacts underwent a transformation that helped to start a series of events that culminated in the creation of southern Africa's first towns and kingdoms and the increasing enmeshment of southern African communities with the wider world.

The Shashe–Limpopo Basin, where Botswana, Zimbabwe and South Africa now conjoin, is the most informative area on the early stages of this process. It is also the area that first emerged as a major player in the networks that brought glass beads and cloth far inland in return for African ivory, gold and other produce. Farmers resettled this area around 1100 BP after a gap of several centuries. One of its attractions was probably the many elephants supported by the local mopane vegetation; the site of Schroda has yielded massive evidence of ivory-working. Hundreds of glass beads attest to the strength of its connections with the trading systems of the Indian Ocean, and a

The conical tower in the great enclosure at Great Zimbabwe.

surprisingly high number of carnivore remains suggest that animal pelts were also processed. It is thus of great interest to read in the works of the early-tenth-century Arabic scholar al-Mas'udi that skins and ivory were well known as exports from southern Africa at that time.

Schroda's size suggests that it was the most important, as well as the largest, settlement of its day in the Shashe–Limpopo Basin. The exceptional number of clay figurines found there confirms this. While some are widely distributed across the site and were probably fertility 'dolls' used in domestic contexts by women and girls, others include relatively large anthropomorphic figures, animals and phallic shapes, all found close to the site's central cattle pen. This setting, and the choice of imagery, suggest that this second group of figurines were probably used in communal initiation ceremonies under the direction of Schroda's leaders, as with similar figurines in recent Venda and Shona initiation ceremonies.

Around 1000 BP a new kind of pottery suddenly appears in the Shashe–Limpopo Basin, which Tom Huffman takes to imply the conquest of the area by people moving up from the south. Contrary to the earlier idea that the people of the Schroda chiefdom (known as Zhizo, from their pottery) moved westward into Botswana, it now seems that a more complex sociopolitical situation developed, with some Zhizo folk remaining in the area. Excavations by John Calabrese have shown that for about 200 years Zhizo-related pottery continued to be made side by side with the new styles from the site of K2, but that the makers of the former style lived in areas of lower status. If he is correct, then ethnic differences may have played a part in one of the key developments of the time a little after 1000 BP in this part of southern Africa, the constitution of an increasingly stratified society.

Good evidence for this comes from the twin sites of K2 and Mapungubwe, a short distance upstream from Schroda. First focused at K2, settlement shifted towards and onto Mapungubwe Hill around 1220, flourishing there for the best part of a century. Both sites have produced extensive signs of trade with the East African coast and they clearly formed successive centres of a major political entity. Burials are one of the best signs of a highly unequal society; some have literally thousands of glass beads and a few from the summit of Mapungubwe Hill also had gold grave goods.

The impression of social difference is reinforced by evidence of differences in diet, by the concentration of copper-working on the hill, and by the much larger quantities of metal of all kind found at these sites compared with their contemporaries. At Mapungubwe this includes bronze and brass, the first time there is evidence of these metals in southern Africa, even though both may have been imported from India. As African exports we again have copious evidence for ivory-working, and the presence of gold at Mapungubwe allows us to consider this too, along, perhaps, with the iron produced in Botswana's Tswapong Hills.

Rare Chinese ceramics from Mapungubwe show how far-reaching southern Africa's connections were by this time. Further into the southern African interior, glass beads and seashells percolated as far as the Tsodilo Hills in Botswana. A series of chiefdoms, archaeologically called the Toutswe Tradition and known for its glass beads and seashells, developed in eastern Botswana, their power probably based more on wealth in cattle and the supply of raw materials to the

Close up of walling at Great Zimbabwe.

Shashe–Limpopo Basin than on direct access to exotic trade goods.

To understand these developments we can use the anthropological concept of a 'prestige goods economy', recalling the foreign origins of both glass beads and imported cloth (the existence of which we surmise from later written sources and the appearance of the first spindle whorls for weaving locally grown, but always monochrome, cotton textiles). Their rarity and the difficulty of acquiring them must not only have made them desirable but also distinguished them from indigenous resources like cattle, control of which had probably been the earlier basis of political power.

Beads and cloth were thus particularly well suited for being used by emerging leaders to reward juniors for their loyalty, a loyalty shown partly by paying tributes of ivory and gold, which were in turn used to keep the inward flows of cloth and beads moving. Archaeology underlines this by illustrating how at K2 glass beads were made even scarcer and more impressive by being melted down and recast into much larger examples, some of which are found up to 450 kilometres away. Restricted access to newly acquired technologies like bronze-working, or more established craftsmanship in making copper jewellery, must also have helped mark out elite individuals.

But we must avoid thinking that trade alone was the basis of their increased – and increasing – power. Cattle were doubtless also accumulated through tribute and in bridewealth payments, and wetter conditions than those of today must have made both cultivation and livestock-keeping easier within the Shashe–Limpopo area itself. Over-hunting of local elephant herds and the consequent release of the Basin's rich, seasonally flooded floodplains to farming may also have been critical in supporting the many thousands of people who lived here during K2–Mapungubwe times. Not only that, but it is by no means self-evident that people should acquiesce in the enrichment of a few at the expense of the many: future analyses would do well to consider how this process may have been resisted and to locate studies of K2–Mapungubwe and its Zimbabwe Culture successors within the broader comparative field of anthropological and historical studies of African political systems.

Hunter-gatherers too have often been overlooked in past discussions of the development of political complexity in southern Africa, although recent work in the Shashe–Limpopo Basin has made their study a priority. The early-first-millennium farmers seem to have attracted hunter-gatherers but Zhizo settlement restricted them increasingly in their use of the landscape; along with that, they allowed – or maybe encouraged or even required – them to supply raw materials, and perhaps labour, for the farming economy.

As trade and elite control of production intensified, however, the San hunter-gatherers seem increasingly to have been relegated to the economic and political margins, their former roles taken over by Bantu-speaking commoners within K2–Mapungubwe society (did the San return to hunting and gathering, living on the outskirts of Bantu-speaking settlements or were they absorbed into working-class sections of Bantu-speaking society?). The appropriation of some formerly inhabited rock shelters such as Little Muck by farmers, and the production of so-called 'late white' paintings that frequently overprint earlier hunter-gatherer art, document the final stages of this process.

Around 1300 Great Zimbabwe replaced Mapungubwe as the major centre of political power in southern Africa. The reasons are still obscure, although Great Zimbabwe's closer proximity to the goldfields of the Zimbabwe Plateau and its easier access to the Indian Ocean may have been among them. Great Zimbabwe itself is the largest and most elaborate of the many dozen stonewalled sites of the second millennium that collectively belong to what is known as the Zimbabwe Culture. Most occur on the Zimbabwe Plateau itself, but they reach beyond this into the eastern Kalahari, southern Mozambique and the far north of South Africa, where Mapungubwe marks the origin of several of the culture's key features.

These features include the construction of stone walls to mark and restrict access to residential areas for the elite, an association between rulers and the hilltops where they lived and (as at Mapungubwe) were sometimes buried, and the presence of an open area below this that served as a court. Lacking from this settlement layout, which extends to peripheral areas of the settlement used by lower-ranking members of the elite and ordinary people, is a central cattle enclosure. The organisation of Zimbabwe Culture settlements that feature stonewalling is thus quite different from the Central Cattle Pattern described earlier, although this structure survived in use at small, peasant settlements such as Vumba in south-eastern Botswana.

Although the Great Zimbabwe site had been occupied earlier, the first stone walls there were built around 1300 and most of the surviving stonework dates from the fourteenth or early fifteenth century. The Hill Complex at its centre comprises a series of stone enclosures linked by walls and natural boulders. This was probably the palace area of the site, and the famous soapstone birds found there may have commemorated royal ancestors. In the valley below lies a series of enclosures, one of which (the so-called Renders Ruin) produced a hoard of valuable items, some of African, others of foreign manufacture, including Chinese and Persian pottery, Middle Eastern glass, and tens of thousands of glass beads.

Nearby is the Great Enclosure, which includes two solid stone towers. Indeed, over 5000 cubic metres of stone were used in the structure to enclose an area of more than 6000 square metres. For Tom Huffman, this building was a centre for communal initiation ceremonies similar to the *domba* of modern Venda people; but Peter Garlake and other archaeologists see it as the royal residence. The enormous destruction wrought by the earliest, non-professional excavations at

Rain power
Mapungubwe and the roots of the first state in southern Africa

MARIA SCHOEMAN

The Shashe–Limpopo river confluence area between 700 and 1100 years ago was a place where not only rivers met, but where people from different cultures and economic backgrounds came together. One of the areas of interaction was ritual: Bantu-speaking farmers and San united in rituals of rain control. Beliefs that germinated in this milieu influenced the choice of location for the centre of the first state in southern Africa: Mapungubwe Hill.

The group who established the centre, known as Leopard's Kopje people after the style of their pottery, first entered the confluence area about 1000 BP. Here they encountered the Zhizo people, whose urban centre, Schroda, was located near the Limpopo River. This incursion ended the Zhizo people's control over the area as well as over the international trade network which the Zhizo elite had steered from Schroda. After the Leopard's Kopje people took command of the area, most of the Zhizo elite abandoned Schroda and moved their capital to Toutswe in Botswana.

Although the Leopard's Kopje and Zhizo people clashed, they were nevertheless both Bantu-speaking farming peoples with similar worldviews. Archaeologists recently discovered that, even though the Zhizo elite left, some commoners chose to stay behind.

After displacing the Zhizo elite, the Leopard's Kopje people established their centre (known to researchers as K2), which housed about 1500 people, at the base of Bambandyanalo Hill. Such a large centre required the production of a substantial agricultural surplus. Leopard's Kopje commoner sites in the river valleys, which were linked to crop farming, spread into areas not previously occupied by Zhizo farmers. The centre of the K2 leaders was also much larger than the Schroda one of the Zhizo.

ABOVE: Mapungubwe Hill.
BELOW: Gold beads from Mapungubwe.

As at Schroda, houses at K2 were arranged around a cattle kraal. The cattle were later removed from the centre. This signalled changes in economic focus, social organisation and religious beliefs, which eventually culminated in the abandonment of K2.

The rain-control sites exhibit changes that parallel the transformations in the society as a whole. At the start of the sequence the Leopard's Kopje people made rain on hills on the plateau. These hills were located away from the settlements, and thus perceived to be close to the natural world. The Leopard's Kopje farming communities included San, who already lived in the valley, in the rain-control process. San were perceived to be close to the natural world and thus able to influence it; they were probably viewed as the symbolic owners of the land. As newcomers to the area, the Leopard's Kopje people would not have had local ancestors. Through using San to control rain, they were accessing the ancestors of the land.

Leopard's Kopje society and settlement did not freeze after they settled in the valley and established their initial relationship with the San. Their occupation expanded and the farmers sought to transform the natural environment into farmland. Elephants were hunted to extinction for the ivory trade by 1000 BP, which opened up new areas for farming and villages. This also created the potential for new farming methods, enabling the Leopard's Kopje farmers to look beyond purely natural resources. They started practising flood-plain agriculture and were thus no longer solely reliant on imme-diate rainfall. The increasing population densities and expansive flood-plain agri-

Great Zimbabwe over a century ago, and the relative lack of effort expended on excavating in those parts of this massive (720 hectare) site inhabited by ordinary people, continue to make it difficult to judge definitively between such competing explanations or to offer a fully rounded interpretation of the life of its inhabitants. It seems likely, however, that Great Zimbabwe was occupied by up to 18 000 people, making it a substantial town by medieval standards and one of the largest precolonial settlements in southern Africa.

Though all the stonewalled sites clearly belong to a common cultural tradition, it is less clear if they ever formed part of a single political unit when Great Zimbabwe was at its peak. The situation recorded in oral traditions and by the first Portuguese visitors to the region in the sixteenth century suggests this may not have been the case. On the other hand, Great Zimbabwe is much larger than any other settlement of this age, has almost all the known imported pottery and locally made gold and bronze items, and was the source of pottery and stonewalling styles introduced later into other areas.

All these facts point to a politically pre-eminent position for its leaders, even if the exact area they controlled may have fluctuated over time for reasons we cannot see now. This position of power was probably created and maintained in several ways, only one of which involved trade with the East African coast. An important factor in that trade must have been the fact that the Zimbabwe Plateau was the only area of eastern or southern Africa to offer traders simultaneous access to both gold and ivory, to which we can add copper from northern Zimbabwe and tin from Limpopo Province. This combination must have been a powerful attraction for Swahili merchants, just as it was later for the Portuguese. Its strength is shown by the simultaneous florescence of Great Zimbabwe and the largest Swahili city, Kilwa (in modern Tanzania), during the early 1300s, when world

culture reshaped the valley completely. Nature was also co-operating, and might have seemed tamed. Rainfall during most of the Leopard's Kopje occupation was above 500 mm per annum.

As the Leopard's Kopje settlements in the valley expanded, and when the valley had been occupied for more than one generation, direct Leopard's Kopje ancestors started multiplying. The ritual need for previous 'owners of the land' consequently diminished. An increase in local ancestors also resulted in changes in rain-control beliefs and practices. This manifested in the transformation of rain-control hills. The Leopard's Kopje farmers started to take control of the areas where rain was made by constructing grain bins on rain-control hills. Building gravel-floored structures soon followed. These structures symbolically marked the hills and signalled Leopard's Kopje ownership and society. Thus the hills had their meanings rewritten; rain-spaces in the natural world that had been controlled jointly by San and farmers were now identified as farming places.

The favourable climatic conditions did not last. Between 750 and 800 years ago a prolonged and severe drought occurred, when rainfall decreased to less than 350 mm per annum. This would have made surplus crops very difficult to produce. The failure of the plateau rain-controllers to relieve this drought provided an opportunity for the Leopard's Kopje rulers to attempt to monopolise the rain-control space. Their effort to own rain control was, however, part of a long-term process of both economic and political centralisation.

Appropriation of rain-control space informed the decision by the elite to abandon K2 and move onto Mapungubwe Hill, less than a kilometre away. The massive political and ideological implications of this step were naturalised through using the physicality of Mapungubwe Hill to symbolise continuity with old rain-control practices. The occupation of Mapungubwe Hill became part of a process that transformed and appropriated earlier social practices and attitudes.

Mapungubwe Hill was chosen as the new royal palace probably because it was a K2-period rain-control site. Like other K2-period rain-control places, Mapungubwe Hill was near a stream, had a shelter at its base, and had two rock tanks on top. Furthermore, it was marked with cup-shaped hollows linked with rain control, including some in a small rock tank. The imagined power that Mapungubwe Hill had, as imbued by the cultural interpretation of its features, was enhanced through rain control and materialised through settlement. This power, especially in the early-thirteenth-century drought, would have made the move of the Mapungubwe elite to the hilltop seem logical and even necessary.

The ruling dynasty on the hilltop were separated physically from their elite and commoner subjects, who resided in the town at the base of the hill. The supporters in turn occupied different areas according to their status. At the zenith of the Mapungubwe state, 5000 people lived in the town. The supporters in turn occupied different areas according to their status. This indicates not just urbanisation but also increasing centralisation, which creates the scope for more intense central control and the ability to extract an agricultural surplus effectively. The new corporate identity associated with the Mapungubwe state was expressed even in changes in ceramic style.

The incorporation of rain-control space into the Mapungubwe royal residence suggests not just a practical move but symbolic alienation from the commoners and a strengthening of royal control over religion. This probably played an important part in the development of sacred leadership, which is a key difference between the pre- and post-Mapungubwe periods.

Yet rain control also continued on the plateau hills, signalling that the Mapungubwe leaders were not entirely successful in centralising everything. In addition, people using the old rain-control hills continued to express their old K2-ness in their ceramics rather than changing to the new Mapungubwe style. Clearly they were choosing not to adopt the new Mapungubwe identity emanating from the centre. Instead, the identity of their K2 ancestors was harnessed in plateau rain-control sites in the Mapungubwe period.

The Mapungubwe regime had lasted no more than 70 years, but the immediate ancestral past survived the time and continued to be important in ritual affairs. The invocation of old identities along with the continuation of traditional rain-control practices implies that, in spite of the radical changes made at the capital by the Mapungubwe elite, traditional beliefs and rituals kept their value for people on the plateau.

OPPOSITE: Game board on stone. Although this game is played throughout the eastern parts of sub-Saharan Africa, game boards also served ritual functions that include rain-control.
BELOW: Gold rhinoceros found at Mapungubwe.

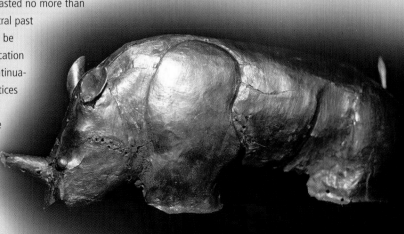

demand for gold increased. A Kilwan coin of this period found at Great Zimbabwe tightens the link still further.

Modern mining has limited our direct evidence of gold-mining on the Zimbabwe Plateau, and gold was almost certainly also panned from rivers. However it was won, it was probably produced by peasant farmers during the agricultural 'off-season' when other labour demands were few. It was thus economically marginal to the majority of Zimbabwe Culture society, an African equivalent of the mass-produced cloth and beads for which it was principally exchanged. Though ivory, like gold, was also valued by the Zimbabwe Culture's elite, it probably fell into this category too: more valuable for ordinary people will have been the meat obtained by killing an elephant and the consequent removal of a potential danger to life and crops. Such points are worth making to contest the view that the export of unworked raw materials placed Great Zimbabwe and other southern African states in a position of economic and political dependency on their foreign trading partners, foreshadowing Africa's colonial and postcolonial situation.

Factors other than trade only reinforce this analysis. A successful agricultural economy, for example, was obviously essential to support a population of the size believed to have inhabited Great Zimbabwe or the many other stonewalled sites, and some archaeologists have suggested that control over prime-quality arable land or pastures seasonally free from tsetse fly infestation was significant in developing and maintaining elite power. Control over iron production may also have been important since this metal was essential for land clearance and cultivation and could be used for bridewealth payments too. Controversial evidence for iron having been smelted at Great Zimbabwe and the mass of iron objects found at Renders Ruin may suggest royal interest in producing this vital commodity, something possibly supported by finds there of iron gongs, symbols of royal status in Zambia and Congo-Kinshasa.

Farmer rock art of Africa

CATHERINE NAMONO

Research on rock art of the Iron Age farmers is still in its infancy compared with what we understand of San hunter-gatherer rock art. Unlike the fine-line brushstrokes and naturalistic imagery of the San, in farmer rock art the images are finger-painted in a white, red or black pigment. In some parts of Africa this tradition is popularly referred to as the Late Whites because images are often painted in a chalky-white pigment and always lie on top of other rock art traditions.

Although farmer and hunter-gatherer rock art traditions occur in the same landscapes, sometimes in the same sites, the contrast between them remains stark. In farmer rock art no attempt is made to capture a true likeness of the 'natural' object. Finger-painting means that attention to fine detail is impossible. In addition, equal attention is not given to all features in an image. Key features are often exaggerated while others are standardised or omitted. The width of an image is often determined by the finger that drew it with paint paste, producing stick-like figures or other designs of the same thickness. Typically these include geometric-like shapes, shapes resembling humans, images with animal characteristics, shapes resembling humans and others that are more definitely people trains, vehicles, wagons, men on horseback, men with guns, men on oxen, and images with hands akimbo. The akimbo stance is interesting as it is an instance of farmers painting 'outsiders'. All images that have this stance also have the accompanying material culture, which is recognisably European – short skirts, pointed shoes, hats, horses, and ox-wagons.

Rock art research to date shows that other farmer rock art traditions are found only in those parts of East, Central and southern Africa where Bantu-speaking farmers are known to have lived. There are at least seven similar farmer rock art traditions there, associated with Bantu speakers, who include among others

What these objects also do is direct our attention to connections between Great Zimbabwe and other parts of the African interior. Access to copper from those more northerly regions, salt production along the margins of the Kalahari, and the large-scale extraction of tin from South Africa's Rooiberg mountains (almost entirely for Indian Ocean trade) all merit more research than they have thus far received.

There is much that we do not yet know about the Zimbabwe Culture, but there is absolutely no doubt (contrary to earlier, racist speculations) that it was wholly a product of African people, the direct ancestors of the modern Shona. What, for example, was the exact relationship between Great Zimbabwe and Mapungubwe, which still seems to have been a focus of settlement in the late fourteenth century? And did Shona-speaking people enter Zimbabwe from the south only at the beginning of the second millennium? Tom Huffman sees the appearance of K2 pottery in the Shashe–Limpopo Basin as an indicator.

And exactly how did the Zimbabwe Culture expand? Was it linked to the movement of a specific ethnic group, as the last hypothesis might suggest, or did it also involve the co-option of other communities whose leaders found that it offered them new ways of consolidating and extending their own power? The latter process may be indicated by the imposition of stone-walled Zimbabwe-type settlements on earlier occupations at sites like Ruanga and Wazi in northern Zimbabwe, an area where ceramics, Portuguese records and features of modern ethnography all suggest that Shona presence has a relatively shallow time depth.

After 1450 Great Zimbabwe entered a decline, though the site may have continued to be a royal centre for another century or so. Whether this was promoted by changing patterns of international trade, long-term ecological degradation, or political events that we cannot recover, is unknown. However, we do know that more than one successor state emerged.

the Warangi of Tanzania; the Chêwa of Zambia, Malawi and Mozambique; the Kalanga of Zimbabwe; the Tswana of Botswana; and the Northern Sotho of South Africa.

Recently researchers have successfully used ethnographic information from the nine-teenth and twentieth centuries to interpret many of the farmer rock art images, providing insight into their possible meaning. Worldwide there are only a few rock art regions that have such detailed sources to use for interpretation. Ethnographic records and local traditions still practised today indicate that what inspired this farmer rock art tradition was its association with secret male and female initiation practices and rituals such as rainmaking. The challenge to the rock art researcher is that the meaning of the imagery is secret and remains the prerogative of the initiated.

A common feature throughout its distribution is the occurrence of a stylised image which is often called the 'spread-eagle design'. It has also been named a 'schematised human being' or a 'saurian motif', or a 'crocodile or lizard', and is now recognised as an important symbol in this rock art tradition. To farmers such as the Northern Sotho the image is known as *koma*, which translates as 'ancestral being'. This spread-eagle design is said to be central to all rituals associated with initiation and is sometimes recognised as the symbol of the chief.

In South Africa, researchers have suggested that some farmer rock art contains pointed humour, a catharsis for coping with and overcoming difficulties that colonial intruders brought to the local people. It reflects a subtle blending of humour with politics. Images in this subcategory are commonly referred to as protest art or art of aggression. There is a predominance of horses, people on horse-back with guns, gun-wielding foot soldiers, figures akimbo, and abstract trains. Such images are also found in Tanzania, Mozambique, Malawi and Zambia. Further research needs to be done to establish whether the painters were driven by the same motivation as those in what is now South Africa.

ABOVE: Human figures in the hands-on-hips posture. OPPOSITE: The so-called 'spread-eagle' design, which represents a crocodile.

The wide distribution of the farmer rock art tradition, from South Africa to Tanzania, provides evidence for a broad similarity in the way African farmers perceive the world around them in East, Central and southern Africa. Important regional variations do exist because of the way in which initiation rituals were perceived and used. Variations also arise from differences within patriarchal and matriarchal farmer societies and in the metaphors that were transferred to the rock art. These differences allow for fertile research in the future.

An example of just one direction that future research will follow is the tantalising finger-painted images of stylised cattle around the shores of Lake Victoria in East Africa. Because these images are very different from other rock art of this historically farmer-occupied area, and are localised and have a focused distri-bution, it is highly probable that the makers of the stylised cattle were not farmers but Nilotic-speaking pastoralists. These people were mobile and it is highly probable that, through interaction, they may have acquired ideas, beliefs, practices and symbols from the farmers.

Farmer rock art traditions, read together with other archaeological data, are highly informative. Their break with older hunter-gatherer traditions confirms their link to migrations of people and ideas. Farmer rock art also reflects the growth of more localised ethnic identities within the broader Eastern and Western Bantu-language cultural traditions, enabling us to reconstruct the ways identities emerged. Across Africa, each farmer rock art tradition has its own particular history because it played a key role in initiation ritual; the rock art thus contains information that is specific to the group that produced it. In such ways, this evidence adds to our understanding of the material and social factors that, in combination, created the rich ethnic tapestry of Africa's modern Bantu-speaking farmers.

ROCK ART RESEARCH INSTITUTE

In north-eastern Zimbabwe the Mutapa kingdom is relatively well known from documents left by the Portuguese, who began trading with (and attempting, at times, to convert and conquer) it in the sixteenth century. Excavations by Innocent Pikirayi show that stonewalling was abandoned here before long, unlike the southwest, where the Torwa kingdom developed. Centred first at Khami, Torwa's capital later shifted to Danangombe after the Rozvi, a lineage originating in Mutapa, conquered it in the late 1600s. Both sites preserve elaborate decorative designs within the walls that demarcated elite residential areas.

Torwa remained largely beyond the reach of the Portuguese and their base on the coast of Mozambique, though it certainly exported gold and was able to acquire new, non-African crops such as peanuts. However, until it collapsed when attacked by Nguni raiders in the 1830s, royal power was firmly based on control of cattle and land rather than long-distance trade. That power reached beyond modern Zimbabwe into what is now Botswana and South Africa, where the important site of Thulamela in the far north of the Kruger National Park has recently been investigated.

With extensive stone walls first built about 1440, Thulamela was occupied until the mid-1600s. Finds of glass beads, seashells and gold- and ivory-working document the presence of high-status people and contacts with Africa's Indian Ocean coast. Two elite burials, later re-interred, recall Venda practice and support the use of Venda ethnography to interpret the Zimbabwe Culture. Indeed, ceramic data parallel the evidence of linguistics to show how the Venda language has roots in both Shona and Sotho. Excavations by Jannie Loubser have also endorsed historical references to the extent and power of the Singo state founded by incoming Rozvi leaders in the late 1600s, and its later dissolution.

Yet it would be wrong to suggest that everywhere between the Zambezi and the Limpopo was intimately associated with trade to the East African seaboard. The Nyanga highlands of eastern Zimbabwe are a good example of a region that was not trading there. Here a highly distinctive set of developments took shape between the fourteenth and nineteenth centuries whose connections with the Zimbabwe Culture remain to be established. Covering around 4500 square kilometres is an extensive area of agricultural settlement still preserving many features designed to conserve and concentrate fertile soil, clear land and facilitate drainage in a high-altitude location otherwise marginal for cultivation. In addition, stonewalled pit enclosures (at one time mistakenly thought to have been used to house slaves) were built to keep a local dwarf breed of cattle so that their manure could be concentrated and put onto fields and gardens. Terracing of hill slopes was also developed, perhaps to free extra land for a growing population.

We must still learn more about the interaction between climate change and human (anthropogenic) effects on the landscape, including forest clearance for cultivation, fuel and building materials. But the work already done here gives a clear model for what could be applied in similar circumstances further south, such as the highlands of Mpumalanga.

Following farmers: agropastoralist settlement in southernmost Africa from 1000 BP

The Mpumalanga highlands, like much of South Africa's north, are the home today of people speaking variants of Sotho–Tswana. Their archaeological signatures and those of their Nguni neighbours to the south and east differ in many ways from the material record of first-millennium farming communities, some of which we have mentioned. Notably, their ceramics do not continue the styles of earlier centuries (the Kalundu and Urewe Traditions). Instead, there is a pronounced stylistic break between these earlier pottery styles on the one hand, and on the other the later pottery associated historically with Sotho–Tswana speakers (the Moloko Tradition that first appeared in Mpumalanga and Limpopo Province in the fourteenth century) and with Nguni speakers (the Blackburn Tradition that appeared a little earlier in KwaZulu-Natal).

This fact suggests that people speaking these languages, the mother tongues of over 35 million southern Africans today, may have been present in the region only since the early second millennium. Moreover, the closest relatives of these languages lie not in southern Africa but in East Africa, where they include Swahili, which even has similar terms for kinship. This evidence suggests, then, that Sotho–Tswana and Nguni were introduced to southern Africa within the last 1000 years, probably from considerably further north; the drier conditions that prevailed in much of East Africa between 1100 and 700 BP may have triggered the movement south.

It is highly desirable to combine the resources of both southern African and East African archaeologists when investigating this scenario, and also in researching the relationships between these new settlers and earlier farming communities. Studies of Nguni have identified loanwords from a hypothetical extinct language similar to Shona, which suggests, unsurprisingly, that contact and presumably intermarriage did take place. That a Shona-like language was once spoken in south-eastern southern Africa neatly matches Huffman's observation that the Kalundu Tradition ceramics of KwaZulu-Natal share origins with K2 pottery, the makers of which created the Zimbabwe Culture.

Sotho–Tswana and Nguni of course do not exhaust the diversity of languages found among Bantu speakers in southernmost Africa. Tsonga, spoken today in southern Mozambique and northernmost KwaZulu-Natal, is another, and work by Fumiko Ohinata in Swaziland has confirmed the existence of a distinct Tsonga identity reaching back beyond colonial era records and further west than their current distribution.

Further south, Gavin Whitelaw is exploring the history of Nguni settlement in KwaZulu-Natal. The earliest sites known are along the coast, but in the fourteenth century people making Moor Park pottery began settling south of the Mtamvuna River and also in the higher-altitude grasslands of the interior. In doing so, they not only had to use stone as a building material but they also opened up new possibilities for economic specialisation and interdependence between communities, not least where a lack of suitable fuel made iron-smelting impossible. Many Moor Park settlements were located on defensible hilltops, perhaps a reaction to the stress and competition for resources that must have been produced by the markedly drier conditions that prevailed from 1320 to 1400.

Another reaction to the drier conditions may have been to encourage some people to cross the UKhahlamba-Drakensberg and settle in the northeastern Free State, an idea supported by the oral traditions of the Sotho-speaking Fokeng and similarities between their pottery and the Blackburn sequence. Early (and still isolated) radiocarbon dates from Tim Maggs's excavations at Ntsuanatsatsi near Frankfort in the Free State, the reputed origin point for the southern Sotho, would fit this scenario. However, other assessments of the available dating evidence argue that more substantial expansion of farming communities into the highveld began as recently as 1640, taking advantage of a wetter, warmer climate and a shift to more regular summer rains that suited the cultivation of sorghum and millet. Yet even now agropastoralist settlement could not spread beyond the 600-mm rainfall line and 1500-metre contour, and the evidence of place names and archaeology suggests that it even contracted slightly in the late 1700s.

The use of stone to build houses and stock enclosures means that these highveld settlements have lasted fairly well and can be readily recognised from the air as well as on the ground. Variations in their organisation and in the pottery associated with them can be reliably linked to

Typical iron hoe.   DAVID PEARCE

known Sotho and Tswana groups and to the oral history of their movements and diversification.

To settle successfully on the highveld, people had to modify their way of life. Livestock gained importance in this grassland environment, as is reflected in numerous cattle figurines and the greater size of livestock enclosures. Increased emphasis on cattle may also have offered more scope for accumulating wealth and creating clientship obligations when cattle were loaned out to others. Cattle also provided an extra source of fuel, in the form of dung, that was of great value in a tree-poor landscape. Consistent with all this, the isotope composition of human skeletons shows an enhanced dependence on animal products compared with people living further north.

The scarcity of wood on the highveld had other consequences. One is the complete absence of evidence of iron-smelting anywhere in the Free State. Not only are metal artefacts rare, with pottery and bone used as alternatives where possible, but it seems that such iron and copper as was used was imported from beyond the Vaal River or from across the UKhahlamba-Drakensberg. In the latter area archaeologists have investigated the mining and subsequent smelting of iron ore around Mabhija in the upper Thukela Basin. This is an area with poor-quality grazing and poor arable soils, and the evidence for concentrated iron production neatly fits oral traditions that recall how people in the Mabhija area exchanged iron for livestock and grain with Sotho speakers in the Free State.

Areas of concentrated production like this, where people had to make the most of limited options, are known elsewhere too – for example, at Itala in northern KwaZulu-Natal. In some cases we know that iron-smelting came to be associated with particular lineages that were the subject of patronage and control by chiefs. The trade links that such specialisations encouraged deserve further investigation, not least because the highveld is not the only area where metal was scarce. South of Durban, for instance, few smelting sites are known, while ore sources were especially meagre in the Eastern Cape. There, Xhosa speakers used wooden spades and stone flakes in partial substitution for iron, something they eagerly sought from shipwrecked Europeans.

Such evidence helps highlight the quite complex networks of exchange that we know existed. Copper, which was produced on a large scale near Phalaborwa and in the Dwarsberge, tin from the Rooiberge, and salt are just some of the items that we know were widely dispersed, along with seashell ornaments, cannabis (dagga) and glass beads. Surviving hunter-gatherer groups may have been important in transporting many of these items as well as more perishable products of their own such as pigments, skins, feathers, and ostrich eggshell beads.

Although nothing on the scale of the Zimbabwe Culture developed south of the Limpopo Valley (Venda excluded), more centralised forms of political organisation did emerge in some places. The Tswana settlements of Gauteng and North-West Province provide some of the best evidence of these processes, as well as for the development of new ways of integrating larger numbers of people together. They have been investigated recently by Jan Boeyens, Simon Hall and Julius Pistorius, among others.

Hall initially argued that the first appearance of stone walls in this area in the 1600s was linked to defining membership of kinship groups more exclusively and to asserting stronger claims to ownership of the landscape. He identified changes in gender relations, with roles becoming more strongly differentiated, women increasingly subjected, and male activities like metal-working and hide preparation brought under more centralised control of the chief. It now appears, however, that population movements associated with a return to a cooler, drier climate may have helped to prompt the initial elaboration of stonewalling and the shift of settlement toward more defensible locations.

The later nucleation into the large settlements reported by early European travellers in the early 1800s probably arose from several interacting factors: periodic drought, conflict, population growth, and a drive toward political centralisation by chiefs. Participation in long-distance trade is so far only weakly visible in the archaeological record, although we know that some Tswana supplied ivory to Tsonga traders linked to the Indian Ocean coast, and that the pursuit of elephant herds was one attraction for the Tswana expansion into the Kalahari in the 1700s and 1800s.

While the archaeology of many Sotho and Tswana groups is (or has the potential to be) relatively well known, the general reliance on perishable constructional materials and a much more dispersed pattern of settlement mean that we still know very little from archaeological sources about the precolonial history of Nguni-speaking people in the Eastern Cape or lowland KwaZulu-Natal. In very general terms, however, it is likely that across this area, and especially at its southern end, there was a gradual continuing expansion of farming communities inland and up valley systems.

This expansion, which was unconnected to any significant move toward political centralisation until the late 1700s, also involved the ongoing assimilation of hunter-gatherer and herder populations. Clan names are one of the lines of evidence for this; but the most obvious one is that of linguistics – one only has to listen to someone speaking Zulu or Xhosa to be aware from the many words containing click sounds of the significance of the Khoesan contribution to

Aerial view of the archaeological remains of an agropastoralist site. The CCP layout is clearly visible.

The pain of entering trance is visible on the face of this San shaman.
RICHARD KATZ

those languages and, by implication, to the history of those who speak them. The intermarriage that this suggests is supported by genetic analyses and by similarities in religious practice.

One good example is provided by the close parallels between San trance dancing and Nguni divination practices, right down to the fact that the Xhosa term for diviner – *igqirha* – is cognate with and almost certainly borrowed from the /Xam San word for shaman, *!gi:xa*. David Hammond-Tooke has convincingly argued that the principal reason for such practices being much more evident among Nguni- rather than Sotho–Tswana-speaking groups lies in the former having a strongly patrilineal, male-dominated kinship system which made female members of their society in particular more receptive to San beliefs and practices. Even today the ochre from San rock paintings has strong spiritual significance for many traditionally-minded Nguni, and so do any individuals thought or known to be of San descent.

The cave, the coast, and ocean links

PAUL SINCLAIR

Many years ago two young lovers were looking for a quiet place to be together. They chanced upon an opening in the rock and entered. They made love and afterwards the young girl being satisfied threw a stone into the back of the cave. She heard a splash and discovered sweet water. They washed themselves and went home reporting the cave they had found and the precious water.
– Traditional custodian of Kuumbi Cave

Kuumbi Cave is set high up, overlooking the surrounding coral limestone landscape about three kilometres inland from Jambiani village on the south-east coast of Zanzibar. Kuumbi Cave (Kuumbi means Great Hall) comprises two large chambers and a number of minor galleries which have been formed over many thousands of years as dissolution cavities from the coral limestone. Stalagmites and stalactites containing useful data on climate change have yet to be investigated. The cave is a valuable source of fresh water.

This place is an important shrine where ancestral spirits are venerated and consulted, attracting visitors from all over Unguja, the main island of the Zanzibar archipelago. There are no obvious rock paintings or engravings and this is not especially surprising given the rapid depositional rate on the cave walls. The cave is guarded by a traditional custodian, continuing the longstanding local bond with this sacred place. The custodian is also a renowned preacher at a mosque in the stone town of Zanzibar. Kuumbi's forested environment has

The entrance to
Kuumbi Cave.

PAUL SINCLAIR

been preserved by the community and provides a welcome and important oasis of plant and animal biodiversity.

Humans have lived in the cave for thousands of years. Archaeological investigations have only just begun but already reveal a long period of occupation in the more than 2.5 metres of cultural deposits in the floor of the outer chamber. The pottery dates from recent times back into the third millennium BP. Stone and bone tools have also been recovered and go back probably some thousands of years. From this evidence we know that hunter-gatherers lived in Kuumbi Cave and represent some of the original inhabitants of Zanzibar, probably from a time in the Pleistocene prior to 15 000 BP when a lowered sea level linked Zanzibar to the mainland. There is good evidence for the existence of early *Homo sapiens sapiens* in both South Africa and Ethiopia, and there seems little reason to doubt the existence of human populations for tens of thousands of years along other parts of the East African coast. It is as well to bear this point in mind when considering the contribution of people from other parts of the Indian Ocean to the cultural and civilisational mosaic of the East African coast.

The deposits at Kuumbi contain debris from daily life, notably preparation of food. There is a range of marine shell fragments and also of *Acatina*, the giant forest snail. Fish bones are less common. Other wild animals represented in the deposit include remains of leopard, zebra, eland, giraffe and small antelope species. Hyrax, rodents, snakes and lizards have also been recovered. Not all of these were consumed by people. Domestic animals include cattle and chicken. Bones of the latter have been dated from deposits in Machaga Cave on Zanzibar to around 2800 BP, making them the earliest known on the East African coast.

Early beads made from glass and carnelian stones, and pottery from India, provide evidence for the early participation of these communities in the trade networks of the western Indian Ocean. After the pioneer work by Felix Chami, caves with similar evidence are known in Zanzibar – at Machaga in Pete

Rock art and oral histories provide further invaluable insights into how hunter-gatherers interacted with farming peoples. We know, for example, that both Sotho and Nguni groups sometimes gave cattle to San clients and forged marriage alliances with them, and that exchange relationships involved the reciprocal giving of game, skins and ostrich feathers for grain and (once it had been introduced from the Americas) tobacco. At least two Nguni-speaking groups, the Mpondomise and the Thembu, also used San shamans to make rain, while far to the north the rock engraving sites at Thaba Sione and Matsieng were appropriated by Tswana chiefs for their own rainmaking ceremonies.

Within areas settled by farmers, assimilation seems to have proceeded fairly rapidly, accelerated perhaps by a denser agropastoralist presence that both physically hindered the movement of foragers across the landscape and brought about reductions in the availability of game and wild food plants as land was taken for fields and pasture. This fragmentation and eventual 'social strangulation' of hunter-gatherer society may be reflected in the proliferation of tiny rock shelters that were ephemerally occupied in Gauteng and Mpumalanga in the mid-second millennium.

Further south, the Caledon Valley is one of the best areas for studying the interactions between farmers and hunter-gatherers. Here, the rainfall requirements of sorghum and millet meant that agropastoralists were largely confined to the area north of Ladybrand and to a 'finger' extending downstream inside western Lesotho. In the north, hunter-gatherer sites disappeared rapidly although they continued to occupy the agriculturally undesirable Maloti Mountains well into the nineteenth century. Rose Cottage Cave near Ladybrand, a major focus of hunter-gatherer settlement in the 1300s and 1400s, also went out of use as smaller sites took its place, some of them very rich in rock art and trance-specific imagery, which perhaps helped substitute for a physical aggregation of what was now becoming a more dispersed population. The substitution of Sotho ceramics for earlier grass-tempered pottery of the kind made by hunter-gatherers further south in

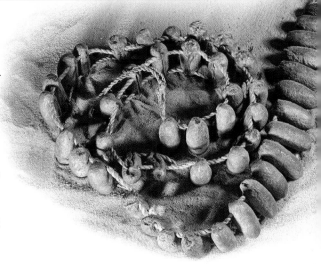

Dance rattles used during the trance dance.
ROCK ART RESEARCH INSTITUTE

the Karoo also speaks of people reorganising their contacts to focus on incoming farming groups.

However, farmers did not penetrate the entirety of the Caledon Valley, the southern half of which boasts many paintings of sheep, cattle and Sotho-type shields which Jannie Loubser has suggested were valued as sources of the supernatural potency that San shamans sought to manipulate. Here, then, hunter-gatherers continued to thrive, as they did in the Lesotho highlands and much of the Karoo. In the western Free State, indeed, they successfully acquired herds of cattle, goats and sheep, something relevant to the discussions about herders and hunter-gatherers in the Western Cape that we considered above. Stonewalled stock enclosures of a kind known to archaeologists as Type R (after the Riet River Valley, where they cluster) and stone burial cairns both attest to this transformation, which was recorded by the British naturalist William Burchell in 1811.

Returning home: the impacts of European trade, colonisation and conquest

All modern humans, including those of Europe, trace their ancestry to a common African source, but it took until 1485 for the European descendants of and on Juani Island near Mafia, for example. On Juani Island, Late Harappan and Early Historic ceramic sherds from India dated to the third millennium BP have been recovered, indicating perhaps some form of direct contact between East Africa and South Asia. Further finds of South Asian early historic period bowls similar to those used by Buddhist monks are also suggestive. Other sherds dated between about 2000 and 1400 BP point to continued contact.

Plants were also conveyed between the continents. It has been known for some time that African sorghum was a key component in the successful agricultural transition from the winter rainfall wheat and barley cropping systems of the Indus River Valley to those better adapted to the drought-prone regions of South Asia from about 4400 BP onwards. This is a different view of Africa – not Africa as the backward dependant but Africa as the provider of an important component of South Asian agricultural strength which, with the later inclusion of rice probably from China, became a fundamental basis of Indian civilisation. Further support for early contact comes in the form of recent genetic evidence which points to early crossings between African and Indian varieties of domestic cattle.

The caves on Zanzibar provide potentially valuable new insights into these questions and are the focus of joint research led by the archaeologists Felix Chami of the University of Dar es Salaam, Abdurahman Juma of the Zanzibar Antiquities Service, and Paul Sinclair of Uppsala University. Similar work is currently under way in southern Madagascar by Chantal Radimilahy and Jean-Aime Rakotoarisoa of the Museum of Art and Archaeology at the University of Antananarivo, among others.

The coastal areas have also been the focus of recent research. Once again, pioneering work by Chami in the Rufiji Delta on the Tanzanian mainland begins to come to grips with this important area, long thought to be one of the most likely locations for Rhapta, the urban centre mentioned in classical sources such as the 'Periplus of the Erythraean Sea'. Juma's research at the early urban settlement of Unguja Ukuu on Zanzibar brings further into focus the potential of trading activities in the period 2000–1000 BP for stimulating urban growth. These ideas – fresh departures and hotly contested as they are, but on balance increasingly supported – strongly suggest a new view of the origins of the Swahili Urban civilisation, with a much stronger African contribution than has been hitherto recognised, both on the mainland and on the offshore islands including the Comores and Madagascar. The prior existence of African iron-using farming communities in the vicinity of nearly all the later urban centres on the mainland, increasingly apparent on the near offshore islands as well, makes it necessary to rethink East African history.

Much has been written of the colonial propensity to underplay the role of Africans in developing the Swahili civilisation of eastern Africa, but it is not only the role of Africans that has been underestimated: the evidence on early contact with India underscores the need to explore this vast source of inspiration and exchange. When the imperial powers divided the Indian Ocean into separate 'African', 'Near Eastern', 'South Asia' and 'South-East Asian' regions in the eighteenth to twentieth centuries, one of

The modern town of Zanzibar.

PAUL SINCLAIR

that population to return home to southern Africa. Their homecoming produced mixed blessings for the region's existing inhabitants, not least those who still followed a hunting and gathering way of life. Seeking a new sea route to India and the Far East, the Portuguese were interested in South Africa only to the extent of acquiring livestock, an interest that waned after the viceroy of India was killed in a skirmish in 1510.

Shipwreck sites, including the camp of the survivors of the *São Gonçalo* (1630) at Plettenberg Bay, dominate the archaeological record which the Portuguese left behind in South Africa and Namibia, as their primary concerns lay further north. Having seized the port of Sofala on the coast of East Africa in 1505, Portugal tried to gain exclusive control of exports of Zimbabwean gold, establishing small trading communities along the Zambezi Valley. Most of this trade soon passed out of government control into the hands of landholders, who intermarried and assimilated with local African communities. Little has been done to explore archaeologically such *prazero* sites, but on the Zimbabwe Plateau trading stations have been excavated at Hartley and Mtoko, the latter with an associated church. Both sites were used to store and sell merchandise, something confirmed by finds of Chinese and European pottery, glass and gold beads and gold dust.

By the late 1500s other European nations were contesting Portugal's supremacy in the Indian Ocean, and English and Dutch ships in particular began to call regularly at Table Bay to trade for livestock. Actual settlement initially took the form of a small station begun in 1652 and designed to provide fresh provisions for Dutch East India Company (VOC) ships sailing between Europe and Indonesia. To facilitate this, the VOC grudgingly allowed a few settlers to become independent farmers, but attempts to develop an intensive agricultural economy met with limited success outside the immediate

the hidden costs was to obscure such links. Their geographical grid has made it much more difficult for scholars to see the connections between regions which are likely to have characterised the trading networks of the Indian Ocean area at least from the period of early agricultural developments in the fifth millennium BP and – as we have seen – quite possibly considerably earlier.

It is worth re-emphasising here that the African inhabitants of the coast probably had a very long presence there (at least 100 000 years) and it seems increasingly likely that they formed the core of the earliest *Homo sapiens sapiens* populations of Europe and Asia. Throughout this exceptionally long timespan the populations of the East African coast could well have been resident, open, dynamic, and potentially in contact with all the major systems of the prehistoric and ancient world – and not backward and isolated, as characterised in colonial and a good deal of more recent scholarship. On the other hand, we should not underestimate the potential bias deriving from overemphasising for instance the Bantu speakers' contribution to civilisation on the coast of East Africa at the expense of, say, the Nilotic and click-speaking populations and the other participants from the wider Indian Ocean region.

We archaeologists in East Africa are in an interesting phase of rethinking basic issues. Previous crude categories such as the Stone Age and Iron Age no longer account for the variability of archaeological data, which often present a mosaic of different ways of life practised contemporaneously. The rather belated realisation that ethnicity is a cultural construct and not a given of objective reality points to the need for deconstructive critique from a post-colonial perspective. Easy correlations between ceramic complexes and peoples backed up by uncritical acceptance of documentary sources and colonial ethnography no longer seem so straightforward, and questions such as what languages were spoken on the East African coast 500, 1000, 2000 and 3000 years ago now seem fraught with uncertainty, not least when it is realised that cultural pride and political standing colour current scholarly assessments today just as they did in colonial times. Earlier usage of migration and invasion as mechanisms for explaining change in the archaeological record seems less than adequate; but to replace these with interpretations based on cultural chauvinism that stress autochthonous development is no better.

It is an unfortunate fact that the amount of primary archaeological research carried out in eastern Africa and especially on the offshore islands of the Comores archipelago and Madagascar is still limited despite the best efforts of a number of excellent archaeologists, notably Pierre Vérin, Claude Allibert and Henry Wright, and the new generation of Malagasy archaeologists led by Jean-Aime Rakotoarisoa and Chantal Radimilahy. The current indications of early occupation of Madagascar – directly in the form of archaeological artefacts dated from about 1300 BP and indirectly from pollen evidence from about 2500 BP onwards – are probably much too recent, given the new findings from Zanzibar and the East African coast.

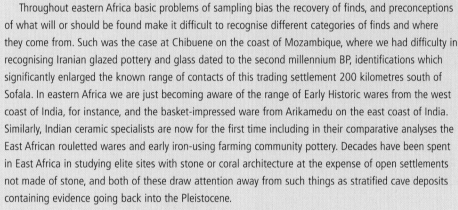

Excavating at Kuumbi Cave.

PAUL SINCLAIR

Throughout eastern Africa basic problems of sampling bias the recovery of finds, and preconceptions of what will or should be found make it difficult to recognise different categories of finds and where they come from. Such was the case at Chibuene on the coast of Mozambique, where we had difficulty in recognising Iranian glazed pottery and glass dated to the second millennium BP, identifications which significantly enlarged the known range of contacts of this trading settlement 200 kilometres south of Sofala. In eastern Africa we are just becoming aware of the range of Early Historic wares from the west coast of India, for instance, and the basket-impressed ware from Arikamedu on the east coast of India. Similarly, Indian ceramic specialists are now for the first time including in their comparative analyses the East African rouletted wares and early iron-using farming community pottery. Decades have been spent in East Africa in studying elite sites with stone or coral architecture at the expense of open settlements not made of stone, and both of these draw attention away from such things as stratified cave deposits containing evidence going back into the Pleistocene.

Becoming aware of some of the biases of previous scholarship should not detract from constructive engagement in fresh empirical field research. Earlier conceptual inadequacies are best understood in relation to the historical context in which they were formed and this awareness should stimulate the incorporation of a broader range of cultural traditions and insights into our own current understanding of the complexities of the history and archaeology of the Indian Ocean region. The quote at the beginning of this essay reminds us that there is more than one form of narrative associated with archaeological sites. Community-based knowledge has insights which often outweigh the pedantic particularism of some scientific discourse. Thus, archaeological sites are not only part of physical landscapes but also feature in intangible cognitive projections which are shared by community members. These cultural views together with the physical remains are crucial for the long-term preservation of one of the richest archaeological heritages of the world.

Special rules apply to visitors to Kuumbi Cave including removal of footwear and particularly the need for respectful behaviour at all times. Please follow the instructions of your guide, do not disturb the plants and animals, and do not leave litter. Enjoy your visit to Kuumbi Cave.

San rock paintings at the site of Tandjiesberg, Free State, South Africa.

environs of Cape Town, for want of capital, labour and ready access to markets.

Settlers moving further into the interior (the *trekboere*) increasingly turned to livestock-rearing, hunting, and trading with indigenous peoples for ivory and skins, while depending upon the Cape for supplies of firearms, manu-factures, coffee, sugar and other necessities but increasingly free of direct VOC control. By 1800, and after a succession of conflicts with Khoe-khoen, hunter-gatherers and Xhosa alike, they had pushed the frontier of European settlement almost to the Gariep River.

The archaeology of this period and of the nineteenth century draws heavily upon textual as well as material evidence for the complexities of the changes that this expansion brought about for both the newly implanted European popula-tions and those already living in southern Africa. One important theme is the study of those sections of the colonial community (women,

slaves, ordinary VOC employees) that receive little mention in official documents, another the analysis of the mental structures through which colonisers and colonised tried to make sense of the new, challenging circumstances in which they lived their lives. For the VOC period, much of the research has centred on and around Cape Town itself. The Castle of Good Hope, Paradise (a timber-cutting station on the slopes of Table Mountain), several house sites within the modern city, and shipwrecks such as that of the *Ooster-land* in Table Bay have all been investigated.

Finds suggest how material culture was used to uphold class distinctions, for example through differential access to high-quality porcelain, glass drinking vessels, or choicer cuts of meat. Such differences could also be developed through architecture: the highly distinctive Cape Dutch-style manor houses that developed in the eighteenth century enabled the rich to impose themselves on the landscape physically and permanently in a way that was impossible to deny, even while the VOC excluded them from political power. Rural settlements have still to be investigated to a comparable extent, but the slightly later settlements built after 1820 by British colonists in the Eastern Cape also marked out a distinctive, if idealised, rural English identity in an initially strange African setting.

A characteristic feature of the Cape colony until abolition in 1838 was that it was a society in which slaves accounted for about half the total population. Since the VOC tightly restricted European immigration and local Khoekhoen were understandably unwilling to turn themselves into labourers, the settlers found an alternative source of man- (and woman-) power by importing slaves, probably a few hundred a year. Coming mostly from Madagascar, India and Indonesia, they were either owned privately or by the VOC. Within Cape Town, they worked principally on Company projects, as domestic servants, and as skilled and unskilled labourers, while in the city's rural hinterland they provided much of the workforce responsible for producing wine and grain.

Archaeologists have tried hard to identify a distinctive slave material culture, in part because its presence would signal a degree of resistance to owner-imposed norms of behaviour. Complicating their efforts is the fact that many Cape slaves were already familiar with the kinds of pottery used in the colony, making the recognition of different ways of preparing or consuming food difficult. Indeed, analysis of pottery assemblages suggests a rapid and widespread adoption of Indonesian and Malay ingredients and cooking styles, though drinking patterns continued to adhere more closely to European customs. The excavation of burials is controversial (being opposed as an indignity to the dead, as in the recent case of Prestwich Cemetery in Cape Town); but it does provide additional information on the slave community of colonial Cape Town, information that would otherwise remain unknown. The mature woman found during

excavations at the Vergelegen estate in Somerset West, for example, had clearly grown up eating tropical grains such as rice before being brought to the Cape and fed a diet rich in temperate grains (like wheat) and fish of the kind known to have been given to slaves.

It would have been naïve of the Dutch to expect the Cape's indigenous peoples to accept colonisation meekly. Two wars in the seventeenth century, however, broke the power of those Khoekhoen closest to Cape Town; and official VOC trading as well as illegal ventures soon led to a permanent loss of their breeding livestock to the colony. European seizure of the best grazing lands, the loss of manpower as people started to work for the colonists, VOC interference in Khoekhoe politics, and outbreaks of smallpox all contributed to the rapid collapse of independent Khoekhoe communities in the southern and south-western Cape.

Survivors had two alternatives, to be incorporated into colonial society as a subordinate labouring class, or to move away. Paralleling the inland movement of 'white' settlers, two main groups chose the latter course. The Oorlams were formed largely of Khoekhoen who left the Cape, while Bastaard communities were typically made up of mixed-race, Christianised and Dutch-speaking individuals. Other groups like the Namaqua were pushed ahead of them. Relevant archaeological studies include that of John Kinahan at //Khauxa!nas, a nineteenth-century Oorlam base in southern Namibia, where architecture mirrors the development of strongly unequal social relations; Sven Ouzman's analysis of finger paintings in the Free State showing horses or riders hunting elephant that may have been produced by Korana groups; and Alan Morris's examination of nineteenth-century Griqua burials, which documented a diet rich in cultivated food and a population of substantially Khoesan and Negroid, rather than European, origin.

As the *trekboere* themselves expanded into

South Africa's interior they competed aggressively with indigenous herders and hunter-gatherers for access to water and grazing, systematically killing or enslaving those who resisted. The Seacow Valley was the scene of a particularly drawn-out struggle from 1770 into the early 1800s. Here Garth Sampson's excavations have traced the gradual appearance of European trade goods in many rock shelter sequences, and the withering away of indigenous bone, stone and ceramic technologies. European destruction of game herds accelerated the transition of San survivors into farm labourers who, as his excavations show, gained increasing access to domestic livestock and cultivated plants by way of replacement resources.

Following the pioneering efforts of Janette Deacon, renewed fieldwork in the Northern Cape may well succeed in identifying comparable data for the /Xam San, whose work with Wilhelm Bleek and Lucy Lloyd provides the foundations for current understandings of San rock art. Although no direct knowledge of that art appears to have survived, Ansie Hoff's studies among the 'coloured' population of the same region reveal a surprising persistence of traditional belief systems despite the loss of language and political independence a century or more ago.

Elsewhere, rock art best records the dispossession of southernmost Africa's hunter-gatherers, most extensively in the UKhahlamba-Drakensberg and Maloti Mountains. Here paintings of elephant hunts may relate to the recorded participation of San in the ivory trade in the 1820s, but scenes showing Europeans, horses or other recognisably colonial imagery cannot simply be read literally. Instead they provide evidence for an intensification of activity by San shamans, who probably used their skills to protect their communities from enemies, make rain (sometimes for Bantu-speaking neighbours), and co-ordinate trade and raids, the latter facilitated by the acquisition of horses between 1840 and 1880. All this may have allowed some shamans to establish new patterns

Saving a tradition

DAVID LEWIS-WILLIAMS

In South Africa in the 1850s, a Thembu man by the name of Silayi left his home and moved eastwards. Repeated conflicts between colonists and indigenous people had made life intolerable on the Cape Colony frontier, where he had been living. When he reached the Tsitsa River he heard about some San families living on friendly terms with Mpondomise people, a group closely related to his own Thembu. In this turbulent time, numerous southern African indigenous communities had become mixed: displaced refugees found themselves moving from group to group.

Amongst the Mpondomise, Silayi met two Khoekhoen, Ngqika and Hans (whose name suggests that he had worked for Boer farmers). They had close contact with the San, and it was in the company of Ngqika that Silayi first met Nqabayo, the San leader. He and his people lived in the Drakensberg near the present-day town of Ugie. He was able to muster 43 men armed with bows and poisoned arrows, though three of them also had flintlock muskets. He was a significant power in the land.

After a while Silayi and Ngqika moved into the mountains where they joined Nqabayo. The San were living in a large rock shelter. They received the two newcomers warmly into their community and presented them with bows and arrows. Silayi thought that Nqabayo was so friendly because of Ngqika's parents. Although Ngqika's mother was a Khoekhoe woman, his father was a San man named Qako.

Silayi and Ngqika discovered that the San still painted – according to Silayi himself, very well. He said that the painters dug their pigments out of the ground and then prepared them in a fire. They made brushes out of hairs taken from a wildebeest's tail or mane which they fastened in small reeds.

Silayi spent three years with the San before returning to his home and to more desperate tragedy. That was in the 1850s. At the end of that century and in the first decade of the twentieth, remaining San families south of the Drakensberg were living in close contact with Nguni people, the name given to all the black farming groups south and east of the Drakensberg. Some of these San were probably descendants of Nqabayo's band. One of the groups was led by Lindiso, who was a rainmaker and a painter. Nguni chiefs often hired San rainmakers in times of drought. After his death, Lindiso's rainmaking powers passed to his daughter, though not his skill as a rock painter: painting was said to be his 'secret'. The rock shelter where he lived is known today, and we can still see his paintings.

Gradually the remnants of traditional San groups including Lindiso's family were absorbed into Nguni communities. Today some people in the area are still known as San descendants, though they no longer speak a San language or practise rock painting. Inevitably, intermarriage eroded the ancient San way of life. On the other hand, long contact between San and Nguni people led to the distinctive San clicks being absorbed into the Xhosa and Zulu languages. Certain beliefs and rituals also passed into Nguni culture. Even today, a Xhosa diviner (*igqirha*) tends to respect memories of San ritual specialists (*!gi:ten*), the ones we call shamans. The Xhosa word derives from the San word.

As their traditional way of life began to crumble, San shamans clung to their ancient belief system. In the 1830s, a missionary learned that the San believed in /Kaggen: 'One does not see him with the eyes, but knows him with the heart.' They appealed to /Kaggen by performing a trance dance 'in times of famine and before going to war'. For thousands of years they had made rain during droughts and had defended themselves against malevolent spirits of the dead, who were said to shoot 'arrows of sickness' into people. Now they tried to ward off the advancing colonists by continuing to invoke beliefs about the spirit world.

This dependence on the old way of life is shown in a rock painting that has become very well known. It depicts 'going to war'. In the centre of the panel are cattle, presumably the focus of the conflict. On the right, colonists advance, some mounted, some dismounted. They shoot with flintlock

OPPOSITE: Manqindi Dyantyi, the daughter of Lindiso, demonstrates how San used to dance in front of rock paintings.
ABOVE: Black and white drawing of San rock painting showing colonists shooting the San.

ROCK ART RESEARCH INSTITUTE

of leadership; our historical sources do indeed hint at non-egalitarian patterns of social organisation among some of these groups as they strove to maintain an independent existence in the face of expansion by European, Sotho and Nguni settlers.

This struggle proved beyond their means, however, and although individuals of San descent survive – and in some areas are seeking to re-engage with their heritage – independent communities were effectively destroyed before 1900. It is in Botswana and Namibia that most San survive today, but compared with areas to the south relatively few archaeological projects have yet specifically targeted the history of peoples like the Ju/'hoansi (!Kung), Nharo, G/wi or Hei//om. In the light of continuing debate over how best to interpret the few historical sources for the period, it is thus uncertain how far some (or all) were transformed socially or economically by participating in local exchange networks, which, in the later 1800s, included supplying ivory, skins, and ostrich feathers to European traders.

Returning south of the Limpopo and Gariep, we must note how European demand for ivory at Delagoa Bay provoked intense competition between local Nguni and Tsonga chiefdoms in the late 1700s. Conflicts deepened between emerging paramountcies, whose leaders sought glass beads, cloth and brass to reward their followers and to acquire still more cattle for themselves.

These conflicts were exacerbated by the rapid shift to maize, which was more productive and demanded less labour than sorghum or millet. Increased numbers of sites and greater use of marginal land, finds of actual maize cobs, and a proliferation of new kinds of grindstones all attest to this change and the population growth that it helped bring about. But maize demands higher rainfall than indigenous African cereals, and in the early 1800s a series of severe droughts and outbreaks of cattle disease afflicted southern

muskets, like those that Nqabayo's men possessed. The unknown San painter depicted flashes from both the pan and the barrel. The fact that some of the riders have dismounted and have left the reins hanging suggests that they are Boers rather than British colonists (the Boers trained their horses to stand still while they fired). To the left of the cattle, San men flee. As they run they shoot arrows at their pursuers.

At first glance we could easily suppose that these images are a simple historical record of a traumatic event. The panel may indeed have derived from a particular cattle raid, pursuit and clash. But there is more to it. A San shaman is depicted on the right, apparently watching over the event. He holds two sticks, the blood of trance falls from his nose, and he has two long feathery attachments on his head: he is entering the realm of the spirits to plead with /Kaggen because his people are 'going to war'. He is calling upon ancient beliefs and rituals to combat new threats.

Tragically, whatever happened in this instance, we know that he was unable to save his people in the long term. These horses, riders, cattle, bowmen, and shamans were among the very last images that the San painted. They have a unique poignancy: bridging the old and the new, they are the end of a long, subtle and truly amazing San artistic tradition.

That tradition may have ended, but it is still remembered and valued. More than that, it lives on in the post-apartheid South African coat of arms. What was once ignored or trivialised is now central to our national identity. In the centre of the coat of arms is a San rock art figure. It comes from a large painted rock crowded with many images that was removed in the early twentieth century from the area in which Nqabayo and his people lived. Today, this artistic treasure may be seen in the Iziko Museum, Cape Town. The designers of the coat of arms duplicated the selected image so that it appears as two people. President Thabo Mbeki explained: 'Those depicted, who were the very first inhabitants of our land, the Khoisan people, speak

of our commitment to celebrate humanity and to advance the cause of the fulfilment of all human beings in our country and throughout the world . . . Through
this new coat of arms, we pay homage to our past . . . It pays tribute to our land
and our continent as the cradle of humanity, as the place where human life first
began.'

When he revealed the new coat of arms, President Mbeki also announced a
new national motto. He had asked that it be in the ancient /Xam San language.
Some nations have their motto in Latin; ours is also in a language that is no
longer spoken, but one that is indigenous to Africa: *!ke e: /xarra //ke* (People who
are different come together).

Of this new motto, President Mbeki said: 'We have chosen an ancient
language of our people. This language is now extinct as no one lives who speaks
it as his or her mother tongue. This emphasises the tragedy of millions of human
beings who, through the ages, have perished and even ceased to exist as peoples,
because of people's inhumanity to others.'

The Origins Centre at the University of the Witwatersrand is dedicated to the
ideals of which President Mbeki spoke. It enshrines the immensely long history of
which South Africans are proud – from the cradle of humanity, to the first art made
by human beings, to the great San tradition, and to images made by Khoekhoe
herders and Bantu-speaking farmers. The Origins Centre also points ahead for us.
As our motto proclaims, the tragedies of the past give way to a diversity-embracing
future.

ABOVE: The new South African coat of
arms. The two images in the centre are
taken from a rock art panel removed in the
early twentieth century to the Iziko Museum
in Cape Town. The panel was removed
from the very area where Silayi lived with
Nqabayo's group of San.
BELOW: San fine-line, shaded polychrome
eland. The painting comes from the very
area occupied by Nqabayo's group of San.

A rider on horseback – either a colonist or one of his indigenous helpers – pursuing San.

Africa. The food shortages that resulted stimulated several groups to reorganise themselves in ways that enabled them to acquire land, women, cattle and grain from others.

Out of the conflict between the three main confederacies present in KwaZulu-Natal around 1810, the Zulu leader Shaka kaSenzagakhona emerged as dominant. Those who refused to accept this new situation moved away to seek refuge elsewhere. These movements produced a period with a very complex pattern of conflicts generally called the *Mfecane* (a Nguni term; *Difaqane* in Sotho). The wider competition for resources, noted above, intensified the struggle, and several other polities developed: the Ndebele kingdom of Mzilikazi, which eventually settled in western Zimbabwe; the Gaza state of Mozambique; a revived Pedi chiefdom in north-eastern South Africa; and the beginnings of today's Lesotho and Swaziland.

Archaeology offers several insights into these processes. In KwaZulu-Natal, for example, it shows how the establishment of Zulu power involved the imposition of a lowland Zulu-settlement style on upland communities that had previously used different kinds of settlement layout. Researchers have also investigated royal capitals such as Mgungundlovu and Ondini, both on the characteristic plan of a Zulu regimental centre, in essence a greatly expanded version of a homestead organised according to the Central Cattle Pattern. In other regions of southern Africa Gaza, Swazi and Basotho royal sites have been little studied, although work has been done at Old Bulawayo, the last Ndebele capital.

The distribution of brass jewellery, which was produced under royal control at some of these sites, was one way in which the Zulu kings could reward their subordinates. Controlling iron production, employing regiments of men and women to tend royal cattle and fields, abolishing traditional initiation schools and placing their female relatives in charge of secondary centres were other means used to impose their authority.

There is good evidence of how some communities were disrupted at this time. One example comes from Alex Schoeman's work among the Ndzundza Ndebele, a Nguni-speaking group that moved north into this part of Mpumalanga some centuries before the *Mfecane*. After their capital kwaMaza was destroyed by Mzilikazi, they moved to a more defensible site and started building their houses more like those of their Sotho-speaking Pedi neighbours, perhaps to differentiate themselves from the linguistically similar invaders. Perhaps unsurprisingly in such troubled times, excavations at kwaMaza also show an increased concern with capping rubbish middens to prevent them being accessed by witches.

Old Bulawayo and Ondini were both destroyed by British forces in the late nineteenth century. Such events marked the terminal phase of European conquest in southern Africa, and archaeology is increasingly able to illuminate aspects of even this very recent past. Examples

include the mid-nineteenth-century Boer ivory-hunting station at Schoemansdal near Musina, at Sandwich Harbour on the Namibian coast (where Euro-American ship crews traded with local Khoekhoen), and military sites from the First and Second South African Wars. More will no doubt be done to investigate the cultural changes brought about by the growth of a capitalist economy and more formalised structures of racial oppression, as well as to study the resistance that developed to this. Another change was the introduction of Christianity. Work at Phalatswe in Botswana, for example, has begun to show how African societies actively incorporated the new religion into their own lives.

Meanwhile European settlers and their descendants were starting to establish archaeology as a discipline that could gather information on the past of all southern Africa's peoples. Today, in a subcontinent liberated from many of the pressures that colonialism imposed, those peoples are themselves active in the archaeological study of their own history and archaeology is increasingly being made accessible to all.

Two San riders on horseback, possibly wearing goat's bladders in their hair.

About the authors

Geoffrey Blundell is Curator of the Origins Centre and a researcher in the Rock Art Research Institute, both at the University of the Witwatersrand. He has published on the interpretation of San rock art, the social production and consumption of the imagery, and the politics of presenting rock art to the public.

Philip Bonner is Professor of History at the University of the Witwatersrand. His research interests cover a wide range of issues from the apartheid era back through the colonial to the pre-colonial period, and he has published extensively on these topics.

Michel Brunet heads the CNRS Research Unit of Human Palaeontology, Poitiers University, France. He specialises in the relationships and palaeo-environments of early hominids in Chad, Central Africa.

Ronald Clarke is Reader in Palaeoanthropology in the School of Anatomical Sciences, the University of the Witwatersrand. He is also Director of Excavations at the Sterkfontein Caves, part of the Cradle of Human-kind World Heritage Site. He is renowned for the discovery of the most complete Australopithecine skeleton yet found.

Nigel Crawhall is currently the Director of Secretariat of the Indigenous Peoples of Africa Co-ordinating Committee. He holds a PhD from the University of Cape Town on the sociolinguistic history of the demise of the !Ui-Taa languages of South Africa.

Janette Deacon has contributed to Stone Age research in southern Africa since the early 1960s. She lives in Stellenbosch and, although retired, remains involved in the conservation of archaeological sites.

Yvette Deloison is a researcher in the National Centre of Scientific Research in France. She specialises in the locomotion and origin of the early hominids.

Christopher Ehret is professor of history and linguistics at the University of California at Los Angeles. He has published widely on African archaeology, with special emphasis on Africa's contribution to world history.

Amanda Esterhuysen is Education Officer in the School of Geography, Archaeology and Environmental Science at Wits University. Her doctoral thesis, submitted in 2006, is on the history and archaeology of Makapan.

Christopher Henshilwood is a Professor at the Centre for Development Studies, University of Bergen, Norway and an Adjunct Associate Professor of Anthropology at Stony Brook, University of New York. He is the Director of the Blombos Cave Project, a major archaeological research programme in South Africa that is contributing significantly to the international debate on the origins of modern human behaviour.

David Lewis-Williams, Professor Emeritus at the Rock Art Research Institute, University of the Witwatersrand, has published extensively on southern African rock art as well as on European Upper Palaeothic and Neolithic archaeology. He is one of South Africa's most widely cited archaeologists and has recently received an 'A' rating from the National Research Foundation in recognition of his global contributions to archaeology.

Peter Mitchell is Lecturer in African Prehistory at the University of Oxford, where he obtained his doctorate in 1987. He has carried out extensive fieldwork in Lesotho and published widely. He is currently President of the Society of Africanist Archaeologists (2004–2006).

Catherine Namono is a Ugandan doctoral candidate at the Rock Art Research Institute, University of the Witwatersrand. Her MA made the first direct link between rock art and girls' initiation among the Northern Sotho in South Africa; and her current research interests include heritage management in Africa and identity in relation to rock art, particularly that of East Africa.

John Parkington is Professor of Archaeology at the University of Cape Town, where he has taught since 1966. His research interests are in southern African Stone Age archaeology and the archaeology of hunter-gatherers. He has been involved in excavations at many Cape sites and in the recording of rock paintings.

David Pearce is a researcher in the Rock Art Research Institute, University of the Witwatersrand. His current research is on southern African Later Stone Age burial practices.

Maria Schoeman is a research officer in the Origins of Mapungubwe programme at the University of the Witwatersrand. At present her focus is on the role that rain control played in ideological changes associated with state formation in the Shashe–Limpopo Confluence Area.

Paul Sinclair has been active in African archaeology for more than thirty years, focusing on human environmental interactions and urban origins through-out eastern and southern Africa. He is Professor of African Archaeology at the University of Uppsala, where he has supervised more than twenty theses in African archaeology.

Benjamin Smith is the Director of the Rock Art Research Institute and Senior Lecturer in the Archaeology Division of the School of Geography, Archaeology and Environmental Studies at the University of the Witwatersrand.

Himla Soodyall is the Director of the Human Genomics Diversity and Disease Research Unit at the National Health Laboratory Service and the University of the Witwatersrand, an enterprise of those two bodies and the Medical Research Council. Her research focuses on examining the genetic variation found in living people to reconstruct population history and origins in sub-Saharan Africa and Madagascar.

Ian Tattersall is a Curator in the Division of Anthropology of the American Museum of Natural History in New York City. His research interests lie in the delineation of species in the human fossil record and the origins of human symbolic consciousness. He has written widely for the public as well as for specialist audiences, and has curated several major museum exhibits.

Recommended reading

Deacon, H and J Deacon. 1999. *Human Beginnings in South Africa: Uncovering the Secrets of the Stone Age*. Cape Town, David Philip

Ehret, C. 1998. *An African Classical Age: Eastern and Southern Africa in World History 1000 BC to AD 400*. Charlottesville, University Press of Virginia

Ehret, C. 2002. *The Civilizations of Africa: A History to 1800*. Charlottesville, University Press of Virginia

Johanson, D and B Edgar. 1996. *From Lucy to Language*. New York, Simon and Schuster

Kingdon, J. 2003. *Lowly Origin: Where, When and Why Our Ancestors First Stood Up*. Princeton, Princeton University Press

Klein, R. 1999. *The Human Career*, 2nd ed. Chicago, University of Chicago Press

Klein, R and B Edgar. 2002. *The Dawn of Human Culture*. New York, John Wiley

Lewis-Williams, JD. 2002. *The Mind in the Cave: Consciousness and the Origins of Art*. London, Thames & Hudson

Lewis-Williams, JD. 2003. *Images of Mystery: Rock Art of the Drakensberg*. Cape Town, Double Storey

Lewis-Williams, JD and G Blundell. 1998. *Fragile Heritage: A Rock Art Fieldguide*. Johannesburg, Witwatersrand University Press

Lewis-Williams, JD and DG Pearce. 2004. *San Spirituality: Roots, Expressions and Social Consequences*. Cape Town, Double Storey

Mitchell, P. 2002. *The Archaeology of Southern Africa*. Cambridge, Cambridge University Press

Mitchell, P. 2005. *African Connections: Archaeological Perspectives on Africa and the Wider World: Archaeological Perspectives on Africa and the Wider World*. Walnut Creek, Altamira

Parkington, J. 2002. *The Mantis, the Eland and the Hunter: Follow the San*. Cape Town, Credo Communications

Potts, R. 1996. *Humanity's Descent: The Consequences of Ecological Instability*. New York, William Morrow

Sykes, B. 2001. *The Seven Daughters of Eve: The Science That Reveals Our Genetic Ancestry*. New York, WW Norton

Tattersall, I, ed. 1995. *The Fossil Trail: How We Know What We Think We Know about Human Evolution*. New York, Oxford University Press

Tattersall, I. 1999. *Becoming Human: Evolution and Human Uniqueness*. New York, Harcourt

Tattersall, I. 1999. *The Last Neanderthal: The Rise, Success, and Mysterious Extinction of Our Closest Human Relatives*. Boulder, Westview

Tattersall, I and JH Schwartz. 2000. *Extinct Humans*. Boulder, Westview

Index